FAIR OF SPEECH

14/7

FAIR OF SPEECH

The Uses of Euphemism

Edited by D. J. Enright

Oxford   New York

OXFORD UNIVERSITY PRESS

Oxford University Press, Walton Street, Oxford OX2 6DP

Oxford New York Toronto
Delhi Bombay Calcutta Madras Karachi
Petaling Jaya Singapore Hong Kong Tokyo
Nairobi Dar es Salaam Cape Town
Melbourne Auckland

and associated companies in
Beirut Berlin Ibadan Nicosia

Oxford is a trademark of Oxford University Press

First published 1985
First issued as an Oxford University Press paperback 1986
Reprinted 1986

British Library Cataloguing in Publication Data
Fair of speech: the uses of euphemism.—(Oxford paperbacks)
1. English language—Euphemism
I. Enright, D. J.
428.1   PE1449
ISBN 0-19-283060-0

Library of Congress Cataloging in Publication Data
Fair of Speech.
1. Euphamism.   I. Enright, D. J. (Dennis Joseph), 1920–
P325.5.E94F35   1986   808   86-18016
ISBN 0-19-283060-0 (pbk.)

Printed in Great Britain by
Richard Clay Ltd
Bungay, Suffolk

CONTENTS

Mother or Maid? An Introduction

D. J. ENRIGHT

As the proverb probably has it, He who looks for offence will find it everywhere. He who concerns himself with euphemism, that mode of avoiding offence, will find it everywhere too, it would seem. Words themselves are in an obvious sense euphemisms for what they represent: sticks and stones may break your bones, but words will never hurt you. As usual, the proverb is true only up to a point. Words can hurt us in diverse ways—by telling the truth, by telling less than the truth, by telling more than the truth. Of course we love words, and sometimes we even think they love us: they are all we have; and *all* means a lot. If we treat them badly, they will take their revenge, for as Karl Kraus put it, 'Language is the mother, not the maid, of thought.' And, quite often, mother knows best.

Having defined the general phenomenon, what we may find tricky is to distinguish for certain between the acceptable and the unacceptable, between that which obeys the truth of the heart and that which tells a harmful or horrible lie. How can we tell, Robert M. Adams asks, 'the fraudulent from the authentic euphemism, the specious moral pickpocket from the considerate and soft-spoken idealist?' The contributors to this book, concentrating on some of the fields in which euphemism nice or nasty thrives, seek to do this. Entertaining though their findings often are, the project (if I dare say so) is of no mean importance at a time when sweet words dance hand in hand with dreadful facts. The present is a quite special, even unique time, in that communications proliferate, people expect to be informed, and the powers that be—however much they would prefer to keep a dignified silence—must find a language in which to inform or misinform, to justify, extenuate or deceive.

Those who complain about the misuse of language, however temperately, are bound to be accused of élitism or (more hurtful) priggishness or (most hurtful) ignorance of how language lives and grows—freely, vigorously, paying no heed to pedants and purists. (Incidentally—a word itself often euphemistic in function—Cyril Connolly wrote that 'pushing up theses' was the euphemism used by men of letters 'for being dead'.) Yet the policy of *laissez-faire*, with its complacent appeal to the past, ignores the unprecedented factors at work today, in particular the effects of television, a forcing-bed of change, coinage, and corruption, such as we have never known before. So words are to be treated like maids?—you can change their duties, sack them, replace them. I have noticed that it is generally intellectuals who take the breezy view, whereas the poorly educated, who respect the education they never got, would like some guidance in matters of language usage, even a degree of firm prescription. Be that as it may—a euphemistic device signifying 'But I'm sure I'm right'—the writers assembled here at times hit hard, at times smile ruefully or laugh aloud, but will never be found to be merely priggish, pedantic or sanctimonious. Nor prudently anodyne: David Pannick, I fear, runs the risk of being struck off the rolls for giving the game away. The human condition—on which euphemisms and their opposites, dysphemisms, cast both light and darkness—is in too grave a condition for such petty self-regard to show its face.*

It would be an egregious pedant, of the most unworldly kind, who could object to euphemism *en masse* as vulgar or pusillanimous prettification. Yet the new edition of *Roget's Thesaurus*, published by Longmans in 1962 and by Penguin in 1966 and subsequently reprinted a number of times, lists 'euphemism' only under the subheads *affectation*, together with 'preciosity', 'cultism' and 'ornament', and *prudery*, along with 'genteelism'. (A lot of recent history seems to have passed unnoticed.) Of the stern or contemptuous opponents of 'pleasant-speaking' one is tempted to observe, They jest at words who never bore a scar. Or, recalling the story of Mrs Shelley, advised to send her son to a school where they would teach him to think for himself and replying 'Oh, my God, teach him rather to think like other people!', we may whisper to

---

* Dysphemisms, the making of things sound worse than they are, may be defined by this somewhat excogitated example: rather than complain that the coffee is weak, tell your hostess that it's like love in a canoe, i.e. 'fuckin' near water'. The locution, supplied by a Californian correspondent, occurs in William Safire, *On Language* (1980).

ourselves, Oh, my God, don't teach people to say what they mean! Barbara Allen was no doubt being frank when she told her unwanted suitor, 'Young man, I think you're dyin'', but we do not admire her for it—better if she had murmured something to the effect of 'I really think you are taking all this a bit too seriously'—and in the ballad she duly gets her come-uppance. Say unto others as you would that they said unto you. Without euphemisms the world would grind, unoiled, to a halt, universal animosity covering all.

Come back, euphemism, all is forgiven! Such is a cry heard in the following pages—but addressed only to the category we might regard as white lies, prompted by compassion, a reluctance to give pain, or a care for another's self-respect, likely to be as battered already as our own. And also to 'euphemism' when it takes the form of hint, nuance or hiatus, the mystery of reticence, in literature. In the course of recent decades the latter has been virtually routed by sexual frankness or 'explicitness'. (The word reminds us of 'adult', as applied, so flatteringly, so insultingly, to certain books, television programmes, and cable channels.) Though at first it promised not only a shot in the writer's bank balance but also a gain in freedom (another word that is too often profaned), explicitness has proved the curse of writing. And, it may well be, no great blessing to sex either.

Inevitably much of this book is given to dysphemism, and much to the other great and concurrent phenomenon of our time: the shift of 'genuine' euphemism into the public sphere, political, military, commercial and social, where it can do much more certain harm than it ever did in the largely private realms of sex, bowel movements, menstruation, money, sickness and natural death. This is the world of black lies, of Newspeak (for Orwell's appendix on the subject has turned out the most truly prophetic part of *Nineteen Eighty-Four*), or—in the putting of a good face on things, the cosmetology of advertising—of grey ones.

We find ourselves in a strange and (some will say) sadly ironic situation. Literature, 'creative writing' we used to call it, once elevated or ennobled or strengthened. With the help of dysphemism, it has now been turned upside-down: motives are customarily mean, the hero is a pathetic neurotic or well-meaning wreck, love is replaced by fornication, the evil may come to a bad end but the good certainly will. You might well suppose that fiction, as we hopefully call it still, is out to destroy the human race by rubbing its nose in its own filth, while only governments, political ideologues, military experts, business men and sometimes psychologists still consider the race worth saving. Why else would social scientists regard the backward as (even so) 'exceptional', and advertisers continually compliment us on our love of excellence, and the military come up at vast expense with a device called 'The Peacekeeper'?

Even crime gets this humanistic treatment, not always self-administered: the 'victim of society' is not necessarily the party who has been mugged, 'insurance' stands in for blackmail and 'aggravation' for violence, while 'light-fingered' suggests a posi-tive admiration for a natural or perhaps hard-won skill, and 'perks' is another word for 'unwritten entitlements', which is another word for something else. Paul Anand, who provided some of these expressions, is an economist and considers euphemism a rightful and even basic aspect of his subject. After all, Proudhon laid down that 'Property is theft.' Mr Anand also offers a family connection of euphemism: the manipulation in international trade of 'hygiene regulations' to get round agree-ments on tariff barrier reduction.

Smiling perhaps through his tears, one contributor mentions the tearing open of whited sepulchres which we have witnessed in the arts and entertainments. And also in biography, which has moved pretty smartly from the pious and prevaricating to the prurient and impertinent. Nabokov's word for its typical practitioner is 'biograffitist'; but 'Truth! stark, naked truth, is the word', its champions will say. Actually those were the words spoken in vindication of *Fanny Hill* by its author. Cle-land, for all that, is praised here by Patricia Beer for employing poetic circumlocution rather than crude among-men talk. Anthony Burgess has commented that the invitations held out in some novels—'Let's fuck, baby'—cause detumescence 'without benefit of what Rabelais's translator Urquhart calls venereal ecstasy'; we are not too surprised to hear that the sexiest book Joseph Epstein knows is *Anna Karenina*.

It is not wholly ludicrous to suspect that, however brave and necessary in its remote origins, this take-over by dysphemism, not only in sexual contexts, can have the effect of further reducing our shaky faith in humanity, in the value of living. Oh, not one's faith in oneself or the worth of one's own being—there could be some point in pulling down individual vanity—but in all those so-called people out there and their so-called lives. It is the more gifted, more persuasive writers who are the most dangerous, but I would not myself be too ready to dismiss the doings of hack pornographers, now no longer restricted to the bare word and the still photograph. The argument that we are free to ignore pornography if we don't like it is hardly more consoling than being told we are not forced to look at an ugly building—we know it is there, and that it might fall on us—while the theory that 'smut' serves a therapeutic purpose (like 'massage parlours', an appellation at once clinical and homely?) is itself an outstanding example of black euphemism. But, oh dear, it takes a saint to condone pornography, and those who object to it can only be self-confessed weaklings in need of careful watching. So let me fall back on the moderate views of Wallace Stevens, writing at an early and relatively innocent stage in the progress of literary frankness and freedom:

We are intimate with people we have never seen and, unhappily, they are intimate with us. Democritus plucked his eyes out because he could not look at a woman without thinking of her as a woman. If he had read a few of our novels, he would have torn himself to pieces.

If Democritus had read a few of our more recent novels, his troubles would have been over.

Jeremy Lewis's phrase, 'the comic villains of the language', could be aptly applied to the class of euphemisms which for one reason or another fail to do their appointed job. A stark case is the euphemizing attempt to erase genitals from statues, which succeeds simply in accentuating the offending members. In the 1939 translation of the sixteenth-century Chinese novel, *The Golden Lotus*, the naughty bits, though mostly hilarious rather than obscene (and often poetic: 'no down concealed it; it had all the fragrance and tenderness of fresh-made pastry'), were rendered into Latin—to save the blushes of the unmatriculated and oblige those with memories of school-Latin to work hard for their pleasures. Well, Colonel Egerton felt the book should be provided in its entirety, and it would have been cheating to leave parts of it in Chinese. When the work was reissued in 1972, these passages were turned into English and patched into the original setting. By a further and inadvertent process of de-euphemization, they can easily be spotted because of their lighter inking.*

The history of the French word *baiser* illustrates what can happen when you use language as a maid-servant, to do a dirty job for you. As a noun it signifies 'kiss', perfectly innocuous; but in its verbal form it became a polite term for 'make love'. Once on the skids, it soon lost all trace of euphemism and turned into a dysphemism; no longer received into polite society, it had to be replaced by *embrasser* (something to do with the arms, like 'brassière'). The death of a verb. . . . We think of the dreaming mind, and how it can drift, so insidiously, from euphemizing to dysphemizing, from tenderness to the most extreme brutishness. Now, to my horror, I see that the *Concise Oxford Dictionary* defines the noun 'embrace' as 'Folding in the arms; (euphem.) sexual intercourse'. Where will it end?

As a contributor notes, you would never buy a used car from a man calling himself 'Honest John'. Nor a household appliance claiming to be 'Made in Britian'; though these days if it is labelled 'Made in Japan' you will jump at it. It is hard to believe that 'automotive internist' will catch on: the job description is too long and unmemorable, unlike the affectionately dysphemistic 'grease monkey'. Nor is it likely that the aggressive 'strike' will be ousted by the managerial sweetmeat, 'volume variance from plan', or that MAD, a nuclear acronym for 'Mutually Assured Destruction', will prove popular: as Vernon Noble observes in *Speak Softly* (1982), it is a little too near the knuckle. Then 'tubesteak', despite the boasting in the second syllable, sounds rather less appetizing than 'frankfurter'; and APT (Advanced Passenger Train) is sheerly unfortunate.

---

* Though the style called 'gallant' was always and everywhere much the same, it is worth culling a few flowers of speech (ornaments? genteelisms?) from the novel, in no doubt literal translation. Thus: 'he asked her to play the flute for him'; 'one other thing there was, black-fringed, grasping, dainty and fresh, but the name of that I may not tell'; 'today I want to play with the flower in the back court'; 'he played with her the game which is called "carrying fire over the mountains" '; 'the time has come, the monk shall smite the timbrel'; 'a stag seemed to leap within her'. It all ends badly, yet, as medical lingo goes, still fairly euphemistically: 'Your vital fluid is exhausted and a furious fever has taken hold upon the instrument of your passion.'

'Lubritorium' is more suggestive of a brothel than a service station: 'Won't be gone long, dear, just dropping in at the lubritorium for a change.' 'Aisle manager' is a pompous substitute for the admittedly rather lowering 'floor-walker'; the latter is uncomfortably close to 'street-walker', which is not itself a euphemism but since *c.*1590 has denoted a particular *modus operandi*. (As does, in its learned way, the French slang, *péripatéticienne*.) The designation 'typing pool' may have been intended to convey happy thoughts of summer bathing, but many of those who have fallen in find it more like a stagnant pond. This may account for the wording of a Canadian government circular of 1976 recorded by Kenneth Hudson in *The Dictionary of Diseased English*: 'vacancies in the word-processing unit'—briskly avoiding both vain promises and the word 'typing'.

Though it survives as the best-known example of Winston Churchill's wit and occasionally surfaces as a well-worn joke, 'terminological inexactitude' never established itself as a euphemism;* and we may doubt that 'strategic misrepresentation' will either. According to William Safire, this is what students of Business Administration at Harvard have been advised to press into service when telling the truth would be bad for business. A regular reader of his *New York Times* column puts the finger on one of those hitherto undetected if minor villains, '*life* insurance', while another proposes a brand-new alternative to 'birth control': 'evading the issue'. We shall wait with interest to see if it enters the language. I suspect it may miscarry.

Was 'anti-Semitic' coined as a gentler way of saying 'anti-Jewish'? If so, whose feelings was it meant to spare? 'Semitic', from Noah's eldest son, Shem, is as much 'Arab' as 'Jewish', and Mario Pei (*Words in Sheep's Clothing*, 1969) remarks on the absurdity that ensues when Arabs are accused of anti-Semitism. 'Aggressive self-defence', US policy in respect of its peacekeeping force in Lebanon (BBC TV news, 13 September 1983), may be justified as convenient shorthand or as conveying a

* Churchill may have been taking off the jargon of bureaucracy. A nice specimen of vogue-word as euphemism is quoted from a cartoon, by Ernest Gowers, in *The Complete Plain Words*: a small girl points to her young brother and shouts, 'Mummy! Johnny's polluted his environment again!'

shade of meaning, possibly ironic as in the couplet '*Cet animal est très méchant, | Quand on l'attaque il se défend*'. But a reference by a former Chief of Defence Staff, Admiral of the Fleet Lord Lewin (*The Times*, 31 December 1983), to the sinking of the *Belgrano* during the Falklands 'conflict' as a 'media embarrassment' will strike some of us as both feeble—like 'near-triumph', as the British 'like to call disaster' (Julian Barnes, of BBC TV's annual 'Sports Review', *The Observer*, 18 December 1983)—and, which is worse, unfeeling. How much nicer to contemplate the villainous words that have managed to get away with a clean sheet. Such as 'death duties' (albeit a sinister combination), which has endured in Britain although in the USA they prefer the relatively emollient term 'inheritance tax'; 'excise', despite the suggestion of cutting away a limb or organ; and 'pencil', whose shared descent from the Latin word for 'tail', *penis*, has gone largely unnoticed. A little knowledge of etymology illuminates the saying about something putting lead in somebody's pencil.

The fox enjoys being hunted. . . . But plainly euphemism cannot be put down solely to hypocritical Albion, to English gentility, that quality we so much despise and would sadly miss should it disappear. The habit as it features in some other languages, including American, is discussed in the following pages; and I imagine that, allowing for local peculiarities, the situation is much the same all the world over. In Proust's novel, Swann's way of hinting that he and Odette should make love was 'do a cattleya' (from the first time, when he began by tucking orchids into her bodice)—certainly a more alluring invitation than that mentioned by Anthony Burgess—while the language of flowers was also favoured by the professional lady who wore a camellia, either white or red, depending. Australian is not exactly a foreign tongue, but it affords euphemisms arising from quite specific local conditions, namely convict jargon. In *Australian Literary Studies*, December 1965, Robert D. Eagleson reports that in the early nineteenth century convicts called themselves 'government people'—he adds that in Australia's early days it seemed 'there was no opprobrium in being attached to the public service'—and also, since they had legal reasons for being in the colony, 'legitimates'. Mr Eagleson points out that while

other members of the community, free settlers, might honour-
ably disclaim any connection with the government, they
hesitated to declare themselves 'illegitimates'.

Just as the ancient Greeks thought it tactful to name the
Furies the 'Eumenides'—a soft salutation turneth away
wrath—so, in hope of averting evil, we incline to number rooms
or floors 12A instead of 13. The number is considered unlucky
because there were thirteen present at the Last Supper, and
hence Friday the thirteenth is at least doubly inauspicious. The
Japanese have a more immediate reason for avoiding room
number 4 in hospitals: 'four', *shi*, is identical in sound with the
word for 'death'. The verb 'to die', as ever, has its softer proxies:
for instance, *kakureru*, to set, as the sun does, to go into the
shadows, is favoured in the case of emperors and the like, while
for more humble folk there is *mimakaru*, to take oneself away.
An acquaintance of mine in Kent has entered into a formal
agreement whereby, 'when Mrs X changes her place of
residence', her house shall pass to the National Trust. It is
understood by all concerned that she has no intention of changing her place of residence until she dies. This is not legal
gobbledegook, but a perfectly acceptable, perfectly decent use of
euphemism.

One of the more picturesque circumlocutions for 'lavatory' in
Japanese evokes a place covered with green camellias (this must
be a peculiarly potent shrub) or, depending on how you construe
the written characters, hidden in snow, but also carrying a
possible allusion to the temple where a priest with a name
similar to 'camellia' once hid himself. The common word for
lavatory is *benjo*, literally 'convenience', and it is interesting to
discover that the expressions in general use (as also in Chinese,
whence they came), *shōben* and *daiben*, where *shō* = little and
dai = big, correspond to our children's terms, 'number one' and
'number two', and to others listed by Catherine Storr. And even
more closely to the French *petit besoin/gros besoin* and the
German *Ich muss nun klein/gross*.

More romantic in aura is the old Japanese name for the gay
quarters, *karyū-kai*, 'blossoms and willows society': whence,
quite naturally, comes *karyū-byō*, 'blossoms and willows
disease'. (Cf. *Kavaliersdelikt*, current in German military
hospitals during the First World War: quasi-stern in that it

carries a suggestion of letting the side down, but thus making every private a general.) Similarly pleasing is a metaphor for 'pimple': *seishun-no-shinboru*, 'symbol of youth'. And since *nashi*, 'pear', is homophonous with the word for 'nothing', you may if you wish have recourse to *ari-no-mi*, 'fruit of something'. Even a pear's feelings ought to be respected.

Catherine Storr also cites metaphorical expressions for menstruation, one of them echoing the grand biblical sentence (Authorized Version), concerning Sarah, quoted by Peter Mullen. 'Flowers' ('monthly flowers', presumably by association with 'flow') must be obsolete. And I doubt that in English there is anything to surpass, for colourful allusiveness and a sense of history, an idiom found among French schoolgirls which, being translated, goes: 'The English have landed' or 'I have my English'. The English are remembered here as 'the redcoats'. If alas the troops fail to disembark, one may have to consult a *faiseuse d'anges* or angel-maker. '*Bénis soient donc les habits rouges,*' Flaubert wrote to his mistress, Louise Colet, after one such scare.

Derwent May touches on the complicity sometimes present between speaker/writer and hearer/reader, the element of shared knowingness. The lady's camellia was a signal to the *cognoscenti*, just as drawn shutters intimate that a shop is closed for the day or a black band on someone's sleeve warns us not to slap the wearer on the back. (In occupied France students might carry two of the long sticks, *gaules*, used to knock down walnuts; they would cry *Vive!* while raising the *deux gaules* in the air. This is the kind of 'signal' which helps the defeated and oppressed to keep their courage up.) Proust's cattleya is more a private endearment, lover's language, than a true euphemism —though I grow increasingly uncertain as to what 'true' means in this connection! And so, to pick one pet name out of many, is 'John Thomas', in this case an endearment passing between lovers or between the owner and the possession. In Goethe's poem, 'Das Tagebuch', which like much of his work is un-'Goethean', John Thomas manifests himself as 'Meister Iste', who 'has his whims and allows himself neither to be commanded nor to be scorned'. Most jokes depend on complicity. In one of the same author's *Venezianische Epigramme* we hear of the pretty girls who take you into their dens '*zum Kaffee*': there is no intent to ward off hurt or horror, we know very well what is meant by 'coffee', and we are meant to smile. Likewise, though the smile will be a sad one, with the low-life *haiku* in which the 'mother' (like 'madam', a euphemism) tells the girl that she will never make a living out of playing her *samisen*, i.e. as a musician.

There may be an element of euphemism in the adoption of foreign words and phrases whereby we imply that what is referred to is so rare among us that we have to import language to describe it. Samples of such transferred shame or uneasiness —not always transferred very far—are 'old Spanish custom' (conceivably a slanderous offshoot of the catch-phrase 'old Southern custom'), 'to welsh', 'to weep Irish' (crocodile tears), 'Indian giver' (US, one who takes his gifts back), 'French leave' (*filer à l'anglaise* is less censorious: if your host has fallen asleep it is permissible to leave without bidding farewell), 'excuse my French!' (i.e. there are no nasty swear-words in our language), and, to go no further, 'French kiss', which the *Concise Oxford Dictionary* bravely attempts to anglicize as 'deep kiss'. As for *double entendre*, it can't actually be found in France, though the phrase *à double entente* can. But the habit of English of continuously pillaging other tongues, though it may betray a deficiency in pride, is a source of strength, variety, and nuance, and we shouldn't be too quick to condemn even its self-defensive manifestations.

The word 'trousseau'—of broader application in French, including the clothes and linen taken by a girl entering a boarding school or convent and by a boy leaving home to start his apprenticeship—was perhaps imported out of delicacy: marriage has something to do with sex. Like the related *enceinte*, it has fallen out of favour these days. Possibly the referent itself has gone, and people get married in what they are standing up in. It is a mortgage that young couples look to equip themselves with now. The term obviously rubbed Dickens the wrong way; in *Little Dorrit* (II. xv) he alludes huffily to

that outfit for a bride on which it would be extremely low, in the present narrative, to bestow an English name, but to which (on a vulgar principle it observes of adhering to the language in which it professes to be written) it declines to give a French one.

In the next sentence the article appears as a 'wardrobe', a good English word; in its origins, if we are to be pedantic, Old French.

The luxuriant and bizarre flowers that spring from too slavish a faith in dictionaries of foreign languages are not properly to be classed as euphemisms, yet—since behind them may lurk the wish to make things sound just a little more delightful than no doubt they are—I shall cite a few examples of promotional prose purporting to derive from innkeepers in the Dolomites eager to attract English-speaking guests. (See the *Spectator*, 22 July 1955.) One of them promised 'two rooms with a vulgar balcony and excommunicating doors' and a convenient shop where 'you can buy jolly memorials for when you pass away' (a conjunction of alarming dysphemisms), while another held out less resistible temptations: 'A vivacious stream washes my doorsteps, so do not concern yourself that I am not too good in bath. Also I am superb in bed.' The same stout all-rounder boasted of 'patty of fungus a speciality. Enjoy it, rest in peace.'

Fair of speech. . . . And sometimes of intention too. But at other times foul of meaning and dishonest in intent. Read further, fair-minded reader, to discover which is which, and why, and where. When I sought to enrol him in this present project, Peter De Vries kindly offered to put the idea 'on the back burner and see if anything comes to a boil'. A watched pot, as we know, does not. And I guess this was a sort of euphemism, a tender-hearted way of saying No. Despite which, and in order to close this overture on a note of comparative uplift, of hope for peace in our time, I shall quote from his novel, *Forever Panting* (1973):

'He's OK. I mean as a husband. But there are these periods of—*he* calls them non-verbal communication.'

'Ah, yes. Complaining mates used to call them prolonged silences. Thank God for jargon, where would we be without it?'

An Outline History of Euphemisms in English

ROBERT BURCHFIELD

i. *Definitions*

WITH the exception of the period before the Norman Conquest, when the evidence is too sparse to reach any reasonable conclusions, all periods of English can be seen to have been characterized by the presence of explicit or neutral vocabulary side by side with synonyms or near-synonyms of varying degrees of inexplicitness. The synonyms that are 'well-sounding' are often but not always euphemisms.

Euphemism is defined in dictionaries as a rhetorical device: 'substitution of mild or vague or roundabout expression for harsh or blunt or direct one' (*Concise Oxford Dictionary*, 7th edition, 1982). It also has a concrete meaning: 'a polite, tactful, or less explicit term used to avoid the direct naming of an unpleasant, painful, or frightening reality' (*Webster's Third New International Dictionary*, 1961). The word *euphemism* is first recorded in English in Thomas Blount's *Glossographia* (1656), where it is defined as 'a good or favourable interpretation of a bad word'. It is derived from the Greek words ευφημισμός 'use of an auspicious word for an inauspicious one' and εὔφημος 'fair of speech'. The employment of euphemisms can be viewed positively as the use of words of good omen, or negatively as the avoidance of unlucky or inauspicious words. Curiously Dr Johnson excluded the word from his *Dictionary of the English Language* (1755) though it had appeared in his main source, Nathan Bailey's *Dictionarium Britannicum* (1730), stressed on the second syllable, and defined as 'good name, reputation, an honourable setting forth one's praise'.

Standard reference works cite *intimacy* as a euphemism for *sexual intercourse, pass away* for *die, underprivileged* for *poor*, and *made redundant* for *dismissed*. Older writers tend to cite somewhat more literary examples, for example *a shorn crown* for *decapitation* and *gentleman of the road* for a *highwayman*.

Dr Thomas Bowdler in his edition of Shakespeare (10 volumes, 1818) removed from Shakespeare's text 'those words and expressions . . . which cannot with propriety be read aloud in a family'. He sometimes did this by substituting innocuous words for unacceptable ones. Thus in *Antony and Cleopatra*, I. i. 10, 'a gipsy's lust' became in Bowdler's version 'a gipsy's will'; in *Othello*, v. i. 36, 'Thy bed, lust-stain'd, shall with lust's blood be spotted' became 'Thy bed, now stain'd, shall with thy blood be spotted'; and in *Hamlet*, v. ii. 64, 'He that hath kill'd my king and whor'd my mother' became 'He that hath kill'd my king seduc'd my mother'. Elsewhere passages were simply removed from the text. Thus 'Royal wench! She made great Cæsar lay his sword to bed. He ploughed her, and she cropp'd' (*Antony and Cleopatra*, II. ii. 230–2) appeared in Bowdler's text only as 'Royal wench! She made great Cæsar lay his sword to bed'. Families needed to be protected from the sexual innuendo of ploughing and cropping.

In the second half of the present century attitudes towards sexual behaviour have changed considerably. The generative organs and their conjunctions have been stripped of immodesty. Instead a marked tendency has emerged to place screens of euphemism round the terminology of politics and race. Key words include *peace, democracy, human rights, freedom, the troubles, emergency, intervention, invasion, campaign,* and *rescue mission*; and *Black*, instead of *Negro, darky, savage, coon,* etc. *Freedom fighters* or *partisans* are seen by their opponents as *terrorists*. Political killers *claim*, or alternatively *admit*, responsibility for assassinating/murdering/killing other people. The terminology arises from the passionate ideological battles of our age. At less bellicose levels, the aged tend to be called *senior citizens*, backward children are said to be *mentally handicapped* or *educationally subnormal*, and juvenile lawbreakers are sent to *approved schools*. Bookmakers tend now to call themselves *turf accountants*, and undertakers have become *funeral directors*.

ii. *Contextual difficulties*

It is impossible at present to write a definitive history of euphemisms. One major impediment is the alphabetical arrangement of dictionaries: no work exists at present in which all the synonyms of a given period of the past can be unscrambled and set side by side. Another lies in the area of contextual interpretation. In 'The deep damnation of his taking-off' (*Macbeth*, I. vii. 20) *taking-off* is sometimes taken to be a euphemism for 'murder'. But Shakespeare does not abjure the word *murder* or its explicit synonyms elsewhere: indeed the word *murderer* actually occurs in the same famous speech ('If it were done when 'tis done . . .'). *Taking-off* is simply a poetical variant in its context, not a true euphemism. Shakespeare is no tenderhearted precursor of Thomas Bowdler.

A further difficulty lies in the interpretation of the complex social arrangements and attitudes of periods before one's own lifetime. It is never easy and often impossible to recognize the true nature of fine distinctions of meaning in the works of writers of the past. In Dryden's *Marriage à la Mode* (1673), a comedy concerned with affairs of love, the words *intrigue* and *amour* are contrasted:

Philotis: 'Tis great pity Rhodophil's a married man, that you may not have an honorable intrigue with him.
Melantha: Intrigue, Philotis! That's an old phrase; I have laid that word by: *amour* sounds better.   (II. ii)

But *intrigue* is now an even older and altogether more archaic word. Allowance needs to be made for the semantic erosions of time.

The language of adversaries has always been just as selectively self-directing as it is at the present time but the subject-matter in the past was often very different. Thus Shylock's *well-worn thrift* is called *interest* by Antonio: the adversarial language (from Shylock's point of view) arises because Antonio 'hates our sacred nation' and 'in low simplicity . . . lends out money gratis'.

Euphemisms of the past are of course often clearly distinguishable and no more so than in some works of the Victorian period. A good many of Dickens's characters display impressive dexterity in avoiding the use of the names of certain articles of dress:

Mr Trotter . . . gave four distinct slaps on the pocket of his mulberry indescribables . . . (*The Pickwick Papers*, ch. xvi)

Other nineteenth-century authors show the same reluctance to employ the word *trousers* or *breeches*:

A fine lady can talk about her lover's inexpressibles, when she would faint to hear of his breeches. (*OED*, 1809)

The priest's unmentionables drying on a hedge. (*OED*, 1883)

In practice, however, trousers and underclothes were doubtless ordered or purchased by name, however 'faint' fine ladies were said to feel when mention was made of them. It was just that it was genteel to assume that there were holes in the language, invisible words, expressions that should be reserved for day-to-day mercantile business but were deemed unsuitable for use in polite circles.

iii. *Scholarly assumptions*

For linguistic scholars a standard example of the ritual avoidance of an inauspicious word lies in the fate of the reconstructed primitive Indo-European word for *bear*, namely *ṛksos*. It survives in Sanskrit (*ṛkšas*), Greek (ἄρϰτος), and Latin (*ursus*), but has disappeared in language areas where the bear was at one time an object of terror, that is in Germanic and Slavonic languages. In the Balto-Slavonic group of languages it has been replaced by the types represented by Russian *medved*́, 'honey-eater' and Lithuanian *lokys*, 'licker'. In the Germanic languages (Old English *bera*, Modern English *bear*, German *Bär*, Dutch *beer*, etc.) it has been replaced by derivatives of the Indo-European noun meaning 'the brown one'.

Another standard example of the avoidance of an ill-omened word is the presence in Old English of the words *swefan*, *sweltan*, and *steorfan*, all meaning 'to die', but originally or also meaning 'to sleep', 'to burn slowly', and 'to grow stiff' respectively. The unrecorded verb *degan*, cognate with Old Norse *deyja*, almost certainly existed in Old English, as the verb corresponding to *dēaþ*, 'death' and *dēad*, *'dead'*, but it was avoided in writing until the taboo on it was lifted by some releasing mechanism soon after the Norman Conquest.

Jonathan Swift says of the Houyhnhnms (*Gulliver's Travels*, 1726) that 'they have no word in their language to express anything that is evil'. By 'evil' he means such things as 'the folly of a servant, an omission of a child, a stone that cut their feet, a continuance of foul or unseasonable weather, or the like'. But among the unmentionables is death. He relates a story of a Houyhnhnm who made an appointment with a friend and his family to come to his house upon some affair of importance:

On the day fixed the mistress and her two children came very late; she made two excuses, first for her husband, who, as she said, happened that very morning to 'shnuwnh'. The word is strongly expressive in their language, but not easily rendered into English; it signifies, to retire to his first mother.

Her husband had in fact died, and the Houyhnhnm wife, like the Anglo-Saxons, was using her own euphemism for 'to die'.

iv. *Substitutions*

One way to sidestep explicitness is to use a range of substitute symbols like asterisks or dashes or to use abbreviations or other semi-concealing devices. In *Tristram Shandy* (1759–67) Laurence Sterne provides a classic example of asterisks replacing an explicit sexual word:

My sister, I dare say, added he, does not care to let a man come so near her ****. I will not say whether my uncle Toby had completed the sentence or not;—'tis for his advantage to suppose he had,—as, I think, he could have added no One Word which would have improved it.

The missing word, contextually, is *pudenda* or equivalent. Sterne teases us by pretending that it is an example of aposiopesis:

Take the dash away, and write Backside,—'tis Bawdy.—Scratch Backside out, and put Covered way in, 'tis a Metaphor; and, I dare say, as fortification ran so much in my uncle Toby's head, that if he had been left to have added one word to the sentence,—that word was it.

The actual conception of Tristram Shandy is also euphemistically presented as a 'little family concernment' between his father and mother, associated with the regular winding of a large house-clock 'on the first Sunday-night of every month':

He had likewise gradually brought some other little family concernments to the same period, in order . . . to get them all out of the way at one time, and be no more plagued and pestered with them the rest of the month.

Other types of euphemistic substitution are very common. Moll Flanders does not have large breasts, but is 'well-carriaged'. She describes her first near-seduction in the following manner:

However, though he took these freedoms with me, it did not go to that, which they call the last favour, which, to do him justice, he did not attempt . . .

And when she eventually succumbs to her first seducer:

I made no more resistance to him, but let him do just what he pleased, and as often as he pleased.

Inauspicious words and unlucky actions are thus skilfully screened by lightly imaginative language.

Henry Fielding softens the barbarousness of the gallows by describing Jonathan Wild's execution 'on the tree of glory' as only 'a dance without music':

This was the day of the execution, or consummation, or apotheosis (for it is called by different names), which was to give our hero an opportunity of facing death and damnation, without any fear in his heart.

Damnation, in more Christian ages than ours, was an ultimate obscenity. So too, more trivially, were and are interjections like *damn*, *Christ*, *Jesus*, and saints' names (*by St ——*). The evasions are of several kinds:

He even went so far as to D   Mr Baps to Lady Skettles . . .
                    (Charles Dickens, *Dombey and Son*, ch. 14)

Though 'bother it' I may
Occasionally say,
I never use a big, big, D—.
            (W. S. Gilbert, *H.M.S. Pinafore*, 1)

Geeze, was that you? What were you doing up there?
            (David Lodge, *The British Museum is Falling Down*, ch. 10)

'Jeepers Creepers!' he said to himself, remembering the expression on Mr Stoyte's face.

> (Aldous Huxley, *After Many a Summer*, part II, ch. 9).

For Chrissake, grow up.

> (J. D. Salinger, *Catcher in the Rye*, ch. 3)

Jiminy Christmas! That gives me the blue creevies.

> (Rudyard Kipling, *Captains Courageous*, ch. 4)

That's what it was—oh, cripes!—awful hole.

> (J. B. Priestley, *Angel Pavement*, ch. 4)

Rhyming slang is another semi-concealing device: *bristols*, 'breasts' (from *Bristol cities = titties*), *cobblers*, 'nonsense, balls' (from *cobbler's awls = balls*), and *Hampton Wick*, 'penis' (rhyming with *prick*). Concealment is also partially achieved by abbreviations and by acronyms: *sweet F.A. =* (politely) *sweet Fanny Adams*, 'nothing at all', (impolitely) *sweet fuck all; snafu =* (politely) *situation normal all fouled up*, (impolitely) *situation normal all fucked up*.

A euphemistic device of an altogether different kind is employed by Thomas Rowlandson (1756–1827). He depicted the brutal and libidinous side of the days of George III and the Regency in a series of erotic paintings with stunningly punning captions like 'The Finishing Stroke' (showing a cuckolded husband about to fire a blunderbuss at his wife's lover caught *in flagrante delicto*), and 'The Country Squire New Mounted' (showing a lecherous squire achieving sexual union while mounted on a horse). Even the notorious libertine, the Earl of Rochester (1648–80), whose usual style lacks disguise of any kind,

> Much wine had past with grave discourse
> Of who Fucks who, and who does worse,

sometimes resorts to euphemistic circumlocutions for parts of the anatomy:

> By swift degrees, advancing where
> His daring Hand that Altar seiz'd,
> Where Gods of Love, do Sacrifice!
> That awful Throne! that Paradise!

v. *Anglo-Saxon Attitudes*

In its earliest form English, like the early forms of many other languages, seems like a restricted, almost a censored, secretion, recorded only in its best regulated form. It is almost as if its main reason for surviving was to supply paradigms and fine-spun sentences for grammarians and literary historians. It is almost certainly right to assume however that the *speech* of our fore-bears in the Anglo-Saxon period, however hedged about by rules and customs, was, as now, untidy, approximate, illogical, and also (when necessary) euphemistic.

However true this general proposition is, one looks more or less in vain for undisputed euphemisms in the central corpus of Old English literary prose and verse. *Sceandword* (opprobrious words) certainly existed, but in medical works and ancient glossaries, not in works like *Beowulf* or the elevated prose of the period.

The vocabulary of the latrine or privy, for example, can be ascertained from Anglo-Saxon works like the *Leechdoms*. Most of the recorded synonyms are based on the notion of 'going' or 'sitting' or of the resemblance of the latrine to a pit or a ditch. The most usual word seems to have been *gang* or *gong* (OED *Gong*[1]), a special use of the same word (OED *Gang* sb.[1]) meaning 'a journeying, a going; eventually, a set of persons, a gang'. Obvious extensions of it occur in *earsgang* (arse-privy, scarcely euphemistic!), *forðgang*, and *ūtgang*; and, with added second elements, *gang-ærn* (ærn place), *-pytt* (pit), *-setl* (seat), *-stōl* (stool, seat), and *-tūn* (separate building). The other main synonyms are abundantly transparent: *ādel(a)* (filthy place), *feltūn* (field building), and *grēp(e)* (ditch, drain).

Of all the Old English words corresponding to Latin *secessus* and *latrina* perhaps only *heolstor* is euphemistic. Its primary sense, recorded several times in poetry and prose, is 'place of concealment', as, for example, when Grendel *wolde on heolster flēon* (*Beowulf*, 755), 'Grendel wished to find a hiding-place', in order to rejoin the *dēofla gedræg* (the company of demons). There is no suggestion whatever of a *double entendre* in any of them. The wide range of euphemistic synonyms to do with easement, privacy, comfort, convenience, running water, separation of the sexes (in public lavatories), and so on, were to come at intervals, as they became released from speech into print, in the centuries after the Conquest. I shall return to them later.

Anglo-Saxon kennings like *mere-hrægl*, 'sail' (literally 'sea-garment'), *freoðu-webbe*, 'woman' (literally 'weaver of peace'—by dynastic marriages), and *hron-rād*, 'sea' (literally 'riding-place of the whale') were not true euphemisms but rather condensed simile-compounds. Litotes (understatement) is fairly common but is usually not marked by the employment of 'pleasant or auspicious' words for 'unpleasant or inauspicious' ones. In *The Dream of the Rood*, for example, the dead body of Our Lord 'remained with a scanty retinue' (*reste he ðær mæte weorode*), that is, by a delicate use of litotes, 'alone'. Only now and then a streak of euphemism is discernible, as in the use of *ellorsīð*, 'death' (literally 'journey elsewhere'):

> Symble bið gemyndgad   morna gehwylce
> eaforan ellorsīð
> $\qquad\qquad\qquad$ (*Beowulf*, 2450–1)

> He is ever reminded each morning
> Of his son's death.

Some other synonyms for *die* (for example, *swefan*, mentioned above) and *death* (for example, *ealdor-gedāl* and *līf-gedāl*, both literally meaning 'separation from life') tend towards the euphemistic. The verb (*ge*)*cringan* 'to fall in battle, to die' may also have been contextually euphemistic. It originally meant 'to curl up' and is related by a slightly devious route to the verb *cringe*. Scholars will doubtless discover other examples of euphemisms in Old English.

The medical writers of the period used a wide range of mostly explicit terminology for the excretory and sexual organs and functions. Synonyms of *ears* (arse) include *ears-endu* (pl., buttocks) and (doubtless euphemistic) *setl* (seat). The anus is *ears-þerl* (*þerl* = *þyrel*, 'hole'). The entrails were *bæc-þearm* ('back intestines', cf. German *Darm*), *smeoru-þearm* (*smeoru*, 'fat, grease', etc.), and *snædel-þearm* (*snæd*, piece cut off, slice). The degrees of intimacy or delicacy implied in such terminology and also in the synonyms for the genitalia are difficult to determine. The etymological meaning of the words is only partially helpful.

Thus *gesceapu* in

> His gesceapu maðan weollon
>
> His private parts swarmed with vermin

etymologically means 'a shape, something made or shaped'. Other synonyms for the male genitalia included *getāwa* ('instruments') and *geweald* (where the underlying sense is 'power, control'). The occurrence of the phrase *geswell þāra gewalda*, 'the swelling of the *geweald*', is a clinical reminder that erection occurred then as now. The normal word for the female genitalia was *gecyndelic*:

Gyf wīf cennan ne mæge, nime þysse wyrte wōs mid wulle, dō on þā gecyndelican.

If a woman cannot conceive, take this herbal extract with wool and apply it to the pudenda.

Testicles were *herðan* (etymologically related to *heorða*, 'deer- (or goat-?) skin'), and the penis is variously *lim* (limb), *teors* (tarse), and *wǣpen* (weapon). Among the synonyms for sexual intercourse are *hǣmed* (the underlying idea being 'cohabitation'; cf. *hām*, 'home'), *hǣmedlāc* (*lāc*, 'play'), *hǣmedðing*, *wīf-gemāna* (*gemāna*, 'companionship, conjunction'), and *wīf-lāc* (*lāc*, 'play'). In the well-known passage in the *Anglo-Saxon Chronicle* about Cynewulf and Cyneheard, the phrase *þā geāscode hē þone cyning lȳtle werode on wīfcyþþe on Merantūne* may mean 'then he discovered the king having intercourse with a woman (rather than 'in the company of a woman') at Merton', but the meaning is disputed.

Arguments based on etymological considerations are in the end indecisive. We may not even conclude that any colloquial connotations were attached to the word *mōnaðlican*, 'menstruation', despite its formal correspondence to modern 'monthlies', nor is it wise to assume any of the informality of the modern expression 'the curse' in the Anglo-Saxon word *mōnaðādl* (literally 'monthly illness').

The absence of any Anglo-Saxon literary works about infidelity or harlotry means that the terminology of Anglo-Saxon debauchery and licentiousness lies buried in obscurity. Not more than about ten synonyms for 'harlot' survive, probably none of them euphemistic. It is of interest to set them down in tabular form beside ten of the more usual terms of the present day.

OLD ENGLISH	MODERN ENGLISH
bepæcestre (seducer; cf. *pæcan*, to deceive)	broad
cifes (concubine; cf. mod. German *Kebser*)	harlot†
cwene*	hooker
firenhicgend (harlot, adulteress)	prostitute
forlig(n)is (cf. *forlicgan*, to fornicate)	scrubber
hōre*	slag
portcwene (town whore)	slut
scand (also 'shame, scandal')	strumpet†
scrætte (from Latin *scratta*)	tart
synnecge (used of Mary Magdalene)	whore

  * Surviving as *quean* and *whore*   † Both now somewhat archaic

Only one word appears in both lists, namely *hōre/whore*. In both groups the apportionment of sin is explicit: there is no holding back and no concealment. The difference is that in Old English these were the *only* recorded words for a prostitute. Old English *cifes* survived in the form *cheve(s)* into Middle English but is not recorded after 1400. With the exception of *cwene* and *hōre* none of the other words is recorded after the Conquest. Social attitudes changed. Prostitution became cloaked in new synonymy.

At all periods hard unforgiving words for prostitute have existed. But, as the centuries passed, evasive alternative words have emerged in profusion, expressions like *call girl, fallen woman, fille de joie, hostess, lady of easy virtue, model, moll, pick-up, street-walker,* and *woman of the town,* brought into being by social exigencies of the time. The mechanisms that released them were the same as those which governed the currency of 'fair-spoken' words for the private parts of the body and their functions. As the urban population increased, and social arrangements became more complex, the heavy sin-based terminology of the Anglo-Saxons went into desuetude. The new seams to be explored and exploited were those of gentility and politeness. New forms of etiquette replaced the old.

vi. *Releasing Mechanisms*

The monks, *scops* (poets), and ordinary citizens of the Anglo-Saxon period went to the *gang* (privy) (or the *gang-pytt*, etc.). Their descendants after the Conquest were able to draw upon a wider range of synonyms, though the native word *gang* remained in use throughout the medieval period:

> . . . bordels of thise fool wommen . . . mowe be likned to a commune *gong*, where as men purgen hire ordure.
>
> (Chaucer, *The Parson's Tale*, 885)

Gallicism in itself was a releasing mechanism: the new language (French) brought new words. In Chaucer's legend of Ariadne, for example, Theseus is thrown into a tower:

> The tour, ther as this Theseus is throwe
> Doun in the botom derk and wonder lowe,
> Was joynynge in the wal to a *foreyne*.
>
> (*The Legend of Good Women*, 1960–2)

The *foreyne* (or *foreign*) is short for *chambre foreyne*, an outer privy. Chaucer, the releaser of so much informal vocabulary that before him was presumably restricted to the spoken language, boldly introduces euphemisms into his works. In *The Merchant's Tale* the young bride May declares that she must go 'Ther as ye woot that every wight moot neede' ('where, as you know, everyone must needs go'):

> And whan she of this bille [sc. a letter from her lover] hath taken heede,
> She rente it al to cloutes atte laste,
> And in the *pryvee* softly it caste.

In *The Prioress's Tale* a widow's seven-year-old son is murdered and his body disposed of:

> I seye that in a *wardrobe* [sc. privy] they hym threwe
> Wher-as thise Jewes purgen hire entraille.

The word *privy* has survived. Chaucer's other synonyms did not.

    Shakespeare's latrine vocabulary is relatively restrained. Costard's use of *Ajax* to mean 'a jakes' is well-known:

> your lion, that holds his poll-axe sitting on a close-stool, will be given to Ajax . . .   (*Love's Labour's Lost*, v. ii. 581)

And the word *jakes* itself is used in an undisguised manner in *King Lear* (II. ii. 70) when Kent says that he will 'tread this unbolted villain [sc. Oswald] into mortar, and daub the wall of a jakes with him'. Less well known are Scarus's use of *bench-hole*:

> We'll beat 'em into *bench-holes* . . .
> *(Antony and Cleopatra*, IV. vii. 9)

and Timon's

> Hang them or stab them, drown them in a *draught*.
> *(Timon of Athens*, V. i. 105)

A *draught* or *draught-house* was an acceptably neutral or even a slightly genteel term to judge from the fact that the compilers of the Authorized Version (1611) preferred *draught-house* (2 Kings 10: 27) to Coverdale's *prevy house*.

After Shakespeare's time releasing mechanisms of one kind or another multiplied the terminology to a quite extraordinary extent. The multiplication of terms and the century in which they were first recorded are shown in the following tables:

1600–1699	*1700–1799*	*1800–1899*
closet	bog(s)	bog-house
commons	dunniken, dunny	convenience
gingerbread-office	head(s) (on a ship)	earth closet
latrine	little house	toilet
necessary house, place, etc.	necessary (as a noun)	WC
	office	
	water-closet	

1900–	
bathroom *	Ladies
can *	lav
cloaks	lavabo
comfort station *	lavatory
Gentlemen	lavvy
gents	loo
geography of the house	men's room *
john, johnny *	public convenience
karzy	rest room *

* Chiefly US

These lists are not exhaustive but they show the outline of the semantic area filled by synonyms for privy, including those that are euphemistic, from Old English *gang* to modern socially divisive expressions like *comfort station* and *rest room* (US genteel), *loo* and *the geography of the house* (UK middle and upper middle class), and *toilet* (UK working class and lower middle class).

The historical trail of the harlot runs from Old English *cifes* and *hōre* to modern English *prostitute* and *whore*. Wave after wave of social prudery at times drove the more explicit terms into retreat, while other social mechanisms brought them back in use and also generated new hard-core words.

In the sixteenth century the following more or less specific synonyms for prostitute came into the language:

baggage	hackney	public woman
cat	*hiren	pucelle
cockatrice	*hobby-horse	punk
cony	laced mutton	*stale (noun)
courtesan	limmer	*stew
doxy	loon	street-walker
drab	minx	tomboy
*driggle-draggle	mort	wagtail
*flirt-gill	mutton	

(Those marked * were short-lived: none of these is recorded after 1660. Others remained in the language for only a slightly longer period.)

Other synonyms or near-synonyms for prostitute were first recorded in the following periods:

1600–1699		*1700–1799*	
buttock	nymph (of the	demi-rep	rake
cousin	pavement)	fille de joie	woman of the
crack	prostitute	lady of easy	town
customer	pug	virtue	
fireship	strum		
flap	tomrig		
lady of pleasure	town-woman		
marmalade-	vizard		
madam	waistcoateer		
night-walker			

1800–1899		*1900–*	
buer	hooker	brass nail	make (noun)
chippy	horizontal (noun)	broad	model
cocotte	horse-breaker	call girl	muff
demi-mondaine	pick-up	demi-vierge	pavement
fallen woman	scarlet woman	demi-virgin	princess
flagger	tart	hostess	scrub
flapper	unfortunate	hump	scrubber
	(noun)	lay (noun)	slag

The language of the sexual organs and of sexual play has darted into and out of the language as puritanism retreated and advanced. The first major unprudish woman in English literature is Chaucer's Wife of Bath. As she observes, the 'membres of generacion' were 'nat maad for noght':

> Glose whoso wole, and seye bothe up and doun,
> That they were maked for purgacioun
> Of uryne, and oure bothe thynges smale
> Were eek to knowe a femele from a male,
> And for noon oother cause,—say ye no?
>
> *(The Wife of Bath's Prologue,* 119–23)

She revels in the language of 'bothe thynges smale':

> For, certeyn, olde dotard, by youre leve,
> Ye shul have *queynte* right ynogh at eve.
>
> (Ibid., 331–2)

Her *queynte* is also, euphemistically, her *bele chose* (447), *quoniam* (608), and *chambre of Venus* (618). It is hardly a circuitous journey from this kind of language and from the euphemistic indirectness of *The Miller's Tale*:

> And thus lith Alison and Nicholas,
> In bisynesse of myrthe and of solas ...   (3653–4)

and of

> And shortly for to seyn, they were aton
>
> *(The Reeve's Tale,* 4197)

to the euphemizing of Dryden, Sterne, and Fielding mentioned above and to that of other writers in later centuries. What changed from generation to generation was the prominence given either to explicit language or to language that was more reserved. Both kinds co-existed but advanced or retreated according to the mode of the writer or the mood of the age.

vii. *The Printed Word Unchained*

The limitless expansion of the printed word in the present century possibly makes it seem as if the proportion of euphemisms (and of every other kind of rhetorical device) has increased considerably. But this is not necessarily so. Previous centuries are now closed periods. For the most part the vocabulary that can be collected in a methodical way from them has been collected. They are not always obliging centuries, and many of the verbal patterns of the past are buried beyond the reach of analysis. In the nine hundred years or so since the Norman Conquest it is easy enough to discern the main forces (or releasing mechanisms as I have called them) which have caused successive generations to bring new 'well-omened' expressions into being and to abandon or suppress other more explicit ones. Avoidance of unseemly words springs from a deeply instinctive belief that by so doing one will gradually cause them to disappear, or at any rate make the concepts denoted by them seem to be less intrusive. War, death, politics, birth, fornication, bodily functions like excretion, reticence, social rank and other social relationships—these and other primary matters have generated 'well-sounding' and 'harsh-sounding' expressions down through the centuries.

Our present age, like those of the past, produces euphemisms to conceal or take attention away from its particular embarrassments and its unsolved problems. In the 1914–18 war *Big Bertha* was the name given, somewhat affectionately, to a field-gun of immense destructive power. In North Africa during the 1939–45 war troops seemed to be forever 'retiring to prepared positions'. Public fears needed to be allayed, at least until the story changed at El Alamein. Our fighter pilots 'bought it' or 'went for a Burton' as they crashed and were killed. The highly vulnerable gunners at the rear end of bomber planes came to be affectionately known as 'tail-end Charlies'. In the Vietnam war the Americans discovered the calming usefulness of expressions like *pacification* (destruction of villages and evacuation of the inhabitants) and *defoliation* (destruction of forests used by the enemy as cover). In the Falklands campaign a cluster bomb used by the RAF consisted of more than a hundred bomblets, each of which when exploded disintegrated into hundreds of high-velocity fragments dispersed over a wide area.

The effect on what are euphemistically called *soft-skinned targets*—a category which includes people—is devastating.

(*London Review of Books*, 15 Sept.–5 Oct., 1983)

None of these processes of soft-naming is new or particularly alarming. Almost any act or deed can be described factually or without connotations of any kind. Equally almost everything can be subtly altered for better or worse if a speaker or writer wishes this to happen. At any given time a battery of substitutional words or phrases exists, to be made use of, kept in reserve, or avoided, at choice. A language without euphemisms would be a defective instrument of communication.

Sir John Betjeman's poem 'Churchyards' reminds us that death is still a primary source of euphemisms:

> Oh why do people waste their breath
> Inventing dainty names for death?
> On the old tombstones of the past
> We do not read 'At peace at last'
> But simply 'died' or plain 'departed'.

Much of the ancient sense of sin has been removed from suicide. Yet Arthur Koestler's death-note written in June 1982 used the euphemism 'seek self-deliverance' as a synonym for 'commit suicide' and 'put an end to my life', both of which phrases also occurred. *Self-deliverance*, taken by Koestler from the vocabulary of the group known as Exit, deserves to be ranked with the funereal vocabulary brought into prominence by Evelyn Waugh in *The Loved One* (1948): The Happier Hunting Ground (for a dead Sealyham terrier), the Slumber Room of the Whispering Glades Memorial Park, the Radiant Childhood Smile restored to the face of Sir Francis Hinsley (who had hanged himself and by doing so grossly distorted his features).

Sexual matters are less hedged about with 'fair-spoken' words than they once were. But race bristles with them, and even the phrase *race relations* itself is seen by Nadine Gordimer as a euphemism. Among the sad figures in her *Burger's Daughter* (1979) is an 'old-maid schoolteacher' anxious to do uplifting work in the black townships of South Africa:

Something less self-defeating than charity, for what (euphemism being their natural means of expression) they call 'race relations'.

There is no shortage of euphemisms in the more casual areas of life. 'Do you drink?' is apparently an underworld expression for asking a policeman if he will take a bribe. Emily, in R. Jaffe's *Class Reunion* (1979), 'hates being "petite", which was a euphemism for getting stuck with all the short boys on blind dates'. A recent issue of the journal *Maledicta* reported that 'a tall building' is sometimes used as a euphemism for an erection. An American bank is said to have avoided the dreaded word 'loss' by calling it a 'net profits revenue deficiency'. In some quarters drug addicts have come to be called 'dependents with a chemical problem'. These minor evasions are of a piece with the avoidance of the word 'leg' a century or more ago:

I am not so particular as some people are, for I know those who always say limb of a table, or limb of a piano-forte.

(Frederick Marryat, *Diary in America*, 1839)

This over-delicate preference has been abandoned. But it has left a tiny legacy in that a common term for an artificial leg (or arm) is still an artificial *limb*, whether it replaces one that had been a 'soft-skinned target' or one that had been removed for some other reason.

For help of various kinds I am indebted to Mr J. Farish (co-editor of the forthcoming *Historical Thesaurus of English*), Miss E. A. Knight, Mr T. F. Hoad, Mrs M. Y. Offord, Miss K. C. E. Vines, and Mr F. R. le P. Warner.

REFERENCES

The Oxford English Dictionary, 1884–1933, and supplementary volumes, 1972–
Eric Partridge, *Shakespeare's Bawdy*, 1947 and later editions
Rochester's Poems on Several Occasions, ed. James Thorpe, 1950
G. L. Brook, *The Language of Dickens*, 1970

The Forbidden Erotica of Thomas Rowlandson, introduced by Kurt
  von Meier, 1970
Ralph W. V. Elliott, *Chaucer's English*, 1974
G. L. Brook, *The Language of Shakespeare*, 1976
Norman Davis *et al.*, *A Chaucer Glossary*, 1979
Hugh Rawson, *A Dictionary of Euphemisms and Other Doubletalk*,
  1981
Judith S. Neaman and Carole G. Silver, *A Dictionary of Euphemisms*,
  1983 (in US, *Kind Words: a Thesaurus of Euphemisms*)

Euphemisms in Greece and Rome

JASPER GRIFFIN

THE word *euphemism* is Greek, and the ancient world was perfectly familiar with both the practice and the theory of the palliative phrase. One very old form was essentially superstitious, arising from the reluctance to utter the real names of terrible and possibly malevolent beings. The ruler of the dead it might be prudent to call Hades, which meant just 'the unseen one'; his sinister realm might be referred to as 'down there', or more simply 'there'. Greeks called the angry goddesses who avenged homicide by such softening titles as 'the Solemn Ones' or 'the Kindly Ones' (*Eumenides*)—a name which might please those grim spirits, imagined as winged like bats and with snaky hair, and which might even have some effect in making them kindly. Romans used a very similar title for the dead themselves: *Manes*, 'the Gentle Ones'.

In the Middle Ages the Portuguese thought it a better omen to rename the Cape of Storms as the Cape of Good Hope. Romans said that the Italian city of Beneventum (modern Benevento) had originally been called Maleventum; but the name was changed, from what sounded like 'Bad Result' to 'Good Result'. Greek mariners facing the stormy and inhospitable Black Sea gave it the auspicious name of the Euxine: the Hospitable, the Welcoming Sea. Since the right hand was the more favoured and more fortunate, it followed that the left was unfortunate. Rather than call it so, it was called in Greek the 'well-named' hand, or even 'the better hand'; in Latin, *sinister* (left) meant originally 'more advantageous'. In retrospect we see that the prejudice against the left hand was too strong to be overcome by euphemisms, so that the Latin *sinister* and the French *gauche* have both become themselves bad words, each with its own specialized derogatory sense.

Euphemisms arising from fear shade off into euphemisms arising from unease. The classical languages do not often substitute a descriptive adjective for the name of something too alarming to be mentioned, unlike our ancestors who refused to utter the real name of the bear and called him 'the brown one' (the original meaning of German *Bär* and English *bear*). The Latin word *serpens*, 'the creeping one', for the snake, is perhaps an exception. But all mankind shrinks from the hateful facts of illness and death, and all men try to avoid speaking of them too bluntly. Particularly inexplicable diseases might be given a name expressing reverence: the mysterious nature of epileptic fits led early Greeks to call epilepsy 'the sacred disease'. In the fifth century BC we find angry intellectuals writing books to argue that it is no more sacred than any other disease, and has in reality perfectly natural causes. In Latin we find 'sacred disease' used of disfiguring skin conditions. In both languages, blunt expressions for sickness are often replaced by words meaning weakness, lack of strength: that is the origin of our words 'invalid' and 'infirmary', both derived from Latin expressions which spoke of disease simply as weakness. As in English, too, one could say at Rome 'I am worried about Fannia's health', meaning her ill health, her lack of health: the word *valetudo*, 'health', from the same root as the English words 'valiant' and 'prevail', meant originally a flourishing condition—not something to worry about, except that it is better not to mention ill health at all, so that even in the context of anxiety one prefers to use a word of cheerful colouring.

Death above all, the intolerable insult to all who live, the reminder of what we all prefer to forget, was infinitely productive of evasive language. The Latin for a death-bed would translate literally as a 'bed of life'. In both Greek and Latin a common way of saying 'if I die' is 'if anything happens to me'. As in English, those slain in battle 'fall'. Others are said to migrate, or to depart, or to 'yield to nature', to 'pay the debt due to nature', to 'breathe their last', and so simply 'to breathe out', *exspirare*—whence the English 'expire'. When traitors were put to death at Rome, the announcement was made in the form of saying 'they have lived'—an elegant way of avoiding the ugly verb of killing or dying. We find Cicero speaking of death in the following terms: 'to fall asleep in the midst of the sufferings of life, and with eyes closed to be lulled in everlasting slumber'. A very common expression was 'to meet one's allotted day', abbreviated by constant use to the pregnant simplicity of 'to meet' (*obire*, whence the English 'obituary'). A dead person (in English 'the dear departed') can be spoken of in Greek as 'the blessed one', or even as 'the hero': attempts to bring into ordinary language optimistic ideas about the posthumous fate of the dead.

In both Greek and Latin the normal word for the conduct of a funeral was to 'carry out' the dead, and a funeral was a 'carrying out': the gloomy goal of the carrying was not expressed. In Greek one could avoid being precise by using a word which meant 'taking care of', or by talking of 'the due ceremony'. In Latin a common word was *exequiae*, which strictly meant 'the cortège which follows'—in this case, which follows the corpse. It was so regularly used in this special sense that it gives us the evasive English word 'exequies', itself an expression used in that elevated and rather shifty style which seeks to conceal the ugly object behind a screen of elaborate Latinities.

We have seen that those put to death at Rome were euphemistically said to 'have lived'. Punishment itself is often referred to as 'taking notice of' the culprit: 'taking notice of a man in the ancestral manner' was a formula meaning capital punishment. The Romans did not use the word 'execution' to conceal the reality of killing, leaving that refinement, like Stalin's favourite 'liquidation', to modern times; but the phrase 'lead away to punishment' was so regular that we find the simple 'lead away' used—'the prisoner was then led away'—to include his being duly beheaded. An irreverent comparison would be with the Chicago phrase 'to take someone for a ride': in each case the spotlight falls on the innocent journey, not on its deadly conclusion, and a sinister resonance is perceptible behind the urbane words. In Greek we often meet expressions for killing which are deliberately abstract and high-sounding: 'dispose of', 'dispatch'. The man responsible for carrying out death sentences was regularly called by the vague and plausible designation of 'the public servant' (*dēmios*).

Death reminds us that beneath our refinements and despite our aspirations we are condemned to the life of the body, undignified and mortal. No less pointed are the reminders which come to us from the physical processes of sexuality. It is sometimes said, by progressively minded agnostics, that before

Christianity came along and made people feel guilty about sex,
there were no obscene words. That is, of course, quite untrue:
both Greek and Latin contained, long before the birth of Christ,
words whose function was to be obscene, and which could only
be used in contexts and companies where obscenity was acceptable. That being so, they needed to have euphemisms as well, for
use elsewhere. The poet Martial wrote an epigram in which he
says to an acquaintance: 'Your expression and your speech are
so modest—I'm really surprised you have managed to become a
father.' Cicero wrote a letter about obscenity and euphemism to
a friend who had used a coarse word in a letter to him. He plays
with the paradox that some actions which are really wrong and
shocking can be discussed without any impropriety, while
others which are in themselves innocent or even desirable can
be mentioned only euphemistically.

'To start a family' is a most respectable phrase: fathers ask their sons to
do it. But they can't bring themselves to call the act of starting it by its
name . . . If we say of someone, 'He strangled his father', we don't say
'Forgive my language', but we do if we are telling some scandal about a
loose woman.

Cicero adds that a heroine in a tragedy can say 'When I was a
virgin Jupiter forced me' (quoting a line of verse), and observes
' "Forced" is well said: if she had used a different word,
everyone would have been outraged.' We can compare the effect
of substituting a four-letter word when Donna Elvira, in *Don
Giovanni*, complains that the Don 'deceived' her. Tragedy,
like grand opera, is a convention which will not tolerate
crudity—though there were high-minded people, then as now,
who argued that obscenity was a sham, and that things should
always be called by their blunt names. Then as now, that
remained a minority view. Another point which Cicero makes
is that the distinction between euphemisms and obscenities is
arbitrary and changes with time. 'Our ancestors called a tail a
penis, and a paint brush is called a "penicillus" because it is like
a tail; but now "penis" has become an indecent word.' The letter
strikes a modern reader as raising very much the sort of points
that a broad-minded but not violently modern man of letters
might make on the subject today; it would still provide the
material, and the tone, for an article in one of the quality Sunday

papers. Like such writers nowadays, Cicero amuses himself with the contradictions and absurdities contained in the idea of obscene language, but concludes 'for my own part, I shall keep my vocabulary as clean as Plato's: that is what I am used to. That is why I have written to you in guarded terms, on a subject where some thinkers say we should call a spade a spade.'

There are euphemistic expressions which aim to avoid impropriety, and there are others which are meant to draw attention to it. The former category includes such decently vague expressions for the sexual parts in Latin as 'the loins', 'the member', or 'the thigh': ' "the thigh" signifies the business of marriage,' says St Jerome, grimly. We find such phrases as 'to be with' a woman, or to 'converse' with her, used to convey intercourse. In Greek, the early epic, a notably chaste form of poetry, regularly uses for lovers the elegant periphrasis 'They were united in love and sleep'. In Latin *amica*, 'friend, girl-friend' normally means 'mistress', while in Greek *hetaira*, with the same meaning, came to signify 'prostitute'. Sometimes an expression intended to be decent finished up as a joke. A Roman orator, having to refer to a freed woman allowing her former master sexual favours, used the phrase 'a dutiful act'. This was found so funny by his audience that for some time, we are told, the words 'duty' and 'dutiful' were in regular use to refer to sexual activities: 'He is very dutiful to her', and so on.

On the other hand, there is enormous wealth of expressions which aim to underline the reality and make it vivid. The metaphor of riding a horse was regularly used in Greek to refer to intercourse with the woman on top; that is what Aristophanes is getting at when a chorus of men say 'A woman is at home on horseback: she never falls off when her mount is at the gallop.' Other forms of athletics could serve the same purpose. The delights of peace and sexual indulgence are enthusiastically listed in his play *Peace*:

And tomorrow you can have some fine sporting events. First wrestling: you can throw her down on her side, force her to her knees and bend her over, go to it manfully, no holds barred: hitting, gouging, using all your limbs. Then the next day will be for the horse races, where one jockey tries to go faster than the next, and the chariot racing—chariots overturned on top of each other, gasping and panting as they come together, while others lie all stiff, losing their grip in the last lap . . .

When the women in the *Lysistrata* take their momentous oath
to abstain from sex until the men of Greece put a stop to the war,
two of the clauses are: 'I will not stretch up my slippers towards
the ceiling—I will not stand like a lioness over a cheese-
grater—', and we are in no doubt what the things are that they
are forswearing. At the end of *Peace* the hero celebrates a
wedding with a glamorous female, and the chorus sing with
him:

> What shall we do to her?
> What shall we do to her?
> We shall harvest her—
> We shall harvest her . . .
> You shall both live happily, free from trouble, picking figs together.
> His is large and thick:
> Her fig is sweet.

All this is in a way euphemistic, but the point is (of course) to
linger on the matter and to visualize it fully, not to keep it out of
sight. The same goes for the countless places where 'knocking',
'digging', 'ploughing', and such metaphors are developed with
more or less enthusiastic and elaborate detail.

A very early example of euphemistic sexual language came to
light ten years ago, when the dry sands of Egypt yielded a
papyrus bearing most of a lost poem by one of the great poets of
archaic Greece, Archilochus (about 650 BC). The poem, which
very much shocked one of its first editors, is a narrative by the
poet of his seduction of a girl. Part of his pleasure in the episode
is that he is able to say some very nasty things about her
sister—'she is past it, and debauched, too,' he tells the girl, 'and I
like you much better'. In the following passage he assures her
that he will limit himself to coitus interruptus: 'There are many
pleasures for young men apart from the divine thing: I shall be
content with one of them. . . . Do not refuse to allow me
beneath the threshold and the gates, my dear; I'll stop at the
grassy garden.' 'The divine thing' is evidently full intercourse;
the other euphemisms are transparent. The effect, again, is
anything but prudish. It is not modesty, either, which makes a
character in a Roman comedy put to another the question 'Did
the soldier's sword fit your sheath?' (*vagina*, one of those
euphemisms which have a great future before them), or a jealous

woman in a Greek mime ask her paramour 'Is it not enough for you to move my legs?' Delicacy, in such cases, is more memorably indelicate than crudity would be.

Excretion is another subject which decency preferred to veil; the Latin word *excrementum* means simply 'what is sifted out'—from the body, that is. Respectable Greek usage was to say 'go aside', 'step off the road', instead of using the coarse words which, of course, existed and were freely used in other contexts.

Sometimes the motive for avoidance of a word was exclusively stylistic, especially in Latin, where the High Style of self-conscious authors attached great importance to avoiding low or ordinary words. French literature has repeatedly shown the same tendency. The subject-matter of my last paragraph recalls a very extreme instance in the great historian Tacitus. He tells of miraculous cures performed by the Emperor Vespasian in Egypt. One was the restoration of sight to a blind man by the application of his spittle. Since so low a word would conflict with the dignity of history, Tacitus writes 'He implored the Emperor to be gracious enough to anoint his eye-sockets with the excrement of his mouth'—for *excrementum* was a large and abstract word. Shakespeare makes fun of the affected Don Adriano de Armado with just the same word in *Love's Labour's Lost*, making him boast of his intimacy with the King by saying 'I must tell thee, it will please his Grace sometime to lean upon my poor shoulder and, with his royal finger, thus dally with my excrement—with my mustachio . . .'. Tacitus also gives us the supreme instance of refusal to call a spade a spade. Telling of a Roman army hard pressed in Germany and forced to dig emergency fortifications by night, he says that in their hasty retreat they had 'to a great extent lost the implements by means of which earth is dug and turf is cut'.

We are here far from any question of superstition or taboo, far in fact from delicacy in the ordinary sense. It leads us on to the next great area of euphemism: the better-sounding word which slips the reality beneath the guard of the audience, the euphemisms of deception and propaganda. Aristotle, who understood everything, knew all about it. He composed his marvellously straight-faced work *On Rhetoric* to show his readers how to use its artful devices. 'If all men were rational,' observes Aristotle wearily, 'there would be no call for rhetoric; but since they are not, this is how it works.' Near the beginning of the book he sets out in analytic form the simple technique of misrepresentation. 'To discredit the cautious man, we can call him cold and calculating. . . . To commend the simpleton, we can say he is frank; the man who is insensible to ill-treatment we can call forgiving; the insanely violent can be called honest and natural. The spendthrift can be called generous, the pig-headed shall be called dignified. And most people', he adds wryly, 'will believe us.'

Such remarks call to mind the fields of politics and advertising, but ancient writers extended the idea to the mind of the lover, too. The poet Lucretius has a striking passage on the folly of passionate love. Men who could escape the snare prefer to trap themselves, ascribing to their sweethearts fantastic perfections which the ladies themselves are well aware that they do not possess. Lovers are blind, and turn their mistresses' defects into beauties by giving them false names.

A girl of dark complexion is called 'honey-golden', a slattern who neglects her toilette is 'natural'; if she is muscular and wooden she is 'a gazelle'. A squat and dwarfish girl is 'one of the Graces: good things come in small parcels'. The unwieldy giantess is 'majestic'. If she is inarticulate and stammers, she 'has a pretty lisp'. She is mute: he calls her 'bashful'. She is a fiery, spiteful gossip: he finds her 'lively and brilliant'. Half dead from anorexia, she is his 'slender darling'.

And so on. In fact, the poet adds sardonically, many a time the besotted lover is leaving flowers at her door and hanging about kissing her doorposts, when if he could be suddenly admitted to find the unsavoury reality, 'he would cast about for a decent pretext to take himself off'.

Both in Greece and in Rome, the upper class, at the beginning of the period, had a virtual monopoly both of wealth and of power. With naive self-approval they called themselves 'the good men', *boni*, and 'the best men', in Greek *aristoi*: whence the English 'aristocracy', literally 'rule by the best men', a fossilized party slogan preserved unwittingly in a modern word. The nobles of Athens were officially known as *Eupatridae*: 'those with good fathers'. Quite consistently, conservatives of the early period refer unselfconsciously to the poor as 'the bad', 'the base'. In its extreme form, the ideology could take on a

racial, almost a zoological, character. Thus the Greek poet
Theognis, an expropriated and embittered aristocrat, speaks of
intermarriage between the old rich and the new rich (still 'base'
to him) in the following terms:

We aim to breed sheep and horses from the best stock: but a good man
does not hesitate to marry the base daughter of a base man, if he gets a
rich dowry with her, nor does a woman decline to marry a base man, if
he is rich. A wealthy husband, not a good one, is what she wants.
Money is all they respect, and good and base intermarry: wealth has
confounded the breed.

The Roman senators felt the same sublime self-confidence.
Cicero uses the words *boni* and *optimi* ('the good' and 'the best')
even in his informal letters to friends, as the titles of the
conservative faction. In a public speech he gives a definition of
his terms. 'Who are the good citizens? . . . All those citizens are
good, who are not criminals, nor naturally wicked, nor mad'
(this term in Cicero means 'radical') 'nor suffering from economic difficulties.' In fact, the supreme good for a Roman is a life
of dignified leisure: all those who are in favour of that are good
citizens. What we have here is, of course, a definition of goodness which calls for two things: to be good, a man must be well
off, and he must not disturb the political system. The only
goodness open to a really poor man (and Cicero would not
pretend to be seriously interested in the virtues of such people)
was to follow the policy of good rich men. Roman unself-
consciousness about identifying wealth and goodness went so
far that the Emperor Claudius, making a speech to a recalcitrant
senate in favour of admitting chieftains from Gaul as senators,
says quite simply that such has always been the wise policy of
Rome: 'Our ancestors admitted to the Senate the local magnates
of the Italian towns, good men and wealthy.' *Good men and
wealthy*: the Latin language endorsed the connection by extending the use of the word for 'wealthy' (*locuples*) to mean 'reliable',
so that it is perfectly natural in Latin to speak of 'a wealthy
witness' or even 'a wealthy authority' for the use of a word or the
text of a law, when reliability was the point. As for political
change, the Emperor Augustus gave the definitive answer to
that when he said 'Anyone who does not want the present state
of society changed is a good citizen and a good man.'

In Greece the lower classes did sometimes get the upper hand, but in Rome, despite intermittent attempts, they never did. That fact, together with the much greater Greek tendency to intellectual analysis and criticism, helps to explain why the old name of 'the good' was much less questioned and ridiculed, as a title for the aristocratic party, at Rome than in Greece. It is not of course peculiar to the ancient world. In one of Trollope's novels we find a publican who has always voted for what the canvassers tell him is 'the gentlemanly party', without having any clear idea even which party it is; and in eighteenth-century Scotland the Jacobites succeeded in getting their party called 'the better cause', so that David Balfour, in *Kidnapped*, says of himself, 'I'm a Whig, or little better'. But even at Rome we find some voices raised in criticism. The historian Sallust, at the opening of his work, described Cicero's generation as one in which a few powerful individuals built up unconstitutional positions of power, and 'men were called good and bad citizens, not because of any good they had done to the state—on the contrary, the more vastly a man was rich, and the more violent he was in crime, provided he was on the side of the status quo, the more he was called a good citizen'. From another side, the euphemistic accounts regularly given of Roman imperialism, as 'bringing the benefit of peace and of law to the subject peoples', are bitterly and memorably undermined by a speech which Tacitus puts into the mouth of a British chieftain, urging his countrymen to resist the Roman legions: 'They use the false name of imperial rule to cover robbery, slaughter, looting: they make a desert, and they call it peace.'

The Greek historian Thucydides gives a more profound analysis of the role of 'newspeak' and of euphemisms in class conflict. Describing the horrors of revolution and counter-revolution in the Peloponnesian War (431–404 BC), he wrote:

Civil war thus ran its course through the cities of Greece, and those places which came to it last, having heard about what had happened already, reached yet greater excesses in the refinement of their schemes, both in the elaborate cunning of their plans and the extraordinary ferocity of their reprisals. As for words, men claimed the right to impose new meanings on them. Reckless audacity was now defined as the courage of a good party man, while prudent hesitation was a mere cover for cowardice. . . . The advocate of violence was thought to be a trustworthy ally, while anyone who opposed it was suspected. . . . The cause of it all was the pursuit of power for the sake of greed and personal ambition: from these passions arose the violence of the contending parties. The party leaders everywhere had high-sounding slogans, on the one side political equality for the masses, on the other wise and moderate aristocratic rule; but they paid only lip-service to the common good and fought for their own profit. . . . So it was that neither side had any care for integrity, but those who succeeded in using fine words to cover some appalling act were highly admired.

The whole account of the supremacy of violent politics, of party loyalty and of terrorism, sounds so modern that it is no surprise to find Thucydides also describing the Spartans 'liberating' cities which did not want to be liberated by them, and which consequently had to be 'forced to be liberated'. It would not be easy to find a slogan or a euphemism in the revolutionary politics of the modern world which was not used and analysed in the fifth century BC.

My last department of political euphemism flourished in the later part of antiquity. Thucydides describes the use of high-sounding language to glorify rival parties and factions; under the Roman Empire there were no parties, all power being engrossed by the Emperor and his increasingly bureaucratic machine. The founder of the Empire showed the course which euphemistic language would take in future, when he chose for himself the extraordinary name Augustus. Its exact tone is hard to convey in English; it was a quasi-religious term, which might mean 'venerable', if that word did not evoke respectable English archdeacons. Nobody had ever had a name like that, and the naked reality of a despotism resting, ultimately, on military force, was brilliantly disguised behind it. We also find Augustus being addressed as 'Your Majesty'—in a world in which, not long before, quite ordinary Greeks had written letters to their kings which started simply 'Apollodorus the son of Athenion to King Ptolemy: Greetings'.

The inflation of titles and language from now on was constant. Augustus' successor, the Emperor Tiberius, told flatterers that he did not relish having his work referred to as his 'divine occupations', but soon everything connected with the Emperor became divine. In the fourth century AD the chief financial minister of the Empire was called 'the Count of the Sacred

Largesses'. Sacred, because concerning the Emperor; largesses, because the Emperor was in principle above the law, and anything he allowed to be paid to anybody was an act of spontaneous generosity, not the meeting of a justified claim or debt. The High Chamberlain was entitled 'The Keeper of the Sacred Bed Chamber' (he was addressed as 'Your Magnificence' or 'Your Greatness'). The Christian Emperor Theodosius says of the holders of this post, 'Their constant care of Our Godhead has placed them among the holders of the highest dignities'; the Christian Emperor Anastasius refers to 'the illustrious man who cares for the sacred chamber of Our Piety'. 'Our Godhead', 'Our Piety': these unclassical expressions are ways by which the Emperor alludes to himself. It only remains to add that the holders of such posts, like the Castellans of the Sacred Palace, could be eunuchs—a sort of person never accepted in the classical period. With the full gorgeous development of such language we have now left classical Greece and Rome behind us for the very different atmosphere of the early Middle Ages. And euphemism, we observe, can be carried no further.

Soft Soap and the Nitty-Gritty

ROBERT M. ADAMS

BECAUSE euphemism, which is an effort to make something sound specially nice, implies that unless prettified it will be specially unacceptable, a euphemistic formation can easily turn into its opposite. That would be a 'dysphemism', a coinage almost as ugly as what it describes.* Easy and obvious examples are found in the troubled area of racial names. For many years, 'Afro-Americans', 'the coloured', and 'Negroes' were prevalent as efforts, more or less high-falutin, to say what it is now accepted procedure to express by the word 'black'. The latest word is notably inexact, since most of the people it designates are different shades of brown, sometimes very light. (It is, to be sure, no more inexact than the word 'white' applied to a spectrum of faces from pinko-grey to swarthy.) But it is a 'genuine' word, implying in its very overstatement rejection of all efforts to mitigate or evade the basic fact; it is, in addition, 'our' word, not the word of outsiders. Recognizing the old euphemisms as really dysphemisms, it confronts and gets rid of them—as in certain social situations it is felt as an insult to use the vaguely honorific word 'lady', where the straightforward 'woman' is called for. (Try programming this into a computer!) There are youthful circles, I learn, which consider it normal to describe a parent as 'my toad'—an interesting euphemism-dysphemism which substitutes frank disgust for the ancient hypocritical professions. It may be ugly, is the implication, but it's honest; in fact, the proof of its honesty is its ugliness.

A leaven of falsity or avoidance is what causes the euphem-ism to exist in the first place; but, given the richness of modern vocabulary, using one word almost always involves avoiding another which might be thought uglier and in some judgements

---

* The coinage owes something to Bentham's 'dyslogism', found throughout the *Table of the Springs of Action*. Direct contraries of Bentham's word would be 'eulogy' and 'eulogistic', which have acquired meanings of their own.

more appropriate. For instance, a particular girl could be called slim, slender, willowy, lithe, svelte, graceful—or skinny or bony. Depending on one's taste in girls, or one's feeling about an individual girl, the first six adjectives might be felt as euphemisms for either of the last.

Occasionally there just is no convenient middle term between a vulgarity such as 'shit' and an artificial learned word such as 'faeces'. (Who ever stubbed his toe in the dark and cried out, 'Oh, faeces!'—or, alternatively, 'Oh, night-soil!'?) Depending on social context, one may have to choose the least unsatisfactory of two evils, or circumlocute, to an inevitably clumsy effect, circumlocution being nothing but euphemism long drawn out. Where there is an unwelcome truth to be hidden from others or oneself, euphemism flourishes, hence its special fondness for situations where codes or ideologies are under pressure. President Reagan, trying to obscure the fact that the MX missile is an awesomely destructive weapon, tries to title it 'The Peacekeeper'. Just so, 'liquidation' used to be a favourite Soviet term for the process of resolving political differences, until the world caught on to what it meant; and Hitler had a 'final solution' for the Jewish problem. 'They make a solitude and call it peace,' said Tacitus of his fellow Romans, noting an uncharacteristic Roman euphemism; it is still available for use in Cambodia. But since politics, above all international politics, is almost exclusively the art of muffling reality in fine words, it would be otiose to multiply examples of this order.

Most of the modern discredit attached to the notion of euphemism stems from use of the formula in service to the proprieties, 'Purity's aged grannams', as Meredith called them. Within the last twenty years a book was published which referred to Fanny Cornforth as Rossetti's 'housekeeper'; that was going half a dozen better than Fowler, who in *Modern English Usage* tells us that 'mistress' itself is a euphemism for 'concubine'. We have euphemisms for our euphemisms; the fact will surprise nobody who reflects on the panoply of euphemisms for referring to homosexuals (gays, fairies, pansies, homophiles, saturnians, uranians, queers, queens, faggots, flits, and so forth), most of which contain elements of derision and contempt, but which can also be thought of as terms for avoiding heavy expressions like 'catamite', 'sodomist', 'pederast', and all the variations to be played on 'buggery'. 'Toilet' is another concept for which there are so many euphemisms, including a French cousin the Vay-say, that one hardly knows which is not a euphemism for the many others.

If the root act of euphemism is suppression or evasion, and therefore untruth, a frequent precondition is some kind of elevation or pretension (whether moral, social, or stylistic) which the euphemism tries to sustain. Classical rhetorical theory, as formulated by Cicero, Quintilian, Longinus, and other legislators, distinguished three levels of discourse, the sublime, the humble, and the intermediate, and insisted that within each mode the style must be appropriate to the subject, the subject accommodated to the style. Thus it would have shocked a classical historian beyond measure to find Gregory of Tours, in a serious history, describing a posse pausing during a manhunt to take counsel: 'dixitque unus, dum equi urinam proiecerunt . . .'. Horses just don't *do* that in a dignified literary work. The same sort of shock, but actual not hypothetical, exploded a Paris audience in 1829 when the fatal word 'mouchoir' was first pronounced during an elevated drama, and a Dublin audience in 1907 when the word 'shift' first sullied, within the fane of a public theatre, the purity of Irish ears. * In all these instances, the elevated style would be expected either to suppress the offensive act or word, or else to circumlocute. 'Poetic diction' is the systematic application of euphemism to maintaining elevation of style, and since nobody to speak of tries to maintain an elevated style any more, this sort of euphemism would seem to be on the verge of obsolescence.

As far as imaginative writing goes, where the exalted style used to be not only accepted but required, this seems to be in

---

* After wrestling for more than half a century with the awful fact that a central property of Shakespeare's *Othello* is a handkerchief (directly equating with French *mouchoir*), the Parisian public was confronted with the fateful word itself in Alfred de Vigny's adaptation, *Le More de Venise*. Previous translators had all used euphemisms: Douin (1773), a bracelet, Butini (1785), a 'beau tissu, précieux et fatal', Ducis (1792), a *bandeau*. The *mouchoir* was impossible only on the tragic stage; more than a century and a half earlier, Molière had introduced the word into *Tartuffe* without rousing any protests —on that score, anyway.

The word 'shift' in Synge's *Playboy of the Western World* offended a rhetorical tradition claiming moral and patriotic sanction, but feeling was inflamed as well by religious and class antagonisms.

good part accomplished fact. For novelists and playwrights, as for movie-makers and constructors of soap operas who follow suit, it seems to have become a formula that every congenial, decorous, 'civilized' situation exists only as a whited sepulchre to be torn open amid shrieks of agony and screams of fury; thus one discovers the authentic, i.e. destructive emotions at the core of it. Wherever exposure is the aim and shock the technique, euphemism (which is placatory and concealing by nature) is bound to be inappropriate. And while this is not necessarily or universally the pattern in poetry, revulsion from an elevated or emphatic style is established there too, and euphemism, as a corruption of 'natural' language, is repudiated.

It is possible, I think, to write a major composition so consistently framed in euphemisms and other avoidance-terms that they will not be recognized individually as such, because they merge into the smear of the style as a whole. That extraordinary lingua franca of cheap nineteenth-century novels, in which most lending-library fiction and even some more pretentious works (as by Edward Bulwer-Lytton) were composed, amounts to an unbroken string of artificial and pompous phrases, amid which mere euphemisms pass almost unnoticed. Even contemporary paperback romances, while drenched in smarmy eroticism, generally slither so moistly through the language of innuendo that they have no use for euphemisms as such, or else submerge them in other forms of evasion and suggestion. For the lightly salacious pornographer, avoidance of the explicit and the crude goes readily with a high level of suggestive titillation.

Certain categories of fictional omission occur so often and go so generally unremarked that they hardly qualify as euphemism. Hardly any characters in fiction have occasion to excrete; in the world they inhabit, such acts would be grossly out of place. Neither do women ever menstruate; the process is no more mentioned in the usual fiction than at the usual dinner-party. In real life, all people secrete various disagreeable effluvia, which most of the time everybody quietly ignores; fiction, having almost total control of its environment, ignores them too, except for special, deliberately chosen effects. Euphemism would enter in only if language, admitting or suggesting the cacodylic hero or heroine, tried to prettify or cosmeticize the effect. You could call euphemism the deodorant of language; if so, a code of silent omissions would correspond to the private preliminary shower-bath that renders anti-perspirants unnecessary.

The reality behind both anti-perspirants and shower-baths is that we naturally stink, and in insisting on that fact much modern literature, which aims at counterstating the accepted conventions and mores, banishes euphemisms from the printed page. Yet in managing its everyday affairs, a complicated cosmopolitan commercial society, which discusses, legislates, and litigates publicly many matters that used to be determined by quiet tradition and domestic consent, needs more euphemisms than ever before. The social sciences, which for years have been trying to develop a sanitized, neutral, and preferably artificial vocabulary, serve as a major source of supply.* 'Senior citizens', for example, is a standard euphemism for the old. There is nothing wrong with the word 'old', or for that matter with the lesser euphemism 'elderly', except that both imply the proximate end of life. 'Citizen' is supposed to suggest active involvement in the affairs of society, and 'senior' the kind of respect given to senators and such. How pitifully far the terms commonly are from reality needs, alas, no demonstration. 'Upwardly mobile' is a similarly sanitized form of 'ambitious', as 'anti-social behaviour' illustrates the power of an indefinite abstraction to subsume numerous ugly particulars by packaging them in a phrase with minor varieties of mischief. The phrase 'different life-styles' practically enforces a non-judgemental attitude, whatever the alternatives one is comparing; 'life-style' itself assumes the individual isn't making any personal decisions, just following a pre-established pattern. The term 'exceptional children' is a particularly brilliant educationist's euphemism, because it lumps together those who are too dull, those suffering from physical handicaps, and those who are too

---

* A related but mostly separate field is the bureaucratic terminology for saying plain and obvious things (or concealing the fact that nothing at all is being said), in pompous polysyllables—gobbledegook, in short. Current flap words are 'the bottom line', 'escalation', 'confrontation', 'counter-productive', and 'revenue augmentation'. There are many, many others, and these are far from the most ridiculous. Whether in any given expression the dominant motive is self-importance or avoidance of uncomfortable reality determines whether it's simple pomposity or euphemistic pomposity.

brilliant to follow the regular curriculum. The democratic objective is to conceal such élitist categories of achievement as better and worse, so as to prevent damage to the self-esteem of the less competent pupil. Perhaps this makes a bit of sense at the early stages of the educational process, though in fact young children are too quick and too cruel in deciding for themselves which of their classmates are smart and which dumb, to be long deceived. Besides, in society at large the democratic mystique creates many purely artificial and heavily discounted terms of avoidance and glorification to prevent invidious distinctions. Thus garbage men become 'environmental engineers', and the sewage disposal plant is the 'waste water treatment facility'. It is the same principle on which, in Britain, garbage collectors are called 'dustmen', though dust is the least of the commodities in which they deal. From the depths of the Victorian era, Henry Mayhew recalls to us a discreet and elegant euphemism among the street paupers of his day: 'pure' collectors were collectors of pure dog-shit, used for various tannery operations. One understands their need for a phrase, however oblique, that would partially disguise their trade.

In despising the dishonesty of euphemisms, as we can and must, we run the risk of overlooking the many destructive and explosive potentialities of language. Though gossip in an infinitely pluralistic society is less deadly than it used to be a hundred years ago, it can still hang a tin can on a dog's tail and rattle him to death. In addition, high-pressure living has added new terrors to the psychopathology of everyday life. The hijacker holding a plane full of terrified passengers under the muzzle of a machine gun, the theatre full of people who must be told there is a fire behind the stage, the potential suicide teetering on a ledge far above the street—in these charged and volatile situations, the pressure on language becomes extreme. One wrong word spoken when a convoy of scabs is confronting a picket line, one foolish expression when racial feelings are inflamed, and men are fighting mad—and half a city may go up in smoke. Euphemisms must be among the expressions used on such occasions: there is no formula for them, and if they make themselves too readily felt as what they are, that's bad. So a natural tendency is to say as little as possible. When calming a restive horse or soothing a fretful cow about to kick over the milk pail, one is free to use a mere tone of voice, murmuring nonsense or something like. With people one must at least seem to make sense. So General de Gaulle, facing an enraged crowd of *pieds noirs* demonstrating against Algerian independence, told them majestically, 'Je vous ai compris', extricated himself from the situation amid cheers, and once in Paris did exactly what they did *not* want, and which he'd intended to do all along.

Euphemisms thus serve as verbal placebos; they are particularly frequent when the ill-timed provocation could expose one to instant retaliation. Sports figures are always careful to speak with respect, even admiration, of their upcoming opponents, however inept. Precautionary and placatory euphemisms include variations on the theme, 'They're a much better team than their record shows', and that minimal, threadbare uncompliment, 'They never give up'. Everywhere except in politics (where it's accepted practice to toot one's own horn as loudly as possible), false modesty is useful protection against overconfidence on one's own part and provocation of the opponent.

Though they commonly involve just language, euphemisms may be expressed in other sorts of signs, as when a hotel numbers its floors '11, 12, 12A, 14', etc., or omits room number 13 entirely. It is a euphemism of sorts when the price of a product is pegged at $9.99—'*under* ten dollars', as the commercials will say. The language of gesture may frequently, though it doesn't necessarily, involve euphemism, as in gestures warding off the evil eye or averting bad luck, which comfort the enactor without requiring him to face or profess a belief of which he is probably ashamed or afraid. Marble fig-leaves on statues and overpainted loincloths on pictures are visual euphemisms; Yahveh or Jhvh, the Tetragrammaton, was such a sacred and terrible name that it must not be pronounced, and eternal penalties were reserved for those who did so: Adonai was substituted as a euphemism, but most commonly mumbled in the public services to prevent anyone from hearing, still less understanding it.

Polite applause at a musical concert one didn't really enjoy, but which showed good will on the part of the performers, is a generally accepted form of social evasion—anywhere but in the opera house at Parma; so is the adjective 'interesting', or one of its many devious equivalents, when one is buttonholed in a gallery by the artist demanding to know what one thinks of his work. Placebo answers to awkward questions are legitimate escape-hatches; but the non-statement may have aggressive aspects too. Pornographic film advertisements ostentatiously decline to list the title of the skin-flick presently showing, on the score that it's too raunchy, too offensive for the public prints. That being just what the owners know their customers want, avoiding real words enables them to have it both ways. And from this moral highland, we look out on the tumultuous ocean of commercial sharp practice, with its 'pre-owned' automobiles (in the last stages of disintegration), its 'cosy' houses (the size of a postage stamp), its 'natural' or 'organic' foods (distinguished from others only by the exorbitant price) and its '40 per cent off' (off what?) sales. Folk wisdom enshrines warnings against many of these euphemistic formulas, as in the excellent advice never to eat in a restaurant that advertises 'home cooking', never to play poker with a man known as 'Doc', and never to buy a used car from a man calling himself 'Honest John' or the equivalent thereof.

Special interest groups require special vocabularies, sometimes active formulas, sometimes avoidance devices, to urge their point of view without presenting it. Stores in America seem to vie with one another in seeking euphemistic variations on the blunt old 'No Smoking' sign. 'Please try not to smoke' is one plaintive formula; 'Thank you for not smoking' assumes you have already obeyed instructions you have not yet received; and 'Our customers thank you for not smoking' puts the whole responsibility on some hypothetical customers who (for all anybody knows) may themselves be sheepish, brow-beaten would-be smokers. The new puritanism implicit in the women's movement shows itself, among other places, in a demand for fresh euphemisms, new restrictions on the traditional English vocabulary. You cannot refer to any female over the age of three as a 'girl'; indeed, even under the age of three, it's better described as a 'child'. You cannot refer to the 'chairman' or even the 'chairperson' of an organization; male, female, or *tertium quid*, it must be the 'chair'—which is not so bad, considering that some of them might just as well be pieces of furniture. You cannot mention 'bluestockings' for literary ladies, even of an age when the term was commonly accepted;

you cannot intimate that Henry VIII found Anne of Cleves physically unattractive, since this is treating her as a 'sex-object'. Marxist or would-be Marxist historians have their taboos and fetishes as well, in equal quantity and of equal grossness. One cannot use the standard eighteenth-century word for a violent crowd, 'mob'—rather, one must circumlocute, periphrase, or euphemize to 'the people', or 'the working class', expressions which don't mean the same thing at all. The same ideologues object to any expression implying disapproval of the Paris massacres of September 1792; large numbers of royalist or accused royalist prisoners were dragged from their cells and murdered out of hand by vigilante gangs. Apparently the proper name for this process is 'people's justice', or something like that.

In the euphemistic expression 'that's a lot of bull' (to make an easy transition), we recognize the operation of that synecdoche where the whole is asked to stand for the part; in a whole range of softened expletives, from 'darn' and 'drat' to 'Jiminy Christmas' and 'by Jove', we recognize deformation. In the 'bl' combination which gives us 'blasted', 'blooming', 'blighter', and 'bloody' we must have something like onomatopoeia at work. (The sound of the word does duty for any sense it might have, as in the 'bleep' which designates an obscenity erased from a tape. Even 'blessed', directly opposite in overt meaning, is sometimes co-opted, because of its sound, to the services of profanity—the ultimate euphemism.) Foreign languages used to, and occasionally still do, provide evasion devices. Latin was retained in translations of ancient texts when one wanted the reader to work so hard deciphering it that all obscene pleasures would be obliterated by the labour of translation. French can also be used to circumlocute English tongue-tiedness in expressions like *ménage à trois* or *double entendre,* and Dickens uses the foreign idiom to bury a faecal joke in the name of Mr Murdstone. Foreign languages reciprocate sometimes by using English expressions where the explicit term in their own tongue would be either unrespectable or illegal. There are cities in Mexico where the expression 'Ladies Bar' is euphemistic for 'whorehouse'. *

---

* 'Whorehouse' has a tease-fascination for Americans. There is a not-inexpensive restaurant in my town called the 'Ore House', and a record shop known

Emerging social customs create situations for which there really are no words other than euphemisms. In modern America, it is a stock dilemma what to call the young man who shares an apartment with one's daughter, or the young woman with whom one's son happens to be cohabiting. 'Lover' and 'mistress' imply high passion where often enough a dominant concern is economy; 'room-mate', 'companion', and 'friend' ignore the sexual component entirely, they are euphemisms simon-pure. Some semi-humorous acronyms have been proposed, but none really satisfactory; the term which finally meets the need may be a euphemism to start, but it will not long be felt as one. If shacking-up persists as a custom, the normal word will have to be created, no doubt with satellite euphemisms and dysphemisms around it. The malady syphilis went through a long search for a proper name, various nations and cities all attributing it to one another, analogies with the smallpox asserting their claim, lues and buboes being suggested (no doubt) by the plague. Only the accident of Fracastoro's erudite pastoral contributed the 'normal' English name of the disease, more than 200 years after this affliction first appeared in the West. (The poem itself was written in 1530; *OED* dates the first appearance of the word in English as 1718.) In fact, 'syphilis' is a rather remote and allusive euphemism, without even the poor excuse that 'St Vitus's dance' has to be the popular name of chorea (prayer to the saint was said to cure it) or that St Cecilia has to be the patroness of music (she was notably incompetent at it).

'Chrétien'—Christian—was a kindly euphemism at first for the goiterous idiots who during the Middle Ages inhabited the high Alpine meadows; they too, the word implied, were members of the Christian community, God's sacred simpletons. Corrupted, adapted to English, and turned to dysphemistic ends, it became 'cretin', a term of generalized abuse for the stupid. When she was thought to possess occult powers, the name of 'witch' may have been a kind of placatory euphemism, meaning 'the person who knows'. As time and competition diminished the witch's prestige, her former euphemism dwindled to a term

as the 'Warehouse'. Flirting with the taboo word apparently makes the name of an establishment particularly memorable; the accepted euphemism in places like Nevada is, I believe, 'Guest Ranch'.

of contempt. Some violations of the taboos cut so deeply against the grain that there is no way to euphemize them. Though we have many alternative ways to take the edge off words like 'murder', 'robbery', and 'fraud', there are no current euphemisms for 'parricide', 'rape', and 'incest'; perhaps in the happier non-judgemental society to come, the gentler formulas will be invented and domesticated.

Evidently, it's better to think of euphemisms as a variety of processes rather than a collection of expressions; and, given the variety of human judgements, it's more than likely that one man's euphemism will be another man's dysphemism. Once in Japan, I attended a concert of gagaku music with a Japanese couple; at intermission, they asked what I thought of it, and with some hesitation over the implied dispraise, I said gently that I thought it was very melancholy and a bit monotonous. They were enraptured. 'Indeed, indeed it is,' they cried, 'Melancholy and monotonous, just so!' And it was clear I could not have paid a higher tribute. Proust's Albertine was an animated euphemism, and it's not hard to think of novels, from *Tom Jones* to *Felix Krull*, where a love affair serves as a euphemistic cover for social ambition. Petrarch used Laura in good part as a euphemism for poetic fame, and poor Charlotte Haze was a social euphemism used by Humbert Humbert to mask his pursuit of her fatal daughter. A living euphemism is sometimes known by the alternative name of a 'stuffed shirt'.

So prevalent and protean is it, that one could argue that euphemism is an essential element of a pluralist society. My particular bent (line of interest, moral slant, or intellectual commitment) is repugnant or ridiculous to others, as theirs are to me. Probably I can learn to tolerate their idiocies; what is much harder to appreciate is that they, in their folly, are politely tolerating me. Euphemisms not only soften disagreeable qualities of the outside world, they may be used to smooth asperities of our own egotistical judgements—thereby keeping us out of jail and on bearable terms with our like-them-or-not associates. The abuse of the process is weaseling, waffling, and something very close to straight lying; its proper use lies in fostering that mutual consideration which underlies civilized conduct and conversation.

Yet a pluralistic society deeply aware of the fragility of its own

conventions—challenged as they have been by wars, holo-
causts, ideologies, social breakdowns, class conflicts, and the
abiding mistrust the society has earned by its endless capacity
for deception and self-deception—cannot help being uneasy in
the presence of euphemisms. That, I suppose, is one rationale
for the present volume. The subject cries out for analysis, and
the question it poses is basic. How do we distinguish the
fraudulent from the authentic euphemism, the specious moral
pickpocket from the considerate and soft-spoken idealist? Since
in their pure form both types are relatively infrequent, the
permutations and combinations are what we must deal with;
and here I confess to feeling the study of language does not help
much. The mind and the intentions behind it are far subtler
than the verbal makeshifts and stuttering formulas with which
we try to define its devious workings. Milton said it once and for
all:

> For neither man nor angel can discern
> Hypocrisy, the only evil that walks
> Invisible . . .

Sex and Euphemism

JOSEPH EPSTEIN

IN the beginning was the Word. There followed, at an un-
determined but one assumes decent interval, private, harsh, and
dirty words. Invention here being the mother of necessity, the
need for euphemism arose. Nowhere could this need have been
greater, or more evident, than in the realm of sex. Euphemism,
so well worth decrying in almost every other sphere of life, is in
the sexual sphere heartily, happily, one is ready to go so far as to
say heathily, welcome. There are times and places where it will
not do to call a spade a spade, let alone other things other things,
and sex surely is one of them.

Remove euphemism from the realm of discourse about sex
and one is left with two possibilities, neither of them very
pretty. One is to speak about it clinically: genitalia, pudenda,
vas deferens, reproductive organs, and all that. The other is to
speak not so much plainly as profanely: to let, so to say, the
most freely used Australian adjective and related nouns and
verbs fly.* There is also the loathsome prospect of speaking in
code, as is sometimes done by coy lovers who christen their
private parts with font- or surnames, and thus utter, as I seem to
recall of a character in a wretched novel whose title and author I
knew years ago and have successfully blocked out, lines such as:
'Will Mrs Featherstone be at home and pleased to receive my
man Andrew this evening?'

Many people have felt—and no small number doubtless still
do feel—that the subject of sex is best dealt with by silence, the
ultimate euphemism. Still, at all times in literature—from
Petronius to Rabelais to the Earl of Rochester to the Victorian

---

* Possibly this instance of ascribing embarrassing phenomena and deplorable
practices to nations other than one's own (Dutch courage, the French disease,
the English vice) needs a word of explanation. It appears that a former captain of
the Australian Davis Cup team admitted in a recent interview that he had had to
fine his players for throwing their rackets about and employing 'the most freely
used Australian noun'. *Ed.*

pornographers to Henry Miller to the work today of nearly every contemporary novelist—silence on the subject of sex has been broken, and is unlikely to be restored. Sex throughout history has perhaps been on most people's minds, but in this century it has increasingly been on almost everyone's tongue as well. Philip Larkin might write:

> Sexual intercourse began
> In nineteen sixty-three
> (Which was rather late for me)—
> Between the end of the *Chatterley* ban
> And the Beatles' first LP . . .

but Freud long before made it difficult to keep the silence on sex; and Freudianism, if not Freud himself, put paid to sexual reticence for all but good. Permit me to quote an American blue eminence, Mr Gay Talese, author of a participatory journalistic study of the sexual revolution, a work entitled *Thy Neighbour's Wife*, who has remarked: 'Sex is so very important; it is probably the most important thing. What is more important? I know of nothing.' Mr Talese's wisdom may be in doubt; his sincerity, never.

How does one talk about this 'most important thing'? The range of possibilities is very great. Sex may be spoken of tenderly or toughly, lyrically or lasciviously, beautifully or brutally, and in all these various ways by the same person on the same day. Because sex can evoke many moods, it requires many distinct vocabularies. This wasn't, of course, always so. For the greater part of the vast history of humankind talk of sex, of bodily love, was distinctly out of bounds. Certainly it was not permitted in polite society; that one could not speak of it there was one of the things that made polite society, well, polite. Talk of sex, when it was talked about at all, tended to be confined to intimate diaries or to blushing utterances made in a physician's office. I recall some years ago coming upon a medical encyclopaedia, published in the United States round the turn of this century, in which the article on masturbation appeared under the rubric 'The Secret Vice'. All sex, though, then seemed, if not a vice, clearly a bit of a secret—D. H. Lawrence's 'dirty little secret'.

Sex is a secret no longer. The unspeakable is nowadays speakable—and spoken. Not to speak of it with a fair frequency is felt to be in the non-speaker a mark of being, in a phrase of the day, 'uptight' (itself, I gather, a vaguely sexual euphemism referring to the condition of one's sphincter). In his article on euphemism H. W. Fowler could complain about the Victorians being 'mealy-mouthed' in using such phrases as 'nether garments' and 'unmentionables' and 'inexpressibles'. But what would he have thought about the female character in a novel I recently read who, noting that she was in her menstrual period, called it 'vampire time'?

The euphemisms of former days have in so many instances been traded in for dysphemisms in our own. My guess is that most people of my generation—I am forty-seven—grew up as I did, with silence on the subject of sex reigning at home and dysphemisms (the opposite of euphemisms) and slang acquired from colourful companions in the schoolyard. I am not quite in the case of the hero of Walker Percy's novel *The Moviegoer* who, when asked by his aunt if he had been intimate with his cousin on a long train ride, answered, 'Not very'; or in that of the bumpkin in an old joke who, when asked if he has slept with a fast woman (there's a euphemism) he had gone out with the night before, answered, 'Slept with her, hell. I didn't get any rest at all. We were up all night screwing.' But I have come to many sexual euphemisms late in life. Only a few years ago did I hear for the first time the euphemism 'an interesting condition' to describe a pregnant woman. More recently than that did I come upon the phrase 'a Boston marriage' to describe a lesbian relationship in which two women love and live with one another but do not engage in sexual relations. Here is a case of a euphemism doing dirty work of its own, and of a snide sort. I, for one, don't hold with the notion of a 'Boston marriage', or at any rate with calling two women who live together, no matter how great their love for each other, lesbians, if in fact they do not have sexual congress (another euphemism, I suppose).

Nor, in the sexual realm, is it always clear when a euphemism is a euphemism. The word 'servicing' is an example. 'Nothing wrong with her that a good servicing wouldn't cure' is the way it is most frequently used. 'I serviced her only two days ago' is another common usage. Obviously 'servicing' is a blunting of the most frequently used Australian participial noun, and hence in a rough sense it qualifies as a euphemism. Yet isn't 'servicing', as a metaphorical term that imputes a mechanistic nature to female physiology, even more brutal than the word it is meant to soften?

The equivalent term for 'servicing' for a male, at least in the United States, is 'having one's ashes hauled'. 'He needs his ashes hauled' is the standard sentence for a man thought to have gone too long without sexual intercourse. This phrase speaks to a supposed deep masculine inner heat that can only be burned out in the furnace of sex—hence those ashes, burned-out coals at the end of a sexual turn, being hauled off. Yet such a phrase demonstrates not only the difficulty of separating euphemism from dysphemism in the realm of sex, but how easily both can slide off into slang. Having one's 'ashes hauled' is clearly a slang phrase, but is it a euphemism or dysphemism? Difficult to say. What can be said, though, is that it does somehow seem an improvement upon 'He acquired sexual relief through fornication.'

'He acquired sexual relief through fornication.' That dreary sentence gives the clue as to why we need euphemisms, slang, even dysphemisms, and anything else we can call to our aid in order to discuss sex. For that sad sentence, straightly and drily phrased as it is, is a highly efficient reminder of that part of human life that is at bottom animal—and of which most of us, thank you all the same, would just as soon not be reminded. From the fact of our animality, of which sex for a good part of our lives can be a nagging reminder, euphemism, dysphemism and slang can afford relief; they permit us to talk about sex less directly. The editors of the *Dictionary of American Slang* are surely correct when they note: 'Slang words for sexual attraction and for a variety of sexual acts, positions, and relationships are more common than standard words. Standard non-taboo words referring to sex are so scarce or remote and scientific that slang is often used in referring to the most romantic, the most obscene, and the most humorous sexual situations.'

Although the editors of the *Dictionary of American Slang* refer to 'the most humorous sexual situations', I would say that almost all sexual situations are humorous—excluding only those that one is oneself involved in. Sex is of course often played as comedy—in certain plays, where the physical stuff takes place off stage, in the novels of such writers as Henry

Miller and Philip Roth, in every dirty joke ever devised—and it is perhaps healthiest when so played. Both animals and human beings feel the need to fornicate; one of the decisive differences between them is that human beings can, sometimes, laugh about it.

Certainly they tend to be more admirable when laughing about sex than when talking about it seriously. When we talk about sex seriously we tend to reveal ourselves as the pathetic, or lying, or hypocritical creatures we are. Consider the term 'open marriage', a euphemism that came into being roughly a decade or so ago through the agency of a popular American manual of sexual advice entitled *Open Marriage*. Stripped of its psychological sham, an open marriage is one in which the partners in a conventional marriage have agreed to give way to the need to copulate with anyone else who will agree to copulate with them. Much better for self-respect to call such an arrangement an open marriage.

Owing to the sexual revolution—itself a bit of a euphemism to denote the freedom from fear of pregnancy that the newer methods of contraception allowed as well as the loss of the power of religion against promiscuity—and to the women's liberation movement, a number of older sexual euphemisms have been marched off the stage and a number of new sexual euphemisms have been marched on. Perhaps no man has ever called his mistress that—'mistress'—to her face, but nowadays the term has an antique quaintness. (Nor has there ever been an equivalent euphemism for men.) 'Room-mate', which once clearly meant someone of the same sex with whom one was living, now no longer so clearly means that. 'Shacking up', once the slightly dysphemistic term for people of the opposite sex living together, is now gone. 'Living together' is now the standard term, although the US Bureau of the Census—and bureaucrats can generally be counted upon to coin good heavy-handed euphemisms—now calls the unmarried person with whom one lives one's 'spouse equivalent'. The most vivid euphemism—or is it a dysphemism?—that has come my way courtesy of the sexual revolution is 'hat trick': a term which in ice hockey means that a player has scored three goals in the same game, under the dispensation of the sexual revolution now refers to a man—or as easily to a woman—who has slept with three different women (men) in the same day. 'Progress', said William James, 'is a terrible thing.'

Historians of the Victorian era are fond of recalling a time when even the legs of pianos were covered. But today, to take a line from the lovely poem of Henry Reed, 'today we have naming of parts'. In a brief essay entitled 'The Lexicon of Prohibition', Edmund Wilson came up with one hundred and five different words and phrases for drunkenness. With a bit of patience one could doubtless come up with a list as lengthy for the male and female genitals and one quite as long again for female breasts. Dick, dong, prick, prong, quim, quiff, boobs, bazooms—private parts nowadays have numerous public names. Boff, bang, plank, hump, the most freely used Australian noun has no shortage of synonyms. The war against censorship is long over, though it is not altogether clear what the victory has brought.

Can it be that the losers in this war have not been the Grundys and the Comstocks but those front-line troops, serious writers, novelists chief among them? Asterisks used to do for what was deemed unseemly language in books, but today an asterisk in a book is as rare as a virgin in life. Malcolm Muggeridge is the last writer I know of to describe himself as 'a man of the asterisk generation'. Of course there have been writers before Muggeridge's generation who had forgone asterisks and chosen instead to mention, to spell out, the unmentionable. James Joyce, for one, whose *Ulysses* provided a landmark legal case in the anti-censorship war. D. H. Lawrence, who could be quite belligerent about such matters, was the General Patton in this war. Henry Miller was perhaps its Ernie Pyle. Since the late 1940s, though, the enemy has been clearly on the run. Such American novelists as James Jones, Norman Mailer and William Burroughs have handled that part of the operation known in military history as mopping up. Today it is apparently difficult to write a novel that is free of two or three hot and heavy sex bouts. Especially does one find, I won't say vivid but certainly elaborate, sexual description in the work of academic novelists. The stakes here go up all the time, and the trend is to greater and greater elaboration. A wag—I, actually—once wrote that the novels of the future are likely to be peopled with genitals sitting around discussing fashionable ideas.

The argument in favour of abandoning euphemism, of treating sex in an open and explicit manner, is well enough known. Sex is a part of life, if Freud is correct a centrally important part, and as such it, sex, calls for candour. To evade candour is to invite dishonesty and, worse, to court repression. Euphemism, in this argument, is both dishonest and ultimately repressive. Sex is a very human activity, and nothing human ought to be alien—that is, hidden, unspoken, pocketed away. To talk candidly, to write openly, about sex is a necessary freedom. And here we come to the knocking over of barriers. Something there is about the modern temperament that cannot tolerate a barrier; it must be pushed against, bulldozed, razed. How easily the barrier against candour in sex fell, or so it now seems; how in restrospect it seems to have been constructed out of marzipan. A few solid shoves and it toppled. Today one can say anything one likes of a sexual kind in print. Only the discretion of editors and publishers stand in the way—which is to say, one can say anything one likes of a sexual kind in print.

To speak autobiographically, here it must be said that growing up under the ancient sexual regime, before the revolution, brought certain benefits. A little smut then went a long way. More precisely, you had to go a long way to get a little smut. To Paris or Mexico City, in fact, where one could bring back those plain-type green-covered paperback editions of Henry Miller's novels published by the renegade firm of Olympia Press. Now one has to go almost quite as far to avoid it. Titillation, in those days, was still possible, whereas today disgust seems endemic. Our age, which treats war, genocide, and tyranny euphemistically, has in sex gone quite the other way.

Sometimes it seems a badge of modernity to speak uneuphemistically about sex. In the United States in recent years we have had the phenomenon of the publication of the journals of Edmund Wilson. I say phenomenon, for what is phenomenal about them is how uneuphemistically sexual these journals from America's most distinguished man of letters are. The closer to our own time Wilson's journals get—thus far publication is up to the 1940s—the less euphemistic they become. In the 1920s Wilson notes, 'I addressed myself to her bloomers'; by the 1940s he refers to 'my large pink prong'. Wilson goes beyond candour, beyond indiscretion, to describe sex with his own wife:

Would always run her tongue into my mouth when I kissed her before I had a chance to do it to her—and would do it so much and so fast that I hardly had a chance to get my own in. Would clasp her legs together very hard when I had my hand or my penis in her—seemed to have tremendous control of the muscles inside her vagina. Her frank and uninhibited animal appetite contrasted with her formal and gracious aristocratic manners.

This is a fairly mild example of the sort of thing that turns up in these journals. It is sex written without euphemism—and it is quite devoid of tenderness, is in fact chilling, even loathsome. What is of interest is that Edmund Wilson himself wished to see such material published. What, one wonders, did he think publication of his sex bouts, written so icily, would demonstrate? His prowess, his humanity, his modernity? After one has read a number of such Wilsonian passages, one is gripped by a single thought—the wish that one hadn't.

Whence does this need for explicitness about sex derive? Does it come from the fact that, the freedom to abandon euphemism now being available, it seems a shame not to avail oneself of it? Does it come from the notion that euphemism no longer, somehow, does the job? Allow me to bring a sexually euphemistic passage in evidence. It is drawn from *Homecoming*, the autobiography of an American literary man named Floyd Dell, in which Dell describes his first love affair (another euphemism). Dell writes:

There was a girl; and we kissed. And then, suddenly, I was in a realm more real to me than the world I had thought of as real—which had now become a shadow, a dream, something remote and dim. I was happy and free; not a literary editor; not a husband; only myself. All the values in my universe were suddenly transvalued. I felt like a wanderer, long absent in alien lands, who sets eyes again upon his native place. Why should I have ever imagined myself that stranger, worn that uniform? This, the realm of liberty, was one in which I could be at ease. There need be no effort here to be what one was not, only infinite sincerity of oneself to another; in love and talk and laughter. We made love happily and solemnly.

Does such a passage seem hopelessly old-fashioned—it was written in 1933—corny, prudish? At the risk of sounding an old-fashioned, corny prude, I must confess it doesn't seem any of those things to me. What I rather like about it is the room it leaves to the imagination. It is very earnest, of course, but then so does love tend to be. It could not, I am confident, be improved by additional detail recounting every chronicle of the crotch, saga of the sack.

In the positive, the glorious sense, the sexiest book I know is *Anna Karenina*, and it is all but shorn of sexual detail. A shoulder is described, eyes, posture, a uniform, tears. 'Anna felt as though she were sinking down. But it was not terrible, but delightful.' These sentences do not refer to a scene of sexual surrender, as they might if they appeared in a contemporary novel, but to Anna Karenina's thoughts about Vronsky as she rides the train back to St Petersburg on her return to her son and husband. There is a great deal, there is everything, at stake in the sexuality in *Anna Karenina*, but sex itself is oh so lightly, so artfully touched upon, hinted at in the novel's pages. It is so sexy almost precisely because it refuses to speak directly—uneuphemistically—about sex. It is sexy because Tolstoy, that instinctual and consummate artist, knew that the best pornographer is the mind of the reader, which in this matter required only the slightest assistance from him.

Did Henry James, whose whole art can be said to be that of euphemism, think much about physical love? The best researches into James's private life conclude that he himself never made bodily love. Yet it is difficult to imagine that a man, as one of his acquaintances once described James, 'so assailed by the perceptions', did not perceive this, too. More to the point, did he imagine his characters, to adopt another euphemism, 'in the act'? Are Chad Newsome and Mme de Vionnet, in *The Ambassadors*, lovers? Are the Princess and Paul Muniment in *The Princess Casamassima*? (In *The Golden Bowl* no doubt about such relationships remains, though the author still feels no need to supply slides.) From James we have nary a direct word, though sufficient reason none the less to believe that they are. Sufficient reason is all James provides—and it is enough. What happens to Isabel Archer after her return to Italy and her betraying husband, Gilbert Osmond, now for ever denied his conjugal rights (to speak once again euphemistically)? How easily she is imagined, long after the novel has been closed, alone and in her bed in her villa, night after night, and what a sad and necessary waste it seems! Henry James, the sexless novelist,

is in many respects the sexiest novelist of all—and further proof
that, in speaking and writing about sex, less can be more.

More, conversely, can be less. The American novelist James
Gould Cozzens was a writer who treated sex neither euphemistically nor dysphemistically but straight on. Yet to treat sex
straight on, as Cozzens must have known, was to treat it
dysphemistically—to make it seem worse than it is. A writer of
dark vision, Cozzens looked upon sex as a solid piece of
evidence arguing against humankind's hope for leading reasonable lives. The least reasonable man, in Cozzens's view, was the
man who set out to be reasonable. In this hopeless endeavour
sex was a sharp reminder of the human link with the animal,
with the irrational. Here, in his somewhat twisted syntax, from
his novel *By Love Possessed*, is how Cozzens makes his case:

His as much as hers, the supple and undulous back hollowing at the
pull of his hands to a compliant curve; his as much as hers, her occupied
participative hips, her obediently divided embracing knees, her parts in
moist manipulative reception. Then, hers as much as his, the breath
got hastily in common; the thumping, one on another, of the hurried
two hearts, the mutual heat of pumped bloods, the start of their uniting
sweats. Grown, growing, gaining scope, hers then no less than his, the
thoroughgoing, deepening, widening work of their connection; and his
then no less than hers, the tempo slowed in concert to engineer a
tremulous joint containment and continuance. Then, then, caution
gone, compulsion in control, his—and hers, as well!—the pace
unreined, raised, redoubled, all measurable measure lost. And, the
incontinent instant brought to pass, no sooner his the very article, his
uttermost, the stand-and-deliver of the undone flesh, the tottered
senses' outgiving of astoundment, than—put besides themselves, hit at
their secret quick, provoked by that sudden touch beyond any bearing
—the deep muscle groups, come to their vertex, were in a flash
convulsed; in spasms unstayably succeeding spasms, contracting on
contraction on contraction—hers! Hers, too; hers, hers, hers!

Less light, less light, to reverse the Goethean request for more.
Such a passage, without a single profane word in it, is extremely
repulsive—enough to put a virile man off his sexual feed for
quite a spell, enough to drive a refined woman into a nunnery.
But James Gould Cozzens had his purposes, and in writing about
sex as he did appears to have accomplished them.

It is not always clear what the purposes of other novelists are in placing elaborately described bouts of sex in their novels. It might be kindest to say that they are, in manifold senses, just screwing around. But I think these writers rather desperately need sex to stay in business as writers. It isn't that sex is all they know; it is merely that sex seems to be what they know best. To restrict myself to American novelists alone, I can think of three prominent figures who, but for the opportunity that the contemporary novel allows them to write about sex, would probably have to go into the dry-cleaning business: John Updike, Philip Roth, and Norman Mailer.

These three gents, to be sure, make quite different use of sex in their novels. For John Updike sexual descriptions often provide an opportunity for a metaphor-soaked, lyrical workout; outside, that is, the frequent sexual paces Updike puts his character Harry (Rabbit) Angstrom through, when it becomes lower-middle-class sex, plain spoken and snarly and nasty. Philip Roth plays the sex in his novels chiefly for laughs, but play it he does, over and over and over. While Updike can be by turns pretentious and loathsome, and Roth depressing while trying for laughter, Norman Mailer, in his handling of the sexual subject, is unconsciously comic (not, I hasten to add, that reading him is likely to cheer anyone up). Sex almost always provides the big moments in Norman Mailer novels; sex, somehow, is always a challenge, a chance for triumph, an over the hill, boys, walk on the moon, bullfight, though when it is over what one mostly remembers is the bull. Quotations on request.

Suffice it to say that in contemporary writing about sex, the stakes rise all the time. We are not talking, and haven't been for some years, about your simple Sunday afternoon off the Grande Jatte fornication. Not only must sex in the contemporary novel grow more regular but it must become more rococo. Thus Mr Updike presents us with an activity known euphemistically as California sunshine (no explanations on request), Mr Roth has a woman in his most recent novel the contents of whose purse include a 'nippleless bra, crotchless panties, Polaroid camera, vibrating dildo, K-Y jelly, Gucci blindfold, a length of braided velvet rope'. Mr Mailer, relying on fundamentals, concentrates on heterosexual sodomy. Ah, me, the literary life.

I have recently been pleased to discover my own ideas better formulated than I myself have been able to formulate them at the hands of a writer I much respect, the poet Donald Davie. In *These The Companions*, a book of memoirs, Donald Davie, at sixty, writes that, though he feels he understands a good deal about the power of love, he also feels he has come to understand the hopelessness of writing about it, except through indirection of the most literarily tactful kind.

But I am less confused about this than I used to be. For I have come to see clearly that there is no way to reconcile the essential and precious privacy of the amorous life, with the unavoidable publicity of print. Or rather there is indeed one way, and of course it is the time-honoured way; by euphemism, which is to say circumlocution, which is to say figurative language. This is what makes Yeats, not Joyce nor Austin Clarke, the most erotic of Irish writers. The handful of poems that he wrote for his wife under the figure of King Solomon addressing the Queen of Sheba are more audacious, under the thinly transparent but necessary veil more 'outspoken', even (if it comes to that) more titillating, than the most notorious passages of *Ulysses* or the most outlandish late poems by Clarke. When Yeats read *Lady Chatterley's Lover* he said that each of the famous four-letter words was like a hole burned in the page; and in saying so he voiced no prissy constraint, but was rather making a technical point, surprised to see so practised a writer as Lawrence falling into a novice's trap, trying to take an impossible short cut.

Are novelists in America and England, as is sometimes said of politicians, out too far in front of their constituents (or readers), or are they fairly representing them and their conduct in their novels? It is not easy to know. It is a tricky question of the kind of which came first, the sick chicken or the bad egg? This much, though, can be said: ours shall not be known as one of the great ages of reticence, especially about personal life. It has been said that many people in our day would sooner tell you about their sexual life than about their financial life. So many people now appear to carry their own psychoanalytic couch on their backs.

We have come a long way from the time when the word 'virgin' was not permitted to be printed in metropolitan newspapers, when syphilis and gonorrhoea (as H. L. Mencken notes in *The American Language*) were referred to as 'vice diseases', when words like whore, homosexual, rape, and sexuality were not used at all. Today, under the new dispensation, we have books with titles such as *The Love Muscle, The*

Sensuous Woman, *The Playboy Adviser*, and *States of Desire: Travels in Gay America*. Obviously, we have come a long way; the only question is, in what direction?

Today people tend to speak plainly or profanely about sex, its parts and their mechanics, and euphemistically about the benefits said to derive from the exercise thereof. As for those benefits, they are frequently described as 'fulfilling', 'growthful', and 'humanizing'; one tends, in these circles, less and less to have sex but to 'experience' it. The people I am talking about here refer to one another as 'feeling', 'caring', and 'loving' people. One of the marks that distinguish them is that they tend to go in for words—some of them euphemistic—whose meaning is harder to capture than a squid in a pool of molasses. Yet these same people have been known to speak right up about their 'clitoris', or 'prostate', and talk in unhushed tones about 'orgasm'. This odd combination of soft words and hard words appears to be at the heart of the sexual liberation movements of our day. These movements—the women's liberation movement, the gay liberation movement—tend to be confessional, anti-repression, and it nearly goes without saying anti-euphemism, except about ends and goals.

Oddly, a good deal of the language used in connection with homosexuality is euphemistic, or at least bordering on the euphemistic. Owning up to one's homosexuality has of course for a great many years now been referred to as 'coming out of the closet'; it is also sometimes said of such a freshly emergent boy or man that he has 'come out', a phrase reminiscent of the American débutante balls of another day, in which young women with social connections would appear formally in public for the first time and hence were said to be coming out. Euphemism becomes slangy, though, when Edmund White, author of *States of Desire: Travels in Gay America*, writes of the city of Cincinnati that 'It's a very sedate, closety city.' 'Cruising', a word that refers to searching around in bars and on the streets for homosexual mates, rides the line between slang and euphemism, leaning over in the direction of euphemism, in my view, because such a 'cruise' can have many a bump in it, including beatings and humiliations certainly not implied in that gentle floating word. I take it to be indisputably a euphemism, though, when it is said of a homosexual man who takes part in sado-masochistic activity that he is 'into leather'. In this realm the largest argument of all, of course, is about whether the self-selected word 'gay' is itself a euphemism. People who oppose it claim it is foremost a misnomer. Misnomer or not, it appears to have stuck, so that nearly all the other uses of gay must now depart. Still, the intention behind the choice of the word was surely euphemistic: the substitution of an agreeable or inoffensive word for one with unpleasant or offensive associations.

The women most ardently engaged in the women's liberation movement like to speak less euphemistically about sex. Women, they feel, have been [most freely used Australian verb simple past] over, and euphemism, they reason, may have provided the screen behind which this was done. Therefore they speak plainly about earthy things: about sex as part of the bill of human rights, about orgasm as an amendment to that bill, about measures of sexual reform to come. One can sometimes watch and listen to liberated women going on in this manner on American television chat shows, with very little diffidence. So little diffidence as is often involved in a wife speaking before an audience of millions about her most private activities can, the first two or three hundred times one witnesses it, provide a bit of a shock. Perhaps, though, it ought not to. We live, after all, in a sex-ridden time in which we have yet to establish a proper vocabulary for our deeds and desires.

Allow me a brief paragraph to back up my statement that we live in a sex-ridden time. It is not, I think, that people are more sex-driven in one age than another; it is instead that in some ages sex seems to be more on the mind than during others. If our euphemisms do not tell much about the quality of contemporary sex, our slang, I believe, does. Getting, sheer getting, seems to loom large in current sexual slang: getting it up, getting it on, getting it off, getting any? getting much? Meanwhile, in universities, for the first time in history, we have women's studies, which means that we have agreed to study literature, history, and society from the standpoint of gender—which is to say, sex. Again, no contemporary biography is considered complete until the subject's sex life is duly accounted for; and here sexual secrets are sought, and, sought arduously enough, often found. More and more the assumption in contemporary life is that sex looms larger and larger.

It is a truism that practice precedes theory, and language often precedes practice. In the language currently used to describe sexual conduct, a language whose most notable feature has been the defeat of the euphemism, both sexual practice and theory reveal themselves. Sexual practice has become easier, less guilty, and from the standpoint of pregnancy less hazardous; sexual theory now deems sex necessary, almost to the point of becoming a rudimentary biological function. As this has come into being, however, an older theory of sexual love has been withering and dying out: the idea—and the ideal—of love as Grand Passion, which derives from a combination of Christianity and Romanticism and which held sway through the nineteenth century. Under the ideal of the Grand Passion, love was thought sacred. Men and women could not talk about sex openly and uneuphemistically and still hold it sacred.

In a suggestive essay entitled 'Fashions in Love', which he published in a collection of 1929, Aldous Huxley remarked that the Christian and Romantic conception of sexual love seemed to have lost ground to a more scientific and psychological conception of sexual love. In his essay Huxley spoke of what was wrong with both conceptions. 'The older conception was bad,' he noted, 'in so far as it inflicted unnecessary and undeserved suffering on the many human beings whose congenital and acquired modes of love-making did not conform to the fashionable Christian-romantic pattern which was regarded as being uniquely entitled to call itself Love.' The new conception, itself the product of the campaign against old taboos and repressions, was also not without its defects. Huxley wrote: 'The new conception is bad, it seems to me, in so far as it takes love too easily and too lightly.' Talking freely about sex might go a long way towards shearing it of its 'guilty excitement and thrilling shame', yet Huxley thought the then current fashion in love-making was likely to be short, 'because love that is psychologically too easy is not interesting'.

Aldous Huxley believed that, with the older Christian-romantic conception of sexual love all but dead and with the new scientific-psychological conception terribly inadequate, it would only be a matter of time before a 'new or revived mythology' arose 'to create those internal restraints without which sexual impulse cannot be transformed into love'. Here

Huxley thought—recall it was the 1920s—that D. H. Lawrence's 'new mythology of nature' was a doctrine 'fruitful in possibilities', which, as we now well know, it hasn't proved in the least. Nearly half a century later, this new mythology, quite as tardy as Godot, has yet to arrive. While awaiting it, most people appear to pass the time sitting around talking all too frankly about—what else but?—sex.

Euphemism and Argot in France

RICHARD COBB

THE chief purpose of a euphemism is to present a situation, a person or an object in a more agreeable, more reassuring or politer light than would be afforded by the hard glare of reality or by crude, direct definition. The lexicographer Littré quotes the example of a working man, presumably an artisan, who, having completed the job for which he was engaged, approaches his *patron* in the hope of being paid. But he is careful not to mention money, tackling the problem obliquely: '*Monsieur a-t-il d'autres ordres à me donner?*' he enquires. *Patron* and *ouvrier* understand each other perfectly, the message has been received. A virtually perfect example of euphemism as a form of disguise or partial disguise, a discreet veil covering something best not named by its name, would be the expression used by Chateaubriand on the subject of the court martial, held at night, and the summary shooting of the unfortunate duc d'Enghien, after he had been kidnapped beyond the French border: an event that he described as *le dépêchement du Prince*, the hurrying-on of the Prince, a masterpiece of the low key.

But if we are to take a euphemism exclusively as an expression designed to clothe something in an ameliorative or lenitive light, we shall be obliged to omit from the discussion some of the most pungent and inventive specimens of popular usage, in particular those calculated to present somebody in a light as ugly as possible. We would lose much by not admitting such pearls as: *se noyer dans un crachat* (to drown in a gob of spittle, of a person who fusses about unimportant matters; cf. to make a mountain out of a molehill), *ne pas se prendre pour de l'eau de bidet* (not to take oneself for the bidet-water, of someone who has a rather high opinion of himself or herself), or *il croit qu'il a chié la colonne Vendôme* (he thinks he has shit the Vendôme Column, again of someone with an inflated estimate of his abilities).

As far as Parisian speech is concerned—and in Europe the language of capitals is always the most ingenious, the least respectful, and the most colourful—it is often difficult to draw a clear distinction between euphemism and slang. Where, for instance, should we place *valseur* (bottom), as cited by Robert Lageat in *Robert des Halles*: *elle était trop frappadingue du valseur* (she was too keen on wiggling her bottom); *dégrafée* (unzipped, for a woman of easy virtue); *uniprix* (for the sort of girl who goes in for beauty contests); *entrée des artistes* (the same part of the body as *valseur*); *baise-en-ville* (overnight bag, for certain occasions); *caleçonnade* (underpants, for the Palais-Royal variety of play: lover caught by husband without trousers); *cinquaseptier* (five-to-sevener, for a libertine who calls in at a brothel after work and before returning home); *pommade* (flattery); *bérésina* and *coup de Trafalgar* (a personal disaster); *rambuteau* (urinal: like *poubelle*, dustbin, named after a Prefect); *nostalgérie* (which Montherlant describes as the attitude of former *pieds-noirs* towards their former home); *tala* (Catholics, *ceux qui vont* à la *messe*); or *massachusetter* (to Americanize)? Similarly, *abîmer le portrait* (to damage the portrait, i.e. to hit someone); *téléphoner à Hitler* (visit the lavatory: cf. to phone auntie; more truly euphemistic forms are *les lieux d'aisance*, the places of easement, 'comfort station', or simply *les lieux*, and *aller où le roi va à pied*, to go where the king goes on foot); *avoir les Portuguaises ensablées* (to have the Portuguese silted up: where 'Portuguese' stands for oysters, and—because of their similar shape—the ears; i.e. to be deaf). I would be most unwilling to let them go simply because they might more accurately be classified as slang.

Both euphemism and slang represent forms of verbal inventiveness that are now fast disappearing from Parisian speech and will soon be only a memory. Robert Lageat is now in his mid-seventies. And of *les Trois Argotiers*, Albert Simonin (best known for his novel *Touchez pas au grisbi*) died in 1980, while Auguste Lebreton (*Du rififi chez les hommes*) and Alphonse Boudard must be in their seventies or eighties. Specifically Parisian forms of speech are dying as a result of the removal from Paris of the central markets and the dispersal over the whole area of Greater Paris of the humbler elements of the original population. There is little trace of inventiveness in the language of present-day *loubards* or teenage villains, or in the cruel age-groupings at one time adopted by conformist *lycéens*: *vestiges*, forty to fifty; *périmés* (expired, like a ticket) or *croulants* (crumbling), fifty to sixty; *son et lumière*, sixty to seventy; *monuments historiques*, seventy onwards—though even these are probably out of date by now. Both *loubards* and *lycéens* employ a language without memory, without antecedents, one that does not look back and is understandable only to a single generation. It is doubtful whether the present teenage generation could make anything of the vocabulary of Villon. So any study of French argot is, unfortunately, likely to be a study of archaisms—one suited, therefore, to *anciennistes*, or historians.

Much of the lightness and vigour of popular language has now gone out of French, to be replaced by the impenetrable and pretentious language of an authoritarian technocracy. Euphemisms have flourished in the neighbourhood of death; but there is something already funereal about the concern to fix them in a point of time. These days we are faced not so much by euphemism and slang as by a constant verbal inflation that, for example, drives out such relatively ancient names of departmental divisions as *Seine-Inférieure*, *Charente-Inférieure*, *Basses-Alpes*, *Loire-Inférieure*, and that makes of everyone a General or a Director. There is no longer any place for diminutives such as *Républiquette* (used pejoratively by Joseph Delteil in his novel *Jésus II*: '*Républiquettes à l'essai, sociétons de hasard . . .*') or *drôlette* (the phoney war of 1939–40). It seems that French is in the process of abandoning mockery and a saving sense of ridicule.

Euphemism must begin with the fact of death, the preliminaries to death, and the instruments of death. Death itself is *la camarde* (the flat-nosed); and there is the much older *trousse-galant*, something that takes off young men in their hundreds and generally refers to cholera or the plague. Death is also *la grande valdingue*, the big cropper, the heavy fall. The dead are *les trépassés*: gone beyond. To die is *casser sa pipe* (to break one's clay pipe, as it falls from the lips), *passer l'arme à gauche* (to transfer one's rifle to the left side), *avaler son bulletin de naissance* (to swallow one's birth certificate), and *souffler sa veilleuse* (to put out one's night-light). *Extrêmiser* (to administer the last rites) comes just before death. To be dead is *manger les pissenlits par la racine* (to eat dandelions by the root; cf. to push up the daisies). *Borlioliser* represents the preparation and burial of the deceased: *la Maison Borniol* is the prince of Paris undertakers. There are innumerable terms for killing: *refroidir*, *suriner* (to knife), *buter* (to knock down), *descendre*. *Verduniser* is to kill on a massive scale. One can be killed with a knife—*eustache, laguiole, lardoir, saccagne*—or one can be *revolverisé* by a *flingue* or a *riflette*.

The guillotine has been extremely well served: *la petite fenêtre* (the little window), *le rasoir national* (the national razor), *le raccourcisseur national* (the national shortener), and the pompous *le glaive* (sword) *de la justice* all date from the Terror of 1793–4. More recent expressions are *l'abbaye de Monte-à-regret, la Veuve* and *la Coupante*. To be guillotined can be *embrasser Charlot* or *monter à la butte* (though this is not *la Butte-Montmartre*). A street on the Right Bank, *la rue de l'Arbre-Sec* (the dry tree), preserves an ancient euphemism for the gallows. During the Revolution, the public executioner enjoyed the inflated title of *l'exécuteur des hautes oeuvres*, though he would probably have been happier with the old and menacing designation of *le bourreau*, from *bourrer*, to hit or pound. (*L'exécuteur des basses oeuvres*, by the way, was the less glorious title of the public torturer.) In the course of the last two centuries the executioner achieved the eminently respectable and rather romantic status of *Monsieur de Paris*. In the eighteenth century there had also been a *Monsieur de Rouen*, a *Monsieur de Lyon*, a *Monsieur de Lille*, a *Monsieur de Marseille*, a *Monsieur de Toulouse*; but the railways, a major instrument of centralization, put these gentlemen out of work, *Monsieur de Paris* taking the train, his machine (*les bois de justice*) placed under a tarpaulin on a special truck. He always travelled first class.

Euphemisms make good use of place-names, though they rarely carry the sort of tourist appeal that a local *syndicat d'initiative* might consider fit to put on a postmark (*Visitez Rouen, sa cathédrale, ses églises, ses musées*). I have already mentioned *verduniser*: before 1914 it referred to a process of water-purification, similar to *javeliser*, from Javel, a village now part of Paris, but after 1916 it acquired a grimmer meaning.

Enversailler (to sadden) is admirably suited to the most depressing town in Europe, with its wide empty avenues and its immense perspectives. *Limoger* (to sack, or at least to demote) derives from Marshal Joffre's action in 1914: he sent a large number of general officers, whom he considered incompetent, to Limoges, the town being sufficiently remote from the front. *Filer en Belgique* is simply to be on the run; the midnight train from Paris to Brussels, from the Gare du Nord to the Gare du Midi, was still known in the 1930s as the *train des assassins*. *Avoir l'air de revenir de Pontoise* (to look as if one has just arrived from Pontoise) is said of some simpleton who thinks he has just discovered the moon; ever since Villon, Parisians have had it in for Pontoise, no doubt because of the description, *Paris-près-Pontoise*. *Aller à la fête à Neuilly* is to put on one's best clothes: a reminder of one of the most popular of Paris fairs in the eighteenth century. *Se porter comme le Pont-Neuf* means to enjoy exceptionally good health with the likelihood of a ripe old age: *le Pont-Neuf* is in fact the oldest bridge in Paris. *Envoyer quelqu'un à Chaillot* (a village) is to send someone packing: not exactly the same as sending him to Coventry. *Bon pour Charenton* is said of someone who is clearly mad; those who have seen the play *Marat/Sade* will be familiar with the place of Charenton in Parisian topography. *Laguiole* (a bone-handled knife) derives from a small town in the Auvergne where such knives are made. *Une contremarque* (counterfoil, ticket stub, pass enabling one to re-enter a theatre) *pour Bagneux* or *pour Pantin* signifies a medical prescription—a pessimistic view in that Bagneux and Pantin are the two principal cemeteries in the Paris region.

Some expressions are outstandingly effective in putting a good face on things. *Être en villégiature* (to be on holiday in the country, to be taking it easy) is a charming way of describing one's sojourn in a prison. *Être dans les vignes du Seigneur* is the nicest possible way of referring to someone who is drunk. And, in a rather different class, *fragonarde* or *prix de Diane* is a flattering depiction of a pretty girl. There is even something affectionate, hinting at long acquaintance and shared domicile, about *gaspard*, the Parisian euphemism for rat, possibly from one of the Three Wise Men from the East.

Homaiserie, from a character in *Madame Bovary*, is a literary allusion to something ponderously self-evident; one could perhaps include *Pétainisme* in the same category. Some institutions are so terrible that it is better not to refer to them directly, as in the case of death. The Gestapo, for instance, is not readily recognizable as such under its Parisian designation of *La Carlingue*: kelson (inboard keel of ship) or cabin of an aircraft. *La maison Pullman facile*, suggestive of luxury and old-fashioned comfort, would seem to relieve the Prefecture of Police, one of the most forbidding buildings of Paris, of much of its menace. *Plastronner* (from starched shirt-front) or *poitriner* is a wonderfully visual evocation of self-satisfaction, of someone puffing out his chest and showing off. *L'ami du clergé* may not be spotted at once as a euphemism for a bottle of calvados: '*Cher confrère, passez-moi donc l'ami du clergé.*' Nor will it immediately spring to mind that when a chauffeur, sitting in a large black car outside an impressive-looking building with a tall green *porte cochère*, explains: '*Ben, j'attends mon homard*', he is referring to a Cardinal of the French Church. (*Homard*, since a boiled lobster is red, is also used of the English, the original 'redcoats'.) Nor are certain saints' days to be found in the religious calendar. *Sainte-Touche* is in fact pay-day. *A la Saint-Glinglin* (probably after the ringing of bells) indicates a very remote time, indeed one that will never come. *Sainte-Nitouche* (*n'y touche*: wouldn't touch a thing, butter wouldn't melt . . .) is a horrible little female goody-goody, an awful little hypocrite.

La Zone (the shanty-town belt between Paris and the suburbs), *être de la Zone*, *zonard*, are now out of use and out of mind; there is no *Zone* any more, only the *Boulevard Périphérique* on the northern rim of the city. But *la grande B* and *chez ma tante* are still very much around, and where they always used to be: the Banque de France and the *mont-de-piété* (pawnbroker), the latter often the only friend of the very poor and the improvident, especially those who cannot keep away from *le turfaga*. The poor, or rather the *économiquement faibles*, live in *HLM* (*habitations à loyer modéré*, moderate-rent housing), and no longer in *HBM* (*habitations à bon marché*, cheap housing). Prostitution too is still around, particularly along the old beat (*macadam*) of the rue Berger. And *être sous presse* (like a newspaper) is a position that could still be ascribed to a *gisquette* (after the Prefect Gisquet, who under the July

Monarchy introduced the *mise-en-carte*, or registration procedures), a prostitute not currently available because engaged
with a customer; as in a Queneau novel: '*Où est Maria?*'—'*Tu
ne peux pas la voir, elle est sous homme.*' *Remonte*, which
clearly was taken originally from the vocabulary of an army still
mainly horse-drawn, refers to the activities of those engaged in
procuring fresh girls for the most ancient profession. As for
Carte de France, an expression once employed by schoolboys to
describe the marks left on a bottom sheet by the process of self-
abuse, it appears to have gone out of use in the period of
L'Hexagone (a term explained by the shape of metropolitan
France). A map, then, to be rolled up and put away for good as, on
a suitably vulgar note, we take our leave of French euphemisms
and slang.

Euphemisms and Children

Catherine Storr

IMAGINE yourself as a small child in unfamiliar surroundings. You may be staying for the first time in the family of a friend or with relations. You may be on a day's outing, a morning's shopping expedition, or in hospital. Although everyone around you is friendly and wants to be helpful, there is no other member of your family present. Your bladder is full and you urgently need to empty it. What do you tell your friend's mum, the rarely seen aunt, the teacher, the doctor, the nurse? Do you say, 'I want hat?' 'I want sit down?' 'I need a daisy?' 'I want chim?' 'I want to make my arrangements . . . I want to go out . . . I want the square root of one?' Or, with peculiar appropriateness to this essay, but quite as incomprehensible, 'Where is the euph?'

I am not inventing. In answer to an appeal in a national newspaper, all these, and many more, expressions for the passing of urine have been sent to me by people of ages varying from eight to eighty-five. I am grateful to each one of them for letting me discover at least a small part of the diverse, ingenious, and often mystifying vocabulary with which children are furnished for making what can be an important and urgent communication.

The topics which are thought to require euphemistic disguises are, of course, limited in the lives of very small children. They will learn first the nursery words for elimination; later there will be words for different parts of the body, and although some of these will not be the correct, current, socially acceptable word, others—like belly-button for navel—will be synonyms rather than euphemisms. These euphemisms will apply almost exclusively to the genitalia and the genital region. Later still, less immediately personal subjects such as death, punishment, truancy, war and crime will be spoken of to and before the child, but my impression is that by this time he or she will adopt any euphemisms the adults are using. There appears to be, today at any rate, no specifically young person's vocabulary in these fields.

Since nursery language exists mainly in the oral rather than the written tradition, it is not easy to know precisely how our forebears were taught to indicate their infantile needs. Adult literature, however, does give us some indication of the general attitude towards the physical needs of the body and what words and phrases were socially acceptable. Whether or not Chaucer or the more explicit poets of the seventeenth century were read, or Shakespeare's plays seen, by children of the time, it seems probable that adults who used such frank language among themselves would have spoken with an equal lack of shame to their children; and certainly children would have heard some straight talk, including several four-letter words which were later banned from polite conversation, when they heard the St James's Bible read aloud in church. Harvey Darton, in *Children's Books in England*, writing about educational books for schoolboys published in the seventeenth century, says:

. . . in these higgledy-piggledy repositories of linguistic lumber . . . you will also discover something which makes the Puritan attitude to a good deal of seventeenth-century education very easily comprehensible. They had plenty to react against. These dialogues [exercises in simple Latin] reveal frankly the coarse truth of English domestic life, with no sign of repugnance. It is necessary to quote a few sentences which children were expected to repeat: they might not be believed without quotation. . . . 'Where do dogs fart? A little above their hams.' 'Why doth a dog, being to piss, hold up one leg? Lest he should bepiss his stockings.'

Darton, writing in 1932, did not spell out his four-letter words; in the last fifty years we have reverted to the greater freedom of expression of our ancestors. Swift, writing nearly a hundred years after the publication of the books quoted above, describes not only the Yahoos defecating on Gulliver's head when he visits the country of the Houyhnhnms, but also how, in Lilliput, he quenched the fire in the King's palace by urinating on it; in Brobdingnag he describes, with his usual obsessive detail, the vast chamber pots, holding 'above three tuns', into which the maids of honour voided their urine in his presence. It was not until 1818 that Dr and Mrs Bowdler published their censored version of Shakespeare for family reading, and even later, in 1833, that Noah Webster undertook the same service for the Holy Bible.

A certain crudity of verbal expression often reflects a considerable tolerance of the more animal side of man's nature; country people who are dealing with the birth, mating and death of animals are notable for their willingness to give a spade its right name. So, as evidence of the change in attitude which overtook this country towards the end of the eighteenth century regarding the body's parts and functions, I should like to quote from three authorities writing on the care of infants. The first, a French surgeon whose treatise on obstetrics was translated into English and published in London in 1736, giving instructions on the handling of a new-born baby, writes:

Let us now see how a Nurse must daily cleanse her Child from the Excrements. As the Young of all other Animals have their Bodies free, without the Trouble of any Coverings, so they easily discharge themselves of their Excrements, without being befoul'd. . . . But it is not the same with Infants, who, (for being bound and swathe'd with Swathes and Blankets, as we are forc'd, to give them a straight figure only suitable to Mankind) cannot render their Excrements, but at the same time they must be befoul'd, and in which (because it cannot be perceiv'd for their Clothes) they often remain, until the ill Scent of it offends the Nurse's Nose; or that she doubts it, because of the Cries and Tears of the Child, which is incommoded by the Moistness and Acrimony of it; to avoid which let the Child be open'd and chang'd at least twice or thrice a Day, and also sometimes in the Night, if necessary. . . .

This tolerance of the 'Excrements' contrasts strongly with the advice of Mr Pye Chevasse, writing almost exactly a century later: '. . . a babe of three months ought to be *held out* [my italics] at least a dozen times during the twenty-four hours. If such a plan were adopted, diapers might be dispensed with at the end of three months—a great advantage. . . . A DIRTY CHILD IS THE MOTHER'S DISGRACE' [author's capitals]. But this, written in the 1830s, was only the beginning of a preoccupation with training, obedience, and strict cleanliness. Here is Nurse Liddiard, a disciple of the Truby King school, writing in the 1930s: 'From the third day the nurse should have a small chamber on her knee, and the baby should be held with the back against the nurse's chest. . . . Many nurses train their babies so that they have no soiled napkins after the first week or so and very few wet ones. . . .' After reading these three extracts, we can hardly be surprised that over a period of 150 to 200 years, between the end of the eighteenth and the mid-twentieth century, books written for children do not concern themselves with matters below the waist. The writers, no doubt influenced by Rousseau's *Emile*, regarded the new-born child as 'innocent', a blank sheet exposed to, and likely to be corrupted by, the world's malignant influence. If they could be protected from corruption, they should be; meanwhile it was the duty of parents and teachers to frighten them into virtue. Euphemisms for the physical body—'the system', 'the private parts', 'down below'—were current where all reference to such coarse subjects was unavoidable; for young readers, the grosser side of life was ignored, but there was no lack of emphasis on death and sin.

Today, the subjects we approach with delicacy when communicating with children are different. Leaving aside the television programmes and 'video nasties' which are ostensibly at least not intended primarily for the under-sixteens, we tend to gloss over the concepts of evil and death. Evil-doing can be explained in psychoanalytic terms as the result of trauma in infancy, and death, owing to the advances made in modern medicine, is no longer a part of the everyday life of most children in this country. But in the early years of the last century, thinking was very different. In the first part of Mrs Sherwood's *Fairchild Family*, published in 1818, the three Fairchild children, aged eight, seven, and six, are taken to see the edifying death—the agonies described in detail—of little Charles, a cottager's child of outstanding piety; and in a better known, and even more horrifying passage, Mr Fairchild takes the children for a walk through a wood, to demonstrate to them the results of squabbling with your siblings—in the case of the Fairchild children, over a doll.

'I will take the children this evening to Blackwood, and show them something there, which, I think, they will remember as long as they live. . . .'
'What is there at Blackwood, papa?' cried the children.
'Something very shocking,' said Mrs Fairchild. 'There is one there,' said Mr Fairchild, looking very grave, 'who hated his brother.'

'Will he hurt us, papa?' said Henry.

'No,' said Mr Fairchild; 'he cannot hurt you now.'

When the children and John were ready, Mr Fairchild set out . . . they came in front of a very thick wood . . . and they walked on for half a mile, going down hill all the way . . . as they went further on, they saw an old garden wall, some parts of which being broken down they could see, beyond, a large brick house . . . fallen to ruin. . . . Just between that and the wood stood a gibbet, on which the body of a man hung in chains: it had not yet fallen to pieces, although it had hung there some years. The body had on a blue coat, a silk handkerchief round the neck, with shoes and stockings, and every other part of the dress still entire; but the face of the corpse was so shocking that the children could not look at it.

'Oh! papa, papa! what is that?' cried the children.

'That is a gibbet,' said Mr Fairchild; 'and the man who hangs upon it is a murderer—one who first hated, and afterwards killed his brother! . . .'

While Mr Fairchild was speaking, the wind blew strong and shook the body upon the gibbet, rattling the chain by which it hung.

'Oh! let us go, papa!' cried the children, pulling Mr Fairchild's coat.

'Not yet,' said Mr Fairchild; 'I must tell you the history of that wretched man before we go from this place.'

I am glad to be able to report that the Fairchild children seem to have survived this ordeal without undue suppression of their animal spirits, and continued to be delightfully naughty on a great many subsequent occasions.

This is a digression; but it does illustrate the changing fashion in the subjects which could not be spoken of openly to children. Victorian writers for children and adolescents could omit any mention of privies and their uses; those writing for older readers were not always able to avoid the advent of babies, but these are heralded, when they do not arrive with extraordinary suddenness, by phrases which can be interpreted correctly only when the event explains all. Amy, the heroine of Charlotte Yonge's best seller, *The Heir of Redclyffe* (1853), widowed during her honeymoon, is asked by her mother, 'And surely, my poor dear child, you have a reason for not risking yourself?' Or, even more cryptically, the flighty Bessie in *The Clever Woman of the Family* (1865), excusing herself for not insisting that her frail, elderly husband should go to London to consult a specialist about his health, tells her brother, 'Just consider, Alick, our own house is uninhabitable . . . my aunt coming to me in a month's time . . .'. The aunt never has time to arrive; Bessie, hurrying away from a former admirer, trips over a croquet hoop, falls, produces a premature baby and dies from 'fatal injury in the fall'. Death in childbirth seems quite as disproportionate a punishment for a very mild flirtation and a passion for croquet, as being hung on a gibbet for the possible consequences of quarrelling with your brothers and sisters.

When we reach the latter end of the nineteenth century we are at last within reach of the memory of people alive today. My most senior informant records that urination was called 'number one' and defecating 'number two'. These expressions survived well into the 1920s, probably much later, judging from the variant sent me by a young man aged nine, 'the square root of one' and 'the square root of four', since he says his mathematician dad invented them for the family's use. My grandmother, born around 1853, used to ask me, at frequent intervals during the day, 'Don't you want to make yourself comfortable?', an expression which I often deliberately misunderstood in order to punish her for interference. Another grandmother, born a decade later, is remembered by a correspondent who was a small child in the 1930s, asking, in the same context, 'Have you taken your precautions?' and from roughly the same period, from a nurse to a child before a day's outing, 'Please make your arrangements' (before we start). Another very common euphemism in the days of outside privies was 'to take a walk'; also 'to go outside', in the right context, had a very specific meaning. Meanwhile the installation of running water, fitted bathtubs and water-closets in middle-class households gave rise to a series of euphemisms taught to children for use when visiting. 'May I wash my hands?' 'May I pay a visit?'—and helpful hostesses often pre-empted the necessity for these requests by offering to 'show you the geography', or 'if you want the smallest room . . .', or 'and that is the room at the end of the passage'. Circumlocutions like these help us to forget that the words which were being avoided—lavatory, toilet—are themselves euphemisms. We speak of the lavatory pan and toilet paper, though the first has nothing to do with washing and the second is not concerned with how we arrange our dress, our hair and faces to appear in public.

It is not difficult to dissociate out-of-date euphemisms from their related objects or activities and to dismiss them as quaint, ridiculous or coy; but when we hear a word consistently applied, we tend to identify the name with what it describes, and to use it and think of it as inseparable from that thing. Words with more than one meaning may cause some confusion in the adult's mind, but the context will generally clarify which meaning is appropriate. Every schoolchild, faced with a textbook containing 'tables' and 'figures', learns within minutes not to turn the pages in search of pictures of furniture or of people.

The very young child, however, as he begins to acquire language, is not offered a choice of meanings for his first learned words, and therefore the identification of sound and object is absolute, and not easily eradicated later. One of my correspondents, to whom I am indebted for the expression for urination 'to do chim', writes that in his nursery days defecating was called 'to do pain', and that now, fifty years later, he becomes vaguely uncomfortable when addressing anyone called Payne or Paine. Another informant who used the euphemism 'tiddles' for urinating was confused to discover that Tiddles was the name of his aunt's cat; and I found it equally hard to learn that 'doing your duty', our family expression for defecation, had other connotations. Nelson's message to his men sounded to me for years like a very public after-breakfast call.

It is because small children accept unquestioningly whatever euphemistic name or phrase is first taught, that these expressions can be extended in a way that makes sense to the child and facilitates communication within the family, but which is logically and grammatically absurd. 'To be excused' was universally understood in schools and adopted by many families as a request to be allowed to go to the lavatory; but the recognition that opening the bowels generally took longer, and was often more arduous than emptying the bladder, led to the former being described as 'to be very excused'. 'I have to retire for a moment' became 'I have to retire seriously', and children who 'spent a penny' several times a day, had, less often but regularly, to 'spend tuppence'. The most striking example of nursery language which has evolved logically into nonsense was sent to me by a lady brought up in Canada, who writes: 'My generation and locale and class used wood or wicker *chaises percées* (commodes). . . . We almost never "went potty" but said, "I have to get on the chair." If the family needed to know "how long", a boy said, "I want to get on the chair to stand up." I, a girl, said that too for years . . . if I needed to defecate I said ". . . to sit down". So did the little boys.'

As the infant grows and acquires language, it is taught to name, among other things, the parts of its own and other people's bodies. Before the nineteenth-century squeamishness set in, it appears that these names were often references to the shape or function of the part; the penis was the 'tool', 'yard', 'prick', 'pizzle', 'cock', 'tail'; there must have been hundreds more in daily use, some humorous, some affectionate, some disparaging, some admiring, just as today's 'dick', 'willy', 'Percy', 'widge' (as well as many of the older examples still in use) represent only a tiny percentage of words which stand for that treasured member. The more reticent genital apparatus of the girl was described less graphically and specifically; 'cunt' is hardly a euphemism and I doubt if it would have been used by children. 'Bottom', 'botty', 'my privates', 'the private parts' or, more ambiguously, 'down below', were allowable expressions before our present age of plain speaking. Today our well-informed schoolchildren have a variety of phrases which seem to me to indicate the same pride in possession which formerly belonged mainly to the male; the vagina is 'minny', 'minge', 'nanny', 'pussy', 'fanny'—though I suspect that this, like 'botty' and 'bottom', covers the whole of the pelvic region. Two odd examples, of very different dates, are 'spider' and 'crockery'. The former was told me by a woman who cannot remember whether or not she coined the word herself, or where or how it arose; she does, however, remember vividly her embarrassment when she was taken to hospital after injuring herself by slipping on the crossbar of a bicycle, and realized that the area she wanted to speak about had a technical name which she didn't know. The up-to-date and, I suspect, better-known example is 'crockery', heard this year in a residential school, when a small girl, seeing some boys at the door of the room where she was being bathed, covered her pubis with her hand and said, 'I don't want them to see my crockery.' I assume this is rhyming slang: vagina—china. I also suspect that the mysterious 'spider' was probably a child's mis-hearing of the anatomical term.

I'm not sure if euphemisms for the female breasts or for menstruation really belong in an essay primarily concerned with children. Certainly both subjects are conspicuously absent from Victorian literature for children or young people. The words 'breast' and 'bosom' were used almost synonymously and for both sexes, often in a symbolic or semi-symbolic sense: 'in Abraham's bosom', or 'he crouched and trembled more and more on his father's breast, till . . . he found the other arm passed round him in support, drawing him tenderly close' (C. M. Yonge, *The Daisy Chain*, 1850). Today there is no such ambiguity—except in the case of a small boy who, admiring his dad's manly chest, refers to his mother's breasts as 'muscles'. A class of fifteen-year-old schoolgirls have sent me various up-to-date words, most in general use: 'boobs', 'melons', 'knockers', 'whips' and, less common but very endearing, 'buzzumbras'. All these show a healthy enjoyment of the female anatomy which contrasts favourably with my own schooldays, when, influenced by the 1920s fashion for the boyish figure, we sympathized with any girl who had well-developed breasts, and tactfully referred to her 'shelf'.

This same Cheshire school class have given me the only new (to me) euphemism for menstruation; besides 'your monthly' and 'coming on', they speak of 'being a woman for a week'. Earlier in the century doctors asked schoolgirls, 'Have your periods started yet?' and among themselves girls and women generally referred to 'the curse'. One correspondent writes that her mother, although not squeamish in general, always called it 'that other business', and this, she believes, was a euphemism confined to her own family. I have also been told that before the days of safe contraception, menstruation was often known —presumably only among women—as 'the wife's friend'; but whether this was because it signalled another month free from unwanted pregnancy, or because it provided a valid excuse for evading the husband's conjugal rights, I don't know. A contemporary of my own mother's used an expression which, as a child, I found slightly improper—'the Colonel's come to stay'. She was an inventive woman, who named urinating out of doors (in the days of skirts sweeping the ground) 'low cunning'.

We are still coy and fearful about death. Although our small children are familiar with death on the small screen, whether it is in classical serials, Westerns, historical dramas, or nearer home, but still 'over there, in another country', we hesitate to inform them of the finality of death when it occurs in the family or among close friends. Children today are told by non-believing parents that grandma or grandpa has 'gone to heaven'. 'Still with you, but you can't see him' is another example provided by girls from the Cheshire school; they also quote 'gone to his Maker', 'gone to a better world'. My stepdaughter, when very young, adopted the first of these phrases in the same unanalytical spirit as those children, and named a hearse a 'gone-to-heaven-car'. But many of these phrases must be in use among people who have no expectation of an afterlife, and who think that by giving the child an expectation of meeting the dead person again at some future date, they are softening the blow. In fact, small children are more realistic (and more ruthless) than their elders often suppose. My own daughter, aged five, when she heard of the death of a well-liked but seldom seen relative, asked, without embarrassment and with a natural interest, 'Will they put his body in the dustbin?' In an excellent book, *A Child's Parent Dies* by Edna Furman (1974), the analysts who con-tributed their case histories of orphaned children—some in treatment before and during, some after the parent's death —found that their young patients could face the fact that death was a final separation, provided that the adults caring for them could help them to recognize the truth and to mourn appropri-ately. They found also that children who were familiar with the deaths of pets, farm or wild animals, were to some extent prepared for the fact that all life ends eventually in death. My editor tells me that his daughter, when aged four, was comforted for the deaths of the birds killed by her much-loved cats, by the ritual of the funerals and by her interpretation of the saying 'up with the lark' as meaning that the buried birds would rise from the dead early the next morning.

Just as it now appears probably kinder to young children involved in broken marriages not to encourage them to hope that the separation may be only temporary and that mum and dad will some time come together again, so the acceptance of death as terminating a relationship for the foreseeable future is better than promises of a reunion hereafter. Of course if the person giving the children the news of the death is personally convinced that this is only a 'passing on', a 'going to a better world' or, as my Canadian correspondent tells me was current in the Salvation Army, 'a promotion to glory', that is quite a different matter; these expressions then become not euphemisms but statements of belief.

The euphemisms used to and by children appear to fall into four categories. The first contains the words and phrases currently being used by others moving in the same geographical and social area; present-day examples are 'pee' and 'wee' for urination and 'poo(h)' for defecation. These—especially the last—are nursery words which seem to be universally understood. In the second category are the expressions coined or adapted by parents or nurses for the child's use, such as 'to try hard', 'to grunt', 'to do a tinkle'. In the third category are the words used by the children themselves, often misunderstandings of words used by the adults, like the girl's 'spider' for vagina, and a delightful example sent me from New Guinea, as follows:

My family call the lavatory 'the euph' . . . (pronounced 'yoof' to rhyme with roof). Why? When my wife was little a slightly older female visitor one evening said she was just going outside. My wife misunderstood what was a euphemistic hint that the visitor was going to the outside lavatory . . . and offered to go out with her . . . there had been, she knew, some rather odd men reportedly hanging around backyards. . . . Eventually my wife was told that the visitor was just going to the toilet and the expressions was a *euphemism*. As this was the first time my wife had heard the word she thought it was a polite term for toilet. It became a family joke, that contracted into 'euph'.

The last category, and it is by far the smallest, consists of euphemisms that children have thought up for themselves. Examples of these are not easy to find; I have been told of a small girl who, having learned to call urination 'tinkle', referred to her father's penis as his 'tinkle tail'. Another correspondent writes:

A friend and his wife, respectively a lecturer and a GP, were embarrassed at the zoo, when their eight-year-old son, pointing at the large penis of an elephant, loudly asked what it was . . . his twelve-year-old sister told him 'You know what it is, Nick, that's its facilities.' The explanation satisfied Nicky . . . but bewildered the parents. Later they asked for an explanation. 'You know,' she said, 'its toilet facilities.'

Finally, two weeks ago, one of my grandsons announced that he had invented a new way of telling someone that his flies were undone. 'I tell him, "You've lost your licence".' But he could not explain how he'd come to think of it, or why this phrase seemed peculiarly appropriate.

It seems clear that most euphemisms are imposed on children in order to save the adult from embarrassment or distress. They are not used to protect the child, who may indeed suffer if he or she is not equipped with a language which can be understood by people outside the family circle. I welcome the return to plain speaking which has taken place during the last twenty-odd years, and the fashion which dictates that children need feel no shame in making known the physical needs which are common to all of us, or in naming correctly and comprehensively every part of the body. I should like to end by quoting from an article by Jane Georges which appeared in July 1983 in the *Guardian* newspaper, which seems to me to illustrate, not exactly the danger or hypocrisy of euphemisms, so much as the sanity and happy effects of encouraging even small children to share as much in adult language as they can, and of forgoing the temptation to enjoy and perpetuate their often charming baby talk. The writer discovered, with dismay, that her two little daughters, aged five and four, had—against strict instructions —accepted a lift in his car from a strange man, who had taken them 300 yards to a park, exposed himself, and then let them go without touching them. The police were called and the older child questioned (the younger after telling the story to her mother had gone to sleep).

The policeman summed up so far. 'So. The man took you and your sister to the park entrance and then stopped the car. What happened then?' For the first time, something like embarrassment crossed her face. 'Just tell me what you told your Mummy,' said the policeman, casually. She pulled herself together instantly and met his gaze head-on. 'He sticked his penis out.'

The policeman flinched, nodded, and after a couple of false starts, wrote something in his book. Leaning sideways over his pen, by this time getting the hang of things, she added, 'He had red knickers on.'

There was a terrible silence in the room while the three adults fought painful inward battles. The policeman collected himself first and abandoned the realm of facts. 'You weren't *frightened*?' She raised her eyebrows. 'No.'

Impossible to say that these children would not have emerged from this experience similarly untraumatized (as their mother believes), if they had been brought up in a home or at a time when the anatomy of the opposite sex remained—for girls often until marriage—a shameful mystery. But it is worth considering whether it is any help to our children if, by implication in the 'double-talk' we use to them, we paper over and half conceal the basic facts of life. The Puritan writers of the seventeenth century wrote that no child was too little to go to hell. In our own society no child is too little to be armed against more immediate dangers.

In the Office

Jeremy Lewis

Euphemisms are widely regarded as the comic villains of the language, whose absurd—if often well-meaning—misdeeds are retold with the ferocious, snobbish derision usually reserved for ruched lace curtains, teak front doors with fanlights cunningly inlaid, and clip-on Tudor beams. They bring out the Pharisee in the mildest of men, and are as integral, as enjoyable and as unkind a part of the English comedy of manners as dropped 'h's, malapropisms, or the bogus family portraits bought in bulk by ambitious City merchants for their brand-new country estates, and so wickedly derided by Surtees in his masterly accounts of mid-Victorian men on the make. There, but for the grace of a finer sensibility or a superior education, go the best of us, asking lady visitors if they would like to 'powder their noses', regretfully reporting that a 'senior citizen' has 'passed on', and anxiously explaining that the dimmest boy in the school is 'educationally disadvantaged' and has problems with his 'communication skills'.

Of course, many euphemisms deserve all the hostility and ridicule they incur: at their worst, they dilute and constrict the language, substituting imprecision for exactitude and the generalized for the particular, doing fine old words and phrases out of a job, and emitting a synthetic and odour-free haze of banality and mediocrity appropriate for an age of 'chat shows', sociologese, and chickens that taste, at best, of nothing at all and, at worst, of South American fish. In their misguided, soggy dishonesty and kindliness of spirit they are, perhaps, the verbal equivalent of the modern mania for giving *all* the children prizes for fear of discouraging the many to the benefit of the few—so rendering the entire exercise futile and raising excited expectations, soon to be dashed by the unhappy realization that, try as one may, sheep and goats must eventually drift apart. Modern man curiously combines a rather dubious cult of frankness and fearless confrontation (usually accompanied by loud beating of the chest and self-congratulatory baring of the soul) with a fearful gentility of behaviour and expression. Such matters as race, religion, intelligence, bodily functions and the differences between the sexes are held at arm's length, and subjected to agonized, dainty circumlocution. Too much time spent in this oddly airless, reverential atmosphere brings out the brute in many of us, provoking a flurry of forceful adjectives and much straight talking about lunatic asylums, lavatories, nature rather than nurture and a thousand and one unwholesome and best-avoided subjects.

But, as we all know, humankind cannot bear very much reality, and only the most robust can survive on a diet of raw truths and untenderized plain talking. Awkward customers who insist on calling a spade a spade and stoutly refuse to make the right noises for the wrong reasons, or for no reasons at all, are invaluable as stimulants or purgatives, but can only be taken in small doses: kindliness and cowardice ensure that, for the rest of us, a mealy-mouthed reticence prevails and that, in public at least, we pick our ways through a familiar swamp of evasions, ambiguities, white lies, hypocrisies and euphemisms, different in detail but not in essence from those we deride or condemn on the lips of others. At home, or with our close friends, we can usually say what we think; in the curious world of the office, so intimate and yet so alien, circumlocution thrives and the euphemism—so irritating, so entertaining, so touching, and so endearingly transparent—comes into its own.

Leaving aside the inevitable distinctions between the rulers and the ruled, office workers fall into two distinct categories: those for whom life is work, and vice versa; and the rest of us, for whom even the most congenial labour seems a tiresome distraction from the true ends of life—widely believed to include such items as cats, children, the seaside, aged relatives, log fires and the novels of Trollope—and whose eyes spend more time than they should gazing out of the office window and sneaking surreptitious glances at the office clock.

Without our first category the rest of us would rapidly grind to a halt and sink into a sloth of amiable but ineffective garrulity and torpor: for it includes among its restricted membership those human dynamos for whom an eighty-hour week is a matter of course, who shame us with their quickness and their concentration, who give their all to the job and get so much from it in return, whose private lives tend to be undernourished or non-existent (or so their detractors like to think), and who regard the bumblings of their milder, less driven colleagues with an understandable and often abrasive impatience. Small firms in particular often depend upon, and revolve around, the character, activities and energy of an obsessive autocrat—monomaniacs of fierce if transient passions, scornful of compromise or consultation except of the most severely practical kind, adept at persuading colleagues and the outside world to share their ferocious conviction that a particular product or course of action is of overwhelming urgency and correctness, and that to doubt it is symptomatic of moral turpitude as well as professional incompetence.

Denizens of a Manichaean world of sharply contrasted blacks and whites, human dynamos have neither the time, the temperament nor the inclination for delicate circumlocution. Business life, for them, is a highly-charged affair of contagious exaggeration, and they bring to it the same heightened emotions and intensity of feeling that a passionate, ambitious, over-protective parent brings to bear on its offspring; and just as the possessive parent feels duty-bound to speak its mind to its long-suffering children, so the human dynamo sees no need to deal in the unreliable, evasive currency of euphemism or ambiguity, or to conceal or disinfect unpalatable verities with a comforting cloud of banalities. As forceful in his language as in his emotions, the dynamo overstates with a passionate conviction—affecting, and no doubt genuinely feeling, a hurt surprise when his bruised attendants occasionally take umbrage. Whatever the dynamo's secret doubts in the small hours of the morning, he needs to exude an infectious self-confidence if he is to activate his fellow men, most of whom he finds distressingly sceptical, bored, idle, dim or disaffected.

Once away from these rarefied heights, however, the searcher after euphemisms will find samples in abundance—very often as direct by-products of the nature and activities of the dynamo, particularly when he (or she) has come to resemble, like P. G. Wodehouse's Mr Bickersdyke, 'an active volcano in the shape and clothes of [a] bank manager'. The dynamo provides the drive and energy needed to get the wheels in motion; his more tactful subordinates apply the lubricating oils and soothing unguents without which the machinery would grind to a resentful halt. Uttering emollient, circuitous words, the lieutenants bind up the wounds of the afflicted and endeavour to place the intemperate but horridly effective onslaughts from on high in a longer, diminishing perspective, and to console themselves and others with reassuring ventures into amateur psychology on the subject of the dynamo's essentially unhappy nature. 'Tell her to get her finger out' is translated into 'Would it be at *all* possible for you to type out five contracts and twenty-four letters before you go home?'—accompanied by an apologetic, winning smile and an explanatory jerking of the thumb in the direction of the smoke seeping under the door of the dynamo's office. So too, 'It's not bloody well good enough, and tell him I said so' will be soothingly rephrased as 'I think we're *almost* there, but if you *could* see your way to . . .'

More often than not, however, the lieutenant fails or forgets to do what needs to be done, in which case yet more indirect speaking is called for. When the dynamo bangs the desk and asks why the report wasn't before him at 9 o'clock that morning, as particularly requested, the shell-shocked lieutenant will mutter nervously about its being 'looked into' or 'in hand': a familiar ploy is to suggest that the matter—like real life (of which, as we know, the dynamo is assumed to know little)—is rather more 'complex' than our impulsive supremo seems to think, and that, being a responsible type, the lieutenant is 'gathering opinions' or even 'setting up a small committee' to investigate the matter. The chances are that since the dynamo is usually a good deal sharper than his subordinates, and even better versed in the ways of the 'real' world, he will immediately recognize this flannel for what it is: but he may well decide to connive at the crime, leaving his subordinate to scuttle away, relieved and mildly triumphant, to remedy matters as best he may.

Kindliness, cowardice, deviousness and lightly-disguised self-interest all have parts to play in the daily output of office euphemisms. Elementary good manners, plus a familiar, even fawning, desire to be liked encourage us to 'ask' rather than order subordinates to do what needs to be done, and to pad out the velvet glove to almost unrecognizable proportions with a

'Would you mind awfully?' or a 'That *is* kind of you' or a 'I *am* sorry to overload you' or a 'What a noble spirit you are': for which of us has not dreaded the withering blast of office disapproval as experienced by that most quintessential of office workers, Sinclair Lewis's Babbitt:

So chill a wind of hatred blew from the outer office that the normal comfort of his home-going was ruined. He was distressed by losing that approval of his employees to which an executive is always a slave. Ordinarily he left the office with a thousand fussy directions to the effect that there would undoubtedly be important tasks tomorrow. . . . Tonight he departed with feigned and apologetic liveliness. He was as afraid of his still-faced clerks—of the eyes focused on him, Miss McGoun staring with her head lifted from her typing, Miss Bannigan looking over her ledger, Matt Penniman craning around his desk in the dark alcove, Stanley Graff sullenly expressionless—as a parvenu before the bleak propriety of his butler. He hated to expose his back to their laughter, and in his effort to be casually merry he stammered and was raucously friendly and oozed wretchedly out of the door.

Rather than risk such disapproval, most office workers will do their best to ensure that uncomfortable confrontations are dodged or defused, ideally by passing the blame to someone else in the manner perfected by Messrs Spenlow and Jorkins in *David Copperfield* ('I will not say what consideration I might give to that point, Mr Copperfield, if I were unfettered. Mr Jorkins is immovable'). 'I'm afraid I couldn't get the support of my colleagues'—or the sales people, or the Managing Director—is often an elaborate way of saying 'no': few of us are brave enough, or crass enough, to say exactly what we think, or to emulate Melville's Bartleby the Scrivener in his polite refusal to do what was asked of him ('I would prefer not to'). Much more recognizable is the brow-beaten hero of Roy Fuller's *Image of a Society*: 'In his office, shrinking from the naked contact with another personality, he would often deal with a situation which demanded a telephone call or an interview by procrastinating or writing a memorandum'—bristling, no doubt, with elaborate circumlocutions. Nor are many of us able to summon up the sense (however insecure) of certainty and self-importance that distinguishes the dynamo from his fellow men: our approach is duller, more sceptical, blighted by a fatal inability to take ourselves and our opinions as seriously as we should and by a glum suspicion that, in the long term, none of it matters a great deal either way. 'Did one then never grow up?' wonders the desk-bound narrator of another of Roy Fuller's excellent, under-rated novels of office life, *The Father's Comedy*: 'Was one never completely guarded by one's personality and beliefs? Even at fifty there were moments when he must pretend to a greater seriousness than he really owned: when a knock on his office door could make his heart jump and his hands conceal a pocket mirror, or a slip of paper on which he had been repeatedly signing his name.'

Office life is mostly a pretty prosaic affair, but since it takes up so much of our time, it's hardly surprising that we wheel out an arsenal of euphemisms to describe what we're up to, and to make ourselves feel more important than we really are. 'Executives', 'directors', 'personal assistants', 'officers', 'managers' and 'researchers' abound, though the 'executive' may as well be in charge of two men as two thousand (a point made by Kenneth Hudson in his entertaining and perceptive work, *The Jargon of the Professions*), 'director' may be a flattering term for 'stooge', the 'personal assistant' may find her life exactly the same as it had been when she was a secretary (in the meantime the copy-typist has probably become a 'secretary'), the 'officer' may be responsible for fire drill and little else, the 'manager (despatch)' may spend his entire career packing parcels, and the 'researcher' may never progress much beyond looking up names in *Who's Who* or addresses in the telephone book. Few of us are really taken in by the futile upgrading of job descriptions, which merely devalues the currency, leaving everyone much as they were before, but with grander-sounding handles to their names: neither the lot nor the status (nor the pay) of the travelling salesman is materially affected by referring to him as a 'travel-ler' rather than a 'rep', though an 'area representative' may feel himself entitled to a superior class of boarding house. Anxious to impress his friend Kit with his standing in the office—he spends much of his day carving his name on his desk—Dick Swiveller talks impressively about 'the firm in which I'm a sort of a—of a managing partner': heirs to a noble literary tradition, few clerks nowadays relish being described as such, and—un-like the unfortunate Swiveller—many of them have official approval for calling themselves 'controllers', 'processors' or 'administrators'. It's the feel of the thing that matters, as Wodehouse's Mike appreciates on his first day in the post-room at the bank:

> 'Jackson, Ah, yes. You have joined the staff?'
> Mike rather liked this way of putting it. It lent a certain dignity to the proceedings, making him feel like some important person for whose services there had been strenuous competition. He seemed to see the bank's directors being reassured by the chairman. 'I am happy to say, gentlemen, that our profits for the past year are £3,000,000—(cheers) —and'—impressively—'that we have finally succeeded in inducing Mr Mike Jackson—(sensation)—to—er—in fact to join the staff!' (Frantic cheers in which the chairman joined) . . .

No sooner has the average office worker hung up his coat and popped his sandwiches into the top drawer of his desk (where they nestle unhygienically alongside an ageing collection of rubber bands, paper-clips, toffee papers and unread memorandums) than he assumes a slightly—sometimes a radically—different personality from that worn over the breakfast table or in the street outside. He learns to feign enthusiasm, excitement, rage and indignation, to wrinkle his brow in simulated deep concern and to clip to his face a fixed grin of eager anticipation; he uses euphemisms and hyberbole to offset the tedium of office life, to persuade himself that filing or writing memos are matters of all-consuming interest, and that he is having the time of his life preparing the annual budget. Most of us are schizophrenic about office life: with one breath we pine for a private income and agitate for the retirement age to be brought down to forty-five, with the next we angle eagerly for the latest office gossip and wallow in the comforting luxury of shop-talk (aptly described by Sinclair Lewis as 'the purest and most rapturous form of conversation'); we curse it daily, but waste away when it is taken from us. At home or on holiday, we groan at the thought of meetings and salesmen and inter-departmental committees, dream of escape to a rustic paradise, and dread, like Babbitt in the woods of Maine, returning to the daily grind:

He saw the years, the brilliant winter days and all the long sweet afternoons which were meant for summery meadows, lost in such brittle pretentiousness. He thought about telephoning, about leases, of

cajoling men he hated, of making business calls and waiting in dirty
ante-rooms—hat on knee, yawning at fly-specked calendars, being
polite to office-boys.

'I don't hardly want to go back to work,' he prayed. 'I'd like to—I don't
know.'

But he was back next day, busy and of doubtful temper.

Once back in those familiar surroundings, we gear ourselves up,
like an actor feeling his way into a part. Within a couple of days
we should be trundling along as normal: for, mercifully, even
the dullest of office jobs has a faint, intrinsic fascination, and if
the bought ledger lacks a certain sparkle, the blandishments of
office gossip, office intrigue and office politics go some way to
redress the balance. Even the cricket-mad Mike 'began to grow
accustomed to the life of the bank, and to find that it had its
pleasant side after all. Whenever a number of people are working
at the same thing, even though that thing is not perhaps what
they would have chosen as an object in life, there is bound to
exist an atmosphere of good-fellowship: something akin to,
though a thousand times weaker than, the public school spirit.'
We learn to relish, and are suitably awed and impressed by, the
hierarchies and the reputations of our own particular trades—so
urgent to those within, so meaningless to those without—and
to tremble at the approach of the mighty (while consoling
ourselves in moments of inadequacy or boredom with the
reflection that, more likely than not, the genius of our particular
profession will cut no ice with the next-door neighbour, in
much the same way that—to Mr Pooter's astonished indignation—Mr Perkupp's hallowed name evoked not a tremor of
recognition at the Lord Mayor's Ball); and, like Babbitt with his
business cronies, we indulge in the endearing, necessary
rhetoric of professional self-esteem:

To them the Romantic Hero was no longer the knight, the wandering
poet, the cow-puncher, the aviator, nor the brave young district
attorney, but the great sales-manager, who had an Analysis of Merchandising Problems on his glass-topped desk, whose title of nobility
was 'Go-Getter', and who devoted himself and all his young samurai to
the cosmic purpose of Selling—not of selling anything in particular, or
to anybody in particular, but pure Selling.

Nor a great deal has changed in the sixty-odd years since Babbitt was bustling about his business somewhere in the Midwest (his admirers may remember that he 'made nothing in particular, neither butter nor shoes nor poetry, but was nimble in the calling of selling houses for more than people could afford to pay'). Only the jargon has altered, for the chances are that his 'young samurai' of today—neatly clad 'young executives' in sober three-piece suits, clutching slim-line briefcases crammed with sales figures, *Management Today*, *Computer Age* and a paperback edition of one of Peter Drucker's books on modern business methods—will be familiar with the horrid terminology of sociologists and management consultants. As Kenneth Hudson points out, we are rapidly adopting the dire American notion that the use of plain English implies poverty or lack of education, and that the more tortuous and indigestible the descriptive verbiage, the more important and 'prestigious' the job must be. The perfect young executive will be—inevitably—'dynamic', 'self-starting' (able to get up in the morning) and 'self-motivating' (ambitious and able to take initiatives), adept at 'decision-making', 'communication skills' (able to speak and write to other people) and 'man management' (telling other people what to do), and capable—like a cleaner, better-paid variety of coal-miner—of 'working at the interface' in a 'multi-use, rapid-growth environment'. It goes without saying that he will be 'profit-oriented' and if, in a 'challenging, turn-round situation', he turns out to be 'something of a grafter, able to follow words with action', so much the better.

This proliferation of odd and ungainly epithets is matched by a wealth of sonorous-sounding job descriptions—many of which, as we have seen, turn out to be old friends togged out in dubious fancy dress. Even the most hard-boiled know that it is bad form to do or say anything that smacks of 'élitism' or a shortage of 'social conscience': heavily influenced by sociologese and the jargons of the 'caring' professions, the authors of job advertisements and job descriptions struggle to avoid any implication that some people will always be brighter, richer, luckier or more agreeable than others, and that—if the world is to go round—some jobs will be more important, better paid, more interesting, and harder to get than others. Not surprisingly, perhaps, this tactful, circuitous manner of speech tends to flourish in firms that are bureaucratic, unionized and relatively democratic (and often rather peaceful and pleasant to work in): office politics in such places tend to be elaborate and Byzantine, calling for greater skill in reading between the lines than is called upon in the more brutal and straightforward world of the domineering autocrat.

For a rhapsodic combination of hyperbole and euphemism, it's hard to better the job advertisement pages of the semi-glossy give-away magazines that are handed to soporific commuters as they stumble off the train at Paddington or Waterloo. Aiming, one would guess, at the goofier kind of shorthand-typist in her late teens or early twenties, plus a smattering of 'mature' secretaries in search of fresh pastures, and exuding a breezy informality ('Call Elaina to find out more'), the employment agencies are as one in their frenzied anxiety to impart glamour, sophistication and a sense of throbbing urgency to the world of filing cabinets and telex machines. Most offices, we learn, are 'plush', 'prestigious' or 'glamorous', offering 'fabulous' but undefined perks (luncheon vouchers, perhaps?), and peopled by a joshing, thrusting 'team' of eager young 'professionals' ('Never a dull moment when you aid and abet a lively, ultra-friendly sales team. They're always popping in and out and your quick thinking and secretarial talents keep them up-to-date and efficient!'). But behind the 'zany' humour and the office pranks lurk coolly efficient business minds: 'This friendly crowd appreciate professionalism, and your lively personality and "people skill" are just the ticket . . .'

As for the boss, he is almost certain to be 'charming', 'involved' (so he should be, one might think) and—once again—'dynamic'; with luck, he may be an Old Etonian as well. Most bosses combine mercurial brilliance with an almost professorial absent-mindedness and inability to make or keep appointments, and the role of the secretary, we're led to believe, is essentially that of a partner-cum-nanny, operating in tandem with the boss and enjoying a good laugh at the same time. 'As his Sec., you'll be called upon to keep tabs on him, relate telexes, organize his diary, arrange the odd luncheon [no suggestion of eating it as well], and basically, enjoy your day!' suggests a firm of absent-minded lawyers, while another advertiser admits that 'Your Director boss finds administration a problem, so total involvement with unlimited scope makes this a position

"extraordinaire".' Just occasionally the mask slips, and the
employer has to admit that, jolly as life is bound to be, the
£6,000-a-year newcomer won't quite be running the show:
'Hopefully you'll be keen to know his work and his clients, as
there'll be plenty of opportunity to chat to them and greet them
[i.e. take their coats and offer them cups of coffee] whilst your
boss tackles the difficult stuff!'

As far as the nuts and bolts of office life are concerned, a
certain obscurity prevails. Much use is made of the verb 'handle', both as a euphemism for 'type' and to hint that the newly-
arrived eighteen-year-old will be a key—perhaps *the*
key—member of the 'team'. 'One day', we read, 'you'll be
handling [i.e. typing] litigation cases, and the next you'll be
putting the finishing touches to [i.e. finishing typing] a major
property deal'; while another tempter promises that the lucky
applicant will 'handle top clients from meeting and greeting to
following through with major decisions'—an offer that could be
open to a rather different interpretation.

More often than not, alas, the humdrum realities of audio
typing and secretarial slog are all too clearly discernible beneath
the over-excited chat and breathless references to the 'media'
and West End fashion houses. 'Secretary required in hectic
world of TV news,' one entry boldly begins—only to reveal,
somewhat lamely, that she will be 'dealing with staff records.
Loads of admin.' It's a long way from Jon Snow in El Salvador or
Martin Bell in Miami. Nor does one need to be a fully-fledged
semiologist to read between the lines of the ad that follows, or to
realize that life in that particular neck of the woods is likely to
be a tedious, lonely affair: 'No pressures, no hassles, no respon-
sibilities—just a straightforward position working for this
friendly City-based audit team. As these guys are out most of
the time, you'll be able to enjoy an easygoing atmosphere, where
you can gauge your own work-load as you look after their day-
to-day workload. . . .'

And once the typist has been offered her 'exclusive' job, or the
brush salesman has successfully applied for the post of
'bristleware executive (merchandising)', what further linguistic
perils lie in their paths? In larger firms, they may well be taken
on an 'induction course' by a master euphemist known as a
'personnel officer'. In the old days, personnel officers tended to

be retired military men, whose job it was to hand out luncheon vouchers, guard the key to the cupboard in which stationery and typewriter ribbons were stored, make sure that the wash-rooms were kept clean and the corridors swept, and keep watch over the white-painted first-aid box, lest a secretary came over faint or a trainee account executive reported in with a curious throbbing about the temples and unfocused, bloodshot eyes. Their modern equivalents plough their way through impenetrable volumes on management techniques, master the hideous complexities of industrial law and labour relations, are privy to the balance sheets and profit and loss accounts, delight in asking staff to spend valuable time filling in 'job description' questionnaires, and are adept in deterring unsuitable applicants ('We feel your experience would be wasted here'), soothing manifestations of discontent ('Salaries are, of course, reviewed every year') and decoding reference letters (does 'steady and conscientious' mean just that, or a bit of a dullard? Is 'lively and unusual' likely to be a demented pest or an export sales manager of the future?).

Should you prove 'inadequate for the job', the personnel officer will come into his own. Gone are the days when the boss—all of a sudden no longer 'charming'—could thump the desk and shout 'You're fired': there's much truth in Kenneth Hudson's claim that 'only those who have made it can be jargon-free', but in a world of industrial tribunals, redundancy pay and compensation for unfair dismissal, even the most direct of dynamos has to mind what he says. Warning shots are fired ('I don't think things are really working out between us' or 'We don't seem to be hitting it off, do we?' or—assuming an expression of kindly concern—'You don't seem to be terribly happy here') in the hope that the victim will take the hint and pack his bags; if he fails to co-operate, some straight talking may be called for ('I honestly feel that, with your talents, you ought to try to widen your experience' or 'We feel you might be happier working for a rather different sort of firm' or—most pleasing of all—'I'm afraid we're going to have to let you go', as though the unhappy worker, faced with a trip to the Job Centre, was a long-caged animal being returned to the wilds, and 'my colleagues and I' its distraught but scrupulous owners).

Once installed, the office worker quickly learns that

unadorned truth can spell trouble, and that the carefully chosen euphemism can be useful in self-defence and in defence of others. Angry, boring or importunate telephone callers are soothed or diverted by a secretary's apologetic explanation that her boss—who is incoherent with drink, or still out at lunch at half-past four, or asleep, or (most probably) hasn't done what he promised and can't face talking to his persecutor—is 'in a meeting' ('in a board meeting' if rank needs to be pulled), 'with a client', or 'a bit tied up at the moment'. 'Can he ring you back?' is a polite form of 'Don't call us, we'll call you', while 'I know he's been trying to call you back' disguises the fact that he has forgotten all about it, or that his secretary never remembered to give him the message in the first place. Blinding headaches, mysterious diseases and cars breaking down in remote parts of the country will explain away a day at the races or a long weekend; a speciality of the publishing firm I work for is to inform callers that the escapee is 'snowbound in Norfolk' —which sounds plausible, but calls for careful checking with the weathermen, and should be avoided in midsummer.

Anyone who has worked for any time in an office will be able to supply his or her own list of particular and professional euphemisms: the office drunk waiting patiently for opening time, and then explaining that 'I'm just nipping out to the bank—I won't be more than twenty minutes'; the farewell toast to the loyal old retainer, 'with the firm, man and boy, for over fifty years' and still earning rather less than the eighteen-year-old typist who joined last week, but duly grateful for the retirement clock and the fulsome prediction by the chairman (who can never remember his name) that 'None of us here will ever forget . . .'; the dishonest, melancholy rhetoric with which subordinates, over a pint in the pub, tell how they had it out with the boss ('And then I told him exactly what I thought . . .'), the full pathos of which was best described in James Joyce's 'Counterparts', where the enormous, bovine Alleyne, tormented and humiliated beyond endurance by his wasp-like superior, boasts of his imaginary defiance in the pub after work before reeling home to vent his frustration on his cowering, unhappy child, or in Roy Fuller's *Image of a Society*:

Ramsden's telephone rang. He put down the remains of his jam puff and picked up the receiver.

'Hello,' he said shortly. His tone changed to one of efficient sweet-
ness. 'Yes, Mr Blackledge,' he said. 'Yes, right away.' He put the
receiver back, looked at Willie and then at his scarcely-touched mug of
tea. 'God's perishing teeth,' he said. 'Why do they always want me at
tea-time?'

Each profession will, inevitably, have its own ways of
sweetening the unpalatable, rounding the hard edges, and exalt-
ing the humble without raising him as far as the soothing
sounds that accompany the operation might suggest. In the
world of publishing—as in any other—the euphemism will be
employed for external as well as internal consumption: particularly when it comes to dealing with authors—including those
the publisher has no intention of publishing—and writing
blurbs. Thus the unwanted typescript will be sent back with a
note explaining that 'after careful consideration', the firm has
decided that it is 'not quite right' or 'not suitable' for the list,
that 'our readers' (useful bogymen, on whose frequent 'illnesses'
can be blamed delays that are, more often than not, entirely the
publisher's fault) 'don't feel sufficiently confident or
enthusiastic to be able to recommend publication', that—much
as the publisher enjoyed reading it—'books of this kind are
impossibly hard to sell in the present state of the market', or
that the author would be 'better advised' to try a publisher
'specializing in this kind of book'. Very often both the excuses
and the regrets are entirely genuine, but euphemisms of this
kind, often set out on a printed rejection letter, may also
disguise the fact that the publisher thinks the book illiterate,
incomprehensible, demented or simply unreadable—and that
he has not, in fact, had to read more than a few sample pages to
come to that conclusion. (Publishers who sense a persistent
author may, if pushed, quote an incident or an opinion from the
middle of the book to give the impression of a thorough reading;
they are well advised to shake the typescript before returning it,
since suspicious authors have been known to insert hairs
between the pages and to expose triumphantly the publisher's
claims to have read their books by revealing that the hairs have
remained undisturbed.)

Once the book has been taken on, the publisher's editor may
well want to suggest cuts or changes to the author—his motives
for which may be literary, or commercial, or a combination of

the two. Some authors may adopt, and expect, a brisk no-nonsense approach; others may need a more tactful, circuitous line. Carefully combining a tentative hesitancy with—he hopes—a clear and sensible idea of what needs to be done, the wise editor will make it clear from the start that he is firmly on the side of both the author and his book (so, indeed, he should be), and that the book will be 'even better than it already is' if such-and-such is done to it. This sense of critical enthusiasm can be particularly necessary when the editor is dealing with —say—a politician's memoirs or the confessions of a reprobate: such books are often full of gripping information appallingly expressed, but their authors may well be far more sensitive about their prose and far less amenable to suggestion than full-time or professional writers. Gazing firmly into the author's eyes, and straining every muscle to look and sound like a metropolitan version of the old-fashioned family doctor, the editor will earnestly explain that, 'fascinating' though that particular passage is, he feels it 'doesn't quite work as it stands' or that it is 'a little bit hard to follow at present': if he can persuade the author to make the necessary changes without having to tell him that large parts of his book are unintelligible, boring or wretchedly badly written, so much the pleasanter for both parties. A useful dodge is for the publisher to pose as the easily baffled general reader—and a perfectly valid one, since most publishers know a little about a good many things and not much about anything, while most writers (including the authors of learned papers on numismatics or hydrodynamics) dream of a wide general readership and hope that their books will be available on the front table in Hatchards in time for the Christmas rush. And a publisher anxious to extract a synopsis or a sample chapter from a reluctant author—'to make quite sure that we're thinking along the same lines'—will, like an old-fashioned schoolmaster flexing his cane, try to persuade him that it is, in fact, in his own best interests to oblige ('It will certainly help you to clarify your own ideas as well . . . ').

Publishers' blurbs are generally a matter of hyperbole, with no adjective left unaccompanied by an equally emphatic adverb ('wickedly comic', 'compellingly readable' and so on). Euphemisms tend to intrude when the publisher isn't quite sure what the book is all about or feels out of his depth ('complex' and 'profound' may indicate bafflement). Curiously enough, a certain prudishness still prevails, with 'sensual' standing in for 'sexy'; 'compelling', 'compulsive', and 'readable' suggest that the blurb-writer is tired, incompetent or can't think of anything more to say, and 'stunning' speaks for itself.

If, as the publisher hopes, the book is a great success, plain language will reign supreme, and the euphemisms can glide away for a well-earned rest. If, on the other hand, things go wrong, they will be urgently summoned up to do their best. Miserable sales will be described as 'respectable' or 'about what we expected' or 'holding up', and likely to 'pick up when the reviews start coming in'; a rotten review is dismissed as 'unrepresentative' ('it's not his sort of book at all') or 'disappointing'; the 'new technology' is entirely responsible for the belated discovery of a rash of printing mistakes; the overdue royalty cheque is, invariably, 'in the post' (although even the most innumerate editors have learnt to introduce 'cash flow' into the conversation, failure to send authors their money is more often the result of incompetence or forgetfulness than of business acumen); the decision not to go ahead and lose more money on the author's next book is blamed on 'the state of the market', and is taken 'very reluctantly indeed'.

In all offices, breaking bad news or getting down to the awkward letter are matters that tend to be postponed for as long as is decently possible: once again, Babbitt's method of dealing—or failing to deal—with the problem is reassuringly familiar, and constitutes a practical euphemism for work itself:

He placed a difficult unanswered letter on the pile of unfinished work, that he might not fail to attend to it that afternoon. (For three noons, now, he had placed the same letter on the unfinished pile.) He scrawled on a sheet of yellow backing-paper the memorandum: 'See abt apt h drs', which gave him an agreeable feeling of having already seen about the apartment house doors.

No doubt Babbitt assured those about him that the matter was 'in hand' and 'being actively pursued'; and that, I suppose, is what office life is all about.

Elizabeth Bennet's Fine Eyes

Patricia Beer

On the whole I am in favour of euphemism. Any manner of speech which aims at avoiding distress to either the speaker or the hearer recommends itself more and more as the years go by. And I am unreservedly in favour of euphemism when I find it in the English novel of the eighteenth and nineteenth centuries, and especially when the subject is the relations between men and women, for it provides a richness, an interest and a complication which unrelieved plain speaking, I think, could never achieve; at all events it never has.

It is impossible to say exactly when euphemism looked like becoming an integral part of the polite speech of actual life. Hugh Rawson in his recently published *A Dictionary of Euphemisms* makes a good guess.

One can only say that fastidiousness in language became increasingly common from about 1750, and that this trend accelerated around the turn of the century, almost as if the incipient Victorians were frantically cleaning up their act in preparation for her ascent to the throne.

1750 is a useful date; not that it marked the appearance of euphemism in the English novel, as before this, without special pleading, there was virtually no English novel for it to appear in, but because the date throws up three novels (in an essay of this length on this subject one has to be arbitrarily selective throughout) which show that at that time euphemism and plain speech could and did exist side by side, sometimes within the same novel, invariably over a range of novels published in any one period. The books to which I allude are Henry Fielding's *Tom Jones* and John Cleland's *Fanny Hill*, both published in 1749, and Samuel Richardson's *Clarissa* which appeared from 1747 to 1748.

'Harkee, Allworthy, I'll bet thee five pounds to a crown we have a boy tomorrow nine months.' Fielding's Squire Western is not in the tavern or at a stag party but in his own drawing-room in the presence of his well-bred daughter Sophia, the temporarily bashful Tom Jones, and Squire Allworthy who has just made a highly decorous speech of congratulation to the betrothed couple on the eve of their wedding. He is not equally forthright about the loss of virginity.

'To her, boy, go to her.' Western has been standing listening outside the drawing-room door and when he realizes that Tom Jones is embracing his daughter he bursts into the room and encourages them, as quoted, 'with his hunting voice and phrase'. The words can hardly be called a euphemism for what he has in mind, as his metaphor is drawn from the activity of chasing and killing, but they are not entirely direct. And in the same sequence he falls back on the conventional slang word of the day: when Allworthy civilly praises Sophia's beauty, Western responds, in a whisper overheard by all present: 'So much the better for Tom, for damn me if he shan't ha' the tousling her.'

On his daughter's wedding night he sings so many 'merry songs' which allude to 'matrimony and the loss of a maiden-head' that Squire Allworthy tries to restrain him. ('Fie, Mr Western!') Yet if he used the word 'maidenhead', that in itself was a euphemism, and no doubt the merry songs were denser with innuendo than, for example, Ophelia's ballad with its forlorn yet witty frankness.

> Then up he rose, and donn'd his clothes,
>   And dupped the chamber door,
> Let in the maid, that out a maid
>   Never departed more.

Squire Western's bawdy seems harmless enough by most standards and it becomes positively life-enhancing when compared with the circumlocutions of Richardson's Lovelace. *Clarissa* is embarrassingly delicate throughout, and nauseatingly so when it comes to the hero's speculation that the heroine may be pregnant: 'I am encouraged to hope, what it will be very surprising to me if it do not happen; that is, in plain English, that the dear creature is in the way to be a mamma.' Not very plain English I should have thought, especially in a letter from one man to another. Neither is this: 'It would be the pride of my life to prove, in this charming frost-piece, the triumph of nature over principle, and to have a young Lovelace by such an angel.' We are in the realm of little strangers and happy events.

Clarissa herself is not much better, though her verbal deviousness is of quite a different sort. Whereas Lovelace's expressions try to diminish and contain the affair in suburban cosiness, hers magnify it with the terms of religious ecstasy: 'For the arrows of the Almighty are within me. . . . The thing which I greatly feared is come upon me.' This sounds like the Virgin Mary; or perhaps St Teresa of Avila: it strongly suggests the Bernini statue. It occurs in a meditation written by Clarissa which finds its way into Lovelace's hands, or, in plain English, is stolen by his friend and posted to him. Lovelace simply cannot believe that anyone raped by him would fail to become pregnant, and these grandiose comments naturally strengthen his assumption.

When it comes to the loss of virginity, of course, Lovelace is in nothing like so strong a position as Sophia's father. Squire Western can afford to be rumbustiously almost-explicit; his daughter's is a case of lawful wedlock, unconsummated before-hand. Lovelace is a rapist, and there is something deadly about his short, smarmy message to his friend: 'The affair is over. Clarissa lives.' Euphemism always misses something. In this case, the affair is not, and Clarissa does not.

From the point of view of this discussion, John Cleland's *Fanny Hill* is much more interesting than either *Tom Jones* or *Clarissa*. As the primary definition of pornography is 'description of the life, manners etc. of prostitutes and their patrons', then this high-spirited, warm-hearted, starry-eyed story has to come into that category. Yet its attempt to maintain verbal decency far exceeds Richardson's. Peter Quennell points out in an excellent introduction to a modern edition that the book

treats of pleasure as the aim and end of existence, and of sexual satisfaction as the epitome of pleasure, but does so in a style that, despite its inflammatory subject, never stoops to a gross or unbecoming word. Fanny Hill would have shuddered at *Lady Chatterley*. The actions described she would have taken in good part . . . but the roughness and coarseness of the dialogue she would have found unspeakably offensive. It includes the kind of phrases and private amatory endearments that Mrs Cole, 'a gentlewoman born and bred', and her school of well-dressed, well-disciplined young beauties would not have considered fit for decent ears.

The subject is indeed inflammatory and the treatment explicit. But no part of the body, and no action or reaction is crudely named. Fanny's references to her maidenhead, though often verging on the cynical, are nearly always ornately metaphorical: 'that trinket of mine which bears so great an imaginary value'; 'that darling treasure, that hidden mine, so eagerly sought after by the men, and which they never dig for but to destroy'.

The book is protected from the coarseness of realism by the fact that a lively set of fantasies is in control. Fanny's description of her initiation by Charles, the 'sweet relenting murderer' of her virginity, is the traditional piece of wish-fulfilment, with streams of blood, yells of agony and dead faints. It is consistent with her comments as to how in matronly middle age lust dies and her hitherto tempestuous blood runs sedately through her veins, and for that matter with her blissful marriage to her beloved Charles, which we may welcome as a happy ending but cannot take for gospel.

Perhaps the heart of the fantasy is the big scene where Fanny and three of her colleagues, each with her 'spark elect', make love successively in the presence of the others. It is all done in a kind of Busby Berkeley way, with pattern, predictability, and smiles. The language is that of kindness and respect. There is no suggestion that Mrs Cole's girls are doing it for the money with men they have never met before, or indeed that Mrs Cole is watching through a spy-hole.

The decency of speech which regulates the goings-on in *Fanny Hill* ('the conversation grew as lively as could be wished, without taking too loose a turn') has very little to do with characterization. The heroine does have a distinct personality: she is generous and gallant, and sensible to the point of wisdom. But her speech is not of her own choosing.

In *Tom Jones* plain speaking *is* a matter of characterization. When Squire Western makes the remark about pregnancy, his three listeners, though they know how to behave in mixed company in a drawing-room, are not really taken aback, however rosy their blushes, for that is the Squire's character.

And presumably contemporary readers accepted his crudity in the same tolerant spirit. There was nothing to worry about; most of the characters spoke respectably.

When it comes to *Clarissa* one hardly knows what to think. Both hero and heroine have a character which is among the most discussable in the English novel. But how does the prissiness of their speech fit in? Clarissa's euphemisms could be said to spring from her personality; she does at times seem to think of herself as the Virgin Mary. Lovelace is more difficult. His would-be delicacy may indeed be a product of character but one fears that the character may be not so much his as Richardson's. If Richardson was consciously intending to create a hero who acted like Genghis Khan and talked like Mr Pooter, this would be fascinating and, as far as one can tell from the newspapers, quite true to life: rapists and rippers are often reported as being very mealy-mouthed in the dock. But one cannot be sure that this effect was intentional.

With euphemism and plain-speaking co-existing in the way they did, eighteenth-century readers were in the strong position of being able to pay their money and take their choice. As time went by, however, the gap widened. Whether society, for non-literary reasons, came to insist on cautiously-worded novels, or whether the cautiousness of some novels brainwashed people, there is no knowing; but by the heyday of Victorianism the choice had become one between respectable family reading and unequivocal pornography.

For several decades the demands of characterization permitted quite considerable licence. In *Sense and Sensibility* (1811) the sedate Elinor Dashwood and Colonel Brandon listen calmly when Mrs Jennings asks the Colonel about the health of her pregnant daughter: 'How does Charlotte do? I warrant you she is a fine size by this time.' Neither Elinor nor the Colonel, we know, would have dreamed of speaking in this way. Poor Elinor makes very heavy weather (the situation is admittedly a most awkward one) of conveying to Edward Ferrars her wish that the living offered him by Colonel Brandon 'were much more considerable, and such as might better enable you to—as might be more than a temporary accommodation to yourself—such, in short, as might establish all your views of happiness'. But Mrs Jennings must be herself; and the speech was presumably as acceptable to the reader as it was to her friends, for she has to be delineated as a vulgarian who has had the nerve to keep up with her city friends.

Nobody needed to fear that Jane Austen or any of her refined characters would speak like that. When Emma Woodhouse is thinking, only thinking, about the pregnancy of her friend Mrs Weston she decides to postpone the announcement of her own engagement until, as she demurely puts it to herself, 'Mrs Weston were safe and well. No additional anxiety should be thrown at this period among those she loved.' One sees what Hugh Rawson means by incipient Victorians. In this passage from *Emma* (1816), with years officially to go, the dark Victorian hint has already arrived.

The fastidiousness of which he speaks may well have affected the novel before it made any general impression on what people actually said to one another. Jane Austen's way of talking in her letters to her sister Cassandra is often quite coarse. On the connection between beds and babies she goes considerably further than Mrs Jennings, and her comments on adultery and mistresses frequently resemble those of Mary Crawford in *Mansfield Park* (1814). It is natural that this should be so. Jane Austen, with quick ears and sailor brothers, must have been as accustomed to worldly vocabulary and sentiments as Mary Crawford; perhaps more so, as her family house was smaller than Admiral Crawford's. Yet Mary Crawford is roundly and consistently condemned. 'My home at my uncle's brought me acquainted with a circle of admirals. Of *Rears* and *Vices* I saw enough, I assure you.' At this daring double pun, uttered at Mansfield Park, and at table too, Edmund and Fanny have to be deeply shocked. They understand it quickly enough of course; 'rear' was well established as a euphemism for 'arse' by their time.

Incidentally, one imagines that Mary may have regarded the name Fanny Price as good for a joke. In British usage, 'fanny' had already acquired its present slang meaning. Lexicographers have suggested that this was a tribute to Fanny Hill, which is interesting; as far as I know, nobody has ever spoken of a woman's clarissa, or sophia.

The dichotomy between private and published speech is one which Jane Austen characteristically puts to splendid use. She

often builds up a character by means of his or her own euphemisms. Mrs Elton in *Emma* is an excellent example: by this
means not only is her social class defined but also her true
attitude to matrimony. Her eagerness to get married herself and
to proclaim the achievement of such of her friends as have
succeeded in doing so ('Mrs Jefferys—Clara Partridge that
was—and the two Milmans, now Mrs Bird and Mrs James
Cooper') is not matched by any real enthusiasm for the actual
state. It is true that the all too demonstrable perils of child-
bearing, tactlessly emphasized by the Anglican service for the
Churching of Women, must have daunted any thoughtful bride,
but Augusta Hawkins shows no signs of being a thoughtful
bride. She simply seems to feel that in every respect except
socially there is something rather nasty about the whole thing.

  Mrs Elton's euphemisms about the courtship are not very
significant in themselves. I say 'Mrs Elton's' though in fact the
account Jane Austen gives of the wooing is, ostensibly, a rendering in indirect speech of what Mr Elton tells the Highbury
gossips, led by nice Mrs Cole. But Jane Austen hardly ever
paraphrases without letting the original voice come right
through, and this particular passage is a wonderful amalga-
mation of author's snide comment on the remarks of one
character who is being influenced by the style of another
character, so that no fewer than three individual voices come
through. Mr Elton of course has never spoken naturally in the
presence of women. As John Knightley points out, to Emma's
annoyance: 'With men he can be rational and unaffected, but
when he has ladies to please, every feature works.' But from the
moment of his becoming involved with Augusta Hawkins his
speech worsens.

The story told well . . . the history which he had to give Mrs Cole of the
rise and progress of the affair was so glorious—the steps so quick, from
the accidental rencontre, to the dinner at Mr Green's and the party at
Mrs Brown's—smiles and blushes rising in importance—with consciousness and agitation richly scattered—the lady had been so easily
impressed—so sweetly disposed—had in short, to use a most intelligible phrase, been so very ready to have him, that vanity and prudence
were equally contented.

This flummery of course may be the effect of bridal nerves

working on innate silliness. But even after Miss Hawkins has safely become Mrs Elton she cannot speak plainly of the married condition. It is impossible for her to say 'my husband'. She is as good as a textbook: the four main expressions she uses in referring to him are perfect examples of four of the main principles of euphemism. They are a vulgarism: 'Mr E.'; a periphrasis: 'a certain gentleman in company'; an archaism: 'my lord and master'; and a phrase from a foreign language: '*cara sposo*' (typically incorrect unless Jane Austen or the printer of the first edition got it wrong).

Even more revealing is what she says when she is telling Mr Weston about the practical delays which beset the preparations for her marriage: 'a certain gentleman in company was apt to despair and exclaim that he was sure at this rate it would be *May* before Hymen's saffron robe would be put on for us'. She is closely following the gutter press of the day. On Fanny Price's visit to Portsmouth in *Mansfield Park* her coarse-grained father shows her a passage from a daily newspaper which it seems only he normally reads.

It was with infinite concern the newspaper had to announce to the world a matrimonial *fracas* in the family of Mr R. of Wimpole Street; the beautiful Mrs R., whose name had not long been enrolled in the lists of Hymen, and who had promised to become so brilliant a leader in the fashionable world, having quitted her husband's roof in company with the well-known and captivating Mr C., the intimate friend and associate of Mr R.

It is all there: *fracas*, Mr R. and Mr C., enrolled in the lists of Hymen, and so on.

Mrs Elton is as dirty-minded as the Bowdlers, and all bowdlerizers. It was a time when straightforward women like Dorothy Wordsworth were saying 'ass' when they meant the quadruped, with no anxiety about the fact that for some years 'ass' had been used in England by those who aspired to delicacy, as a polite pronunciation of 'arse'. Mrs Elton is more delicate still and says 'donkey'; and says it unnecessarily often in the course of the strawberry-picking expedition to Donwell. She also over-reacts when Jane Fairfax, planning to go as a governess, says that there are offices in London for the sale not quite of human flesh but of human intellect. She plunges into references to the slave trade, about which one can be reasonably certain she does not give a damn, presumably because Jane's phrase about the sale of human flesh to her means prostitution.

It is tempting to make something of the fact that on her arrival in Highbury the first adjective she uses to describe Mrs Weston is 'motherly'. Mrs Weston, married on the first page, is pregnant throughout most of the book, but beyond one or two unobtrusive references to her getting tired nobody openly mentions her condition. Is Mrs Elton showing that she has spotted it? Certainly nobody in Highbury knows better than herself how to use delicacy as innuendo.

As the nineteenth century went on, it became less and less possible to assign outspoken remarks to outspoken characters; everybody had to talk cagily. A subject like pregnancy obviously had to be mentioned sometimes, if only in the interests of plot. The major novelists meet the challenge in various ways. Wilkie Collins, who cares for nothing so much as plot, is briskly opportunistic about the birth of his protagonist's child in *The Woman in White* (1860).

In the February of the new year our first child was born—a son. My mother and sister and Mrs Vesey were our guests at the little christening party, and Mrs Clements was present to assist my wife on the same occasion. Marian was our boy's godmother, and Pesca and Mr Gilmore (the latter acting by proxy), were his godfathers.

This is masterly. He has distracted our attention from the actual event, except perhaps in the phrase about Mrs Clements, by reintroducing no less than seven of his characters, rounding up Mrs Vesey and Mrs Clements who have been lost to sight for some time, and indicating that his mother and sister have accepted his wife, that Pesca has not suffered for his part in events and that Mr Gilmore is still abroad but that he is now well enough to undertake both godfatherhood and his turn in the narrative.

Towards the end of *Daniel Deronda* (1876), George Eliot has to impart the information that Gwendolen Grandcourt, recently widowed, is *not* pregnant (much trickier), as the terms of her husband's will are drastically governed by the possibility. She ingeniously invents a conversation between men, who speak unemotionally as though it was a subject of purely testamentary interest:

'Any prospect of an heir being born?'
'From what Mr Gascoigne said to me, I conclude not. He spoke as if it were a question whether the widow would have the estate for her life.'

As the plot of *The Woman in White* depends on the fact of illegitimacy and so to a lesser extent does that of *Daniel Deronda*, it is worth mentioning here that the nineteenth-century novelists seem to have felt less need to be euphemistic about a child's being born out of wedlock than about its being born at all. Bastardy for them is often not so much a sexual happening as a question of inheritance and money and physical appearance.

Dickens, who rose to and surmounted so many more challenges than most novelists, on the subject of pregnancy makes life particularly difficult for himself; and for us sometimes, as in the excruciating chapter—and I think it must have been excruciating even in its own day—in *Our Mutual Friend* (1864) in which Bella is given six pages, ripe with suggestive words and actions, to work up to telling her husband that 'there is a ship upon the ocean . . . bringing to you and me . . . a little baby'. Its being little apparently makes it more delicate as a subject: a stock technique of euphemism.

Much more successful is the circumlocution used in *Bleak House* (1852/3) when Ada's unborn baby is described as 'the help that was to come to her' in her struggle to reclaim her young husband from his ruinous delusions. There is dignity and pathos in the picture of her standing at his death-bed, heavily pregnant, trying to appear calm: 'so serene and beautiful, with the help that was to come to her so near'. But Dickens's greatest success in the treatment of this subject is when he makes it comic. The conversation between Mr and Mrs Sparkler in Chapter 24, Book II, of *Little Dorrit* (1855/7) is the apotheosis of a nudgy deviousness which is thoroughly vulgar; but funny.

'Calculated to shine in society,' retorted Fanny, with great irritability; 'yes, indeed! And then what happens? . . . Why, I find myself at the very period when I might shine most in society, and should most like for very momentous reasons to shine in society—I find myself in a situation which to a certain extent disqualifies me for going into society. It's too bad, really!' . . .

Mr Sparkler submitted that he had thought 'it might be got over'.

'Got over!' repeated Fanny, with immeasurable scorn.

'For a time,' Mr Sparkler submitted . . .

'However,' she said, when she had in some measure recovered from her sense of personal ill-usage; 'provoking as it is, and cruel as it seems, I suppose it must be submitted to.'

'Especially as it was to be expected,' said Mr Sparkler.

In the nineteenth century there were no euphemisms that were euphemistic enough to describe, in print, a wedding night. Dickens does his excellent best but even he can get no nearer than rhapsody.

So she leaning on her husband's arm, they turned homeward by a rosy path which the gracious sun struck out for them in its setting. And oh, there are days in this life, worth life and worth death. And oh, what a bright old song it is, that oh, 'tis love, 'tis love, 'tis love, that makes the world go round.

This reticence would be no disadvantage at all in itself, but it does lead to perverse misinterpretation on the part of readers who have come to depend on complete explicitness. Casaubon's alleged impotence is a case in point. Someone was telling me that nowadays they positively teach students doing *Middlemarch* (1871/2) for A-levels that his marriage to Dorothea was not consummated. This is nonsense. The text is discreet, certainly, but I should have thought unequivocal: 'He had not found marriage a rapturous state but he had no idea of being anything else than an irreproachable husband, who would make a charming young woman as happy as she deserved to be.' Casaubon was not so unworldly as to think that a bride who was still virgin after six weeks of marriage would not be bewildered and distressed. Even Ruskin in such circumstances was ready with self-justification. And it is expressly stated that Dorothea 'had no distinctly shapen grievance that she could state even to herself': non-consummation would have been one. The passage which I suppose teachers are thinking of is 'He determined to abandon himself to the stream of feeling, and perhaps was surprised to find what an exceedingly shallow rill it was.' But this is said of Casaubon before the marriage; and before Freud.

No one would dispute that he is presented as an inexperienced and not very ardent lover, or doubt that he finds sexual intercourse disappointing, but Dorothea is no Effie Ruskin; her troubles are more complex.

Nineteenth-century writers often got round taboo by making use of what the twentieth century calls body language, which could express what neither they nor their characters were free to say. *Cranford* (1853) is often thought of as a study in sexual frustration with roses round the door, yet Elizabeth Gaskell includes in it an exciting picture of sexual fulfilment: the romance of Lady Glenmire and Mr Hoggins. That Lady Glenmire is a sexy woman is established by Miss Pole's surprisingly daring comment: 'Well, there is a kind of attraction about Lady Glenmire that I, for one, should be ashamed to have.'

We are told nothing else, but shown it. A watchful servant describes how her ladyship, on her first Sunday in Cranford, 'looked up and down the church, like a bird, and nipped up her petticoats when she came out, as quick and sharp as ever I see'. A watchful Elizabeth Gaskell describes how Mr Hoggins, the village doctor, a large man, has a habit of crossing his legs in a way which disturbs the Cranford spinsters. After this the affair develops mostly out of our sight, though there are two or three good clues, usually missed, but we can assume that the birdlike survey of the church included Mr Hoggins, a noticeable man, and that the brisk nipping-up of petticoats may have been a reaction to his presence and perhaps gaze, and that the way he crossed his legs did not repel the experienced and frisky Lady Glenmire. So we arrive without an unseemly word spoken at the day when the engaged couple appear in public.

Her face seemed to have almost something of the flush of youth in it; her lips looked redder and more trembling full than in their old compressed state, and her eyes dwelt on all things with a lingering light, as if she was learning to love Cranford and its belongings. Mr Hoggins looked broad and radiant, and creaked up the middle aisle at church in a brand-new pair of top-boots.

The day had clearly not arrived when in polite society no legs would be mentioned at all, from Mr Hoggins's to a piano's; nor the day when a writer—in this case the Revd Sabine Baring-Gould—would speak of 'certain heavily-frilled cotton investitures of the lower limbs', meaning petticoats; he must have meant petticoats because otherwise he would have alluded, as he does elsewhere, to 'the bloomer arrangement in the nether latitude'.

Legs and bosoms were the only parts of the female body that ever needed euphemisms at all in the nineteenth-century novel, as read at family firesides. The others were either considered harmless or so unmentionable as never to be approached, however deviously. For most writers, and Dickens especially, bosoms were principally objects for dying husbands to rest their heads on, though there are occasional hints as to the breast-feeding of babies. One of the few cases where a bosom is spoken of as a sexual asset is in Thackeray's *Vanity Fair* (1847/8): 'Green eyes, fair skin, pretty figure, famous frontal development.' Two men are discussing Becky Sharp, which is not surprising. The surprise is that they are medical men, Mr Clump and Dr Squills, who might have been expected to manage without phrases like 'famous frontal development' when talking to each other. The family novel has to be like a film where two foreigners converse in their common language with foreign accents.

In the nineteenth century plain terminology passed into the novels that were read when none of the family was about: which is euphemistic for erotica, which is euphemistic for pornography. Yet there are surprises even in this genre, in that there is great inconsistency. One moment the writer is saying 'cunt' and the next using some sickly periphrasis like 'Holy of Holies' or 'Maltese Cross', for no artistic or technical reason that I can see. Euphemism must be its own reward if writers use it when they need not. It must be a natural human instinct.

I cannot say that such instincts should not be investigated, as I have enjoyed Hugh Rawson's dictionary and also that of Judith S. Neaman and Carole G. Silver, which came out in 1983. Yet such investigations can be disquieting.

Jane Austen's novels are full of oglers—Mr Darcy, Sir Walter Elliot, Sir Thomas Bertram—who look girls up and down as they walk along the streets of Bath or around the drawing-rooms of the stately homes ('very refreshing after sitting so long in one attitude'). What Mr Darcy sees as he watches Elizabeth Bennet is a pretty girl with a pretty figure whose face is 'rendered uncommonly intelligent by the beautiful expression of her dark eyes'. Interrogated by Miss Bingley at a party he boldly speaks of the great pleasure which a pair of fine eyes can give, and even more boldly identifies the owner of the eyes. From that moment Elizabeth Bennet's fine eyes become a leitmotiv in Miss Bingley's conversations with Darcy.

Ms Neaman and Ms Silver have now forced on me the knowledge that 'a fine pair of eyes' is a euphemism for 'big tits'. They assure me that American soldiers introduced the expression into Britain during World War II and that it has since become quite common. I am doubtful about this. There was an American base very near here during the war and no American soldier ever made the remark to me or even to my better-endowed friends; and none of my younger friends has ever come across it, except one who thinks she once heard it in a TV sitcom. But no euphemism springs from nowhere, and the history of surrealism shows that there was a connection between breasts and eyes long before World War II; think of Shelley's dream. If that was what Darcy meant all along, fine; but I think we should have been told.

Euphemisms and the Media

DERWENT MAY

ADVERTISING, the press, television—there are times when it seems that what they have created between them in these last years of the twentieth century is a whole culture of euphemism, a world where everything is presented as slightly better than it is. An artist I know was invited by a wine merchants' to draw a vignette of their premises for their wine list. When it was ready for distribution, they sent out a press release saying that this decoration of their list was 'by the well-known artist, —— ——'. At that moment, the artist told me, he realized that the one thing he was not was 'well-known'. If they had thought he was, they wouldn't have felt any need to say so.

Whether what the wine merchants' wrote was exactly definable as a euphemism, I am not sure. But I think it was: the individual who wrote the hand-out, when he chose the phrase 'well-known', was thinking to himself something like 'not all that well-known—as you'll naturally know, readers—but deserving to be, as you'll see when you look at the picture'. The case illustrates a genuine difficulty, however, which is where to draw the line dividing euphemism from sheer exaggeration. Exaggeration in advertising is commonplace: it is, one might say, the soil in which the fine flower of euphemism grows. Exaggeration—or 'hype' as the current phrase has it, which is itself a disarming euphemism for 'hyperbole', a word that doesn't sound so good—is simply reckless. It makes its claims as if they were to be taken at face-value, as if there were no doubt about their truth at all.

But euphemism, as I see it and have presented it in this essay, requires some recognition by the writer or speaker that the person he is addressing will feel some doubt, some resistance, some distaste even, when these particular matters are mentioned, or these claims are made; and a deliberate, often somewhat uneasy attempt to overcome this resistance by his choice of language. It always contains a touch of complicity with the reader or listener. In fact it tries to put down resistance precisely through the implicit and sometimes good-humoured acknowledgement that the resistance is there.

The advertising of certain goods takes us straight to the heart of the matter. These are such things as lavatory paper, sanitary towels, contraceptives, and substances for cleaning or fixing false teeth. All of these are perfectly respectable products, but the mention of them inspires distaste or disgust in many people. The commercial names of many of these products are the first euphemisms used in the selling of them. Durex contraceptive sheaths, Andrex toilet rolls, Tampax sanitary tampons—that little Latin 'x' in the suffix associates them all with science, and so with emotional neutrality and cleanliness instead of uncomfortable emotion and biological dirt. 'Ex', you might say, cleans up the spot. (One sales name, however, seems to me to suffer from a backlash effect here. Estate agents sometimes call small, self-contained parts of a house a 'granny annex', or more recently just a 'grannex'. I can't help feeling that potential house-buyers might be put off a 'grannex' by association with the names—and in the end the inescapable character—of these other wares.)

There is an odd piece of social history connected with the marketing of some of these products. The Independent Broadcasting Authority has decided that the advertising of contraceptives as such (though not of official family planning centres) offends against taste, so does not allow it on television. The advertising of sanitary towels and tampons is also forbidden on Independent Television (though not on Independent Radio); however, there have been two recent experiments in advertising sanitary protection on television, in 1979 and 1980. For three months in 1979 and six months in 1980, transmission of advertisements for these goods was allowed after strict inspection by the IBA. (The IBA, at home, uses its own euphemistic acronym when discussing the subject—'Sanpro'.)

A riot of euphemisms burst on to the television screens of Britain: not so much verbal ones as—often far more interesting—visual ones linked with the words. In one advertisement, promoting Vespré sanitary towels, the spoken commentary ran: 'When science improves things, they often get slimmer, more useful, and more convenient. And that's exactly what's happened to the press-on towel. . . .' Direct enough words, it might be thought. But the pictures accompanying them were not of sanitary towels: they were pictures, first, of a Brownie camera, then a slim, modern camera; next, of a thick, ordinary wrist-watch, then a slim quartz watch. The slim camera clicked, the slim watch ticked; only then did a packet of Vespré appear, being picked up by a female hand and put into a shoulder-bag.

Kotex Mini absorbency towels used a euphemism of abstractions. 'There are times when full absorbency towels are too large,' the commentary went. 'For those times Kotex introduce new Kotex Minis. Smaller, slimmer. . . .' Meanwhile one saw a black outline rectangle being drawn on the white screen, followed by a smaller rectangle drawn inside the larger one; again, only at the end did a packet of Kotex Minis come on, filling the space in the small rectangle.

However, all these inventive euphemisms were of no avail. Too many viewers wrote in to say they were disgusted even by these advertisements, and the advertising of sanitary protection continues to be forbidden on Independent Television.

Good visual euphemisms are to be found in advertisements concerned with false teeth—something that no one wants to see. An advertisement for one fixative simply shows two beautiful slim blue cylinders fitting together perfectly, as a voice praises the efficiency and salubriousness of the product. Steradent, a product for cleaning false teeth, shows us a glass full of the liquid—but what is sitting in the glass is not the dreaded dentures, but a solid object just fleetingly reminiscent of them, a kind of white sculpture of the word STERADENT itself. Harpic lavatory cleaner keeps us in mind of its powerful effect, while attracting our thoughts away from other associations, by identifying its action with the great dramas of *Star Wars*—'May the bleachmatic force be with you,' a deep voice booms. A whole atmosphere of euphemism is wittily used in an advertisement for Andrex lavatory paper. A dog is seen playing in a garden with a roll of the stuff, winding it round the trees on a summer's day. 'Soft, strong, and very long' is the point—'soft' gets into the advertisement through the balmy weather (and also the soft-definition filming), 'strong and very long' are qualities that make the toilet roll a perfect toy for a dog. The real advantages of these qualities are left to filter romantically into the mind.

Before leaving these delicate topics, we must turn briefly to Durex contraceptives, banned from the air but appearing to great effect in newspaper advertisements. Durex pride themselves, rightly, on not being indirect or mealy-mouthed about what they are selling. (Some other firms, aspiring to that goal, do indeed get their effects by the startling frankness of their advertising—a fact which may alert us to how used we have become to euphemisms. 'Pregnant executives!' begins an advertisement in the *New Yorker*, from an organization that finds work for women kept at home; it is in the starkest contrast to the advertising all round it.) However, even the Durex advertisements cannot resist a touch of euphemism to distract us from too close pondering on what happens when you use their product. They say, for instance, with admirable accuracy and plainness, that 'Durex Nu-Form Extra Safe has its own spermicidal lubricant making it as reliable as the Mini Pill —that means 97 per cent effective'. But when they go on to say 'the sheath of today has been specially shaped to offer supreme sensitivity', there is a distinct air, in the rhetorical vibrations of 'supreme' and 'of today', of getting away from the 'shape' as quickly as possible. There is also a euphemistic suggestion —hardly to be taken literally, that is—that all this will be mainly of interest to married couples seriously planning their families. Finally, the advertisements are brightened up with cartoons of a quaint, fat-nosed couple in bed, in one case with the woman beginning to lean hungrily over the man, who shrinks away saying 'Not tonight dear, I've got a headache!' In such a joke the real advantage to women of contraceptives is allowed to be glimpsed, but only through a euphemistic veil of comic allusion and distraction.

An aspect of life rather different from these, that nevertheless sometimes meets with resistance when it is mentioned, is money. For advertisers, the tension can appear when they want to allow for the fact that their customers may not be very well off, but do not want to upset them by reminding them of it. I saw an Underground poster for Listerine Antiseptic Mouthwash that tackled the problem by very ingenious euphemistic invention. The first thing, of course, was to associate the product not so much with the unpleasant business of purifying one's bad breath with a liquid that itself has an uninviting taste, as with the luxurious eating and drinking that may make such a performance necessary. At the same time, the advertisement had to appeal to potential customers for whom luxury is not all that easily come by. So it showed a table laden with strong-flavoured items for a kind of student dinner-party—and described these alluring goodies as 'kipper dips, spring onions and wittily cheap wine'. That 'wittily cheap' seemed to me a brilliant specimen of euphemism, combining all the elements that the advertisement needed. Whether, of course, it worked on the people who read the advertisement on the Underground platform is another matter. In such a poster, the uneasy feelings of the advertiser may be getting more attention than the resistance of the prospective purchaser.

In fact, in every sphere of advertising we find goods being bumped up in ways that can be distinguished as euphemism rather than exaggeration. Airlines call their first-class seats 'de luxe', which means they can call their second-class seats 'first class' or 'club' or 'clipper'; then they pass off their third-class seats as 'tourist'. Estate agents turn a terrace house into a 'town house', probably doing much better with that than with the 'grannex', though the absurdity is plain to any house-buyer. Even the BBC joins in the game when it is selling its own video-cassettes and wants to suggest that it is to be taken just as seriously as straight commercial firms in the same business: 'Auntie Strikes Back' is the slogan at the head of one advertisement, a double euphemism, combining its own staff's affectionate name for the BBC with an image of power from the same *Star Wars* series of films that we saw Harpic employing. Another poster, this from one of the public services, with death as the subject to be both advertised and avoided: the London Fire Brigade, warning people against the dangers of double glazing, shows a woman ineffectually hammering at a double-glazed window with a chair, to the accompaniment of the euphemistic legend 'Double Glazing That Won't Let You Out Could Keep You In For Good'. And before we leave the realm of advertising, we might note that euphemism has even invaded one branch of that earnest group of bookshops, Collet's Books: on a shelf in Gray's Inn Road in London, beneath the History shelf, appears a line of feminist books hopefully labelled 'Herstory'. Perhaps, however, this is a case where, with our doubts about the soundness of what is being offered, we see the word as a euphemism, when the bookseller really sees it as an expression of the truth.

In newspapers, and in television and radio news, most euphemisms have a different origin. A reporter said on BBC Television News, when President Reagan was visiting South Korea, that 'the South Korean government is careless of civil liberties and human rights'. 'Careless': that is the one thing we know that the South Korean government is not, and cannot be, in such a matter. If it refuses its people certain civil liberties, it knows exactly what it is doing. It may be wise, it may be wicked, to act as it does; but the situation has certainly not come about through inadvertence.

Why should a BBC correspondent say this, when we practically all perceive it to be a euphemism? What one is bound to conclude is that reporters live close to politicians and official spokesmen, and absorb from them the euphemisms which they feel their job requires of them. When Reagan is visiting South Korea, the Americans must release some praise of the South Korean government on the world; but it must not appear gullible, so it must also offer some muted criticism of what is undoubtedly a severe regime. Out of such compromises are political euphemisms born.

They differ from advertising euphemisms in that the act of complicity here is more on the part of the listener or reader than on the part of the progenitor of the euphemism. Advertisers are implicitly saying, 'We know that there are other aspects of (say) sanitary towels that we're not reminding you of, but you'll understand why we adopt the euphemism, so let's smile at that together.' Politicians have less of a smile on their faces: they keep them straight. This time, the willing listener is the 'guilty' party, if that is the right word (and it generally is). It is the listener who implicitly responds, 'We know it's worse than you say, but we're happy to go along with your softening of the ugly facts; it makes it easier for us to live with them.'

Of course, it is particularly deplorable when newspapers go along with such euphemisms: it is the task of the press, in my view, to scrutinize and explode them. Nevertheless we all know how frequently they do creep in, even into what seems at first the most objective of reporting. Leader-writers often use them as blandly as government spokesmen.

Most of them consist of attempts to diminish people's awareness of the degree of violence being used somewhere or other. 'Pacification' has usually meant the death of many rebels or dissidents, or (as Orwell observed) the bombardment of defenceless villages and the machine-gunning of cattle; the Vietnam war itself was often described simply as a 'police action' in the press. Great Britain had its 'Malayan emergency', which entailed a fairly ruthless war against Malayan communists. Political rights or wrongs are not the question here; whatever those may be, it always seems wrong for governments to conceal their actions and purposes under euphemisms, and for newspapers to co-operate with them in doing that.

Potential disasters also give rise to political euphemisms. Probably not many defence correspondents would allow themselves to use the phrase 'all-out strategic exchange' to describe nuclear war; but comforting acronyms derived from military sources are often found in their reports. Examples of these are MIRV for Multiple Independently Targeted Re-entry Vehicle, itself something of a euphemism for a missile with several warheads, each 'homed' (yet another euphemism, full of bitter irony) on a different target; MARV for Manoeuvrable Re-entry Vehicle, a variant of MIRV (Mervin and Marvin are of course the names of nice American boys); and PAR for Posture of Acceptable Risk, for a situation where one side has enough nuclear weapons for a relative increase on the other side not to lead to absolute superiority, and therefore not requiring any action.

I have also come across BEST for Behavioural Skills Training—i.e. learning how to kill; and, in the same vein, a CIA assassination unit called the Health Alteration Committee. Perhaps the last two are intended less to appease anybody's fears than to enable the trainees and employees to live a little more comfortably with what they are doing—or at any rate to ease the tension they must sometimes feel.

The language of political campaigning also slips only half-noticed into pure euphemism at times, and is picked up by press commentators. 'Campaign rhetoric' itself is really a euphemism for 'the kind of lies and exaggerations you expect politicians to use'. As an example, 'There is an active possibility that we may do such and such' generally means that there is not the least intention of doing anything about it. 'That's a value judgement', when thrown as a reply to a heckler, means 'I'm not interested in your criticisms and I'm certainly not going to argue with you'. 'We've been perfectly candid' may mean 'We've been caught lying and we shall now see how little of the truth we need tell'. President Nixon is, fairly or not, associated with much of this kind of language, and gets his reward in a euphemism heard among drug-takers, where a 'Nixon' means a drug which claims high potency but in fact has very little. Without doubt, the Russian press is full of similar euphemisms, and I imagine similar cruel jokes circulate in Russia about Brezhnev or Chernenko.

One political area (if it can be dignified with that description) has spawned a famous group of euphemisms in the press, all of which I think are really pernicious. These are ways of describing killings by the IRA. Sometimes we read or hear on the news that the IRA has 'admitted responsibility' for a murder; at other times, that it has 'claimed responsibility'. Each of these phrases—used for reasons that I must admit are deeply obscure to me—is an absurd euphemism that not only casts an unjustifiably favourable light on the IRA, but also factually misrepresents the IRA's own attitude. What the IRA does on these occasions is announce with satisfaction that they killed the victim. 'Admitted responsibility' suggests an acknowledgement of guilt on their part that is not the case; 'claimed responsibility' is an altogether ridiculous euphemism, 'claimed' hinting at the IRA's satisfaction in the killing, 'responsibility' acknowledging the common perception of it as a crime, the two words coming together in a meaningless pairing that seems to indicate utter confusion in the authors of the phrase.

Crime euphemisms echoed in the popular press tend to show complicity with the criminal rather than the reader. They are drawn from criminal slang, in which we see the familiar attempt to joke about one's behaviour, in order to protect oneself from examining it too closely. 'Straightening a policeman out' is a euphemism coolly based on the use of opposites—it means bribing him. 'There was a drink in it for him' also means that the policeman, or whoever else is being referred to, was bribed. 'A couple of right-handers' is a cheerfully euphemistic version of a beating-up, never heard, one imagines, from the person set upon.

Illness, too, leads to euphemisms in newspapers. Here we come back to something a little closer to euphemistic advertising. As with such advertisements, the newspapers wish to speak of upsetting but interesting subjects without upsetting their readers too much. 'On sick leave'—universal office jargon, these days—allows people to avoid thinking of the power of illness: leave, after all, is taken voluntarily. 'A heart condition' is something we presumably all have, so if someone's heart attack is described in those terms we need not think too hard about his perhaps fatal difference from us. 'Negative patient-care outcome' is a hospital euphemism for the end, but one hopes no self-respecting newspaper would fall for it. Other organizations, incidentally, have their self-protective euphemisms for illness and misfortune: 'motion discomfort' for sea-sickness and air-sickness, 'a water landing' for a crash in the sea.

Also closer to advertising in its relation to the reader is the kind of feature about film or rock or television stars that one gets in a magazine like *TV Times*, or the glamour columns of the tabloids. The problem here is to describe extravagant or immoral goings-on in a way that excites the reader without shocking him too much. We read in *TV Times*, for instance, how Miss Jerry Hall, Mick Jaggers's girl-friend, 'took a brief excursion' with a millionaire racehorse-owner. That discourages anyone from thinking that Jerry Hall's glamorous life could be marred by anything as unpleasant as promiscuity or infidelity. Two song-writers, according to the same publication, 'live in the Hollywood hills, their peace disturbed only by the rustle of royalties falling through the letter-box'. A complicated euphemism, this: it goes so far in its attempt to subdue envy on the part of its readers that it seems to twist round and end up as rather sour irony. The reader can settle for the reaction he chooses, at different points along the emotional movement of the sentence. Sometimes, however, such features have to rescue the actors' glamour. When *TV Times* has an article in which fat actors from the serial *Coronation Street* talk about their weight problems, we get, according to the report, 'a calorie countdown with the Street's chubby stars'.

Readers' own lives and problems can get similar treatment. What Women's Lib militants would describe in their own prim euphemism as 'sexual harassment' is carried out, according to feature-writers, by 'office Romeos'. These are the same writers who will try to blunt the sharp edge of life by calling pregnant schoolgirls 'gymslip mums', but also appeal to the reader to 'stroll down memory lane' to the supposedly pastoral time when such problems were undreamt-of.

One last form of newspaper euphemism that should be mentioned takes exactly the opposite form from those we have discussed so far. This is a way of writing about behaviour that might otherwise shock or dismay in such neutral—practically anthropological—tones that normal reaction is inhibited. A good example of this is an article in the *Observer* magazine by Peter Crookston, describing the life of some young, unemployed 'Mohicans'—that is to say, 'punks' with their head shaved so that the remaining hair forms a line of spikes along the top. One of them, 'Spider', is in Trafalgar Square on a hot day in August, 'showing off to a couple of girls on holiday from Scotland. . . . Within minutes of meeting the girls he had one of them spreadeagled against the parapet of a fountain in a passionate kiss. Spider is 16 and is believed to live with his parents in North London.' Another is called 'Rat': 'he is 20 and local legend has it that he ran away from home at nine, lives in a squat in Woolwich and has three girls in the family way'. As for Keith, the main subject of the article: 'Yes, he takes drugs, but not very much now.'

This seems to me very distinctly a euphemistic way of writing. As with many of the other examples we have seen, it shows an implicit awareness that its subject-matter might provoke a strong reaction. But it tries to damp down that reaction, and to create in its place an unemotional acceptance of what it is describing, not by mincing its words or by any jollity or jokiness, but by the very flatness of its precision.

It might be said that items like the 'Deaths' column of *The Times* or the *Daily Telegraph* do the same thing. Recently, that aspect of *The Times*'s column was highlighted in a novel way. When the actor John Le Mesurier died, he left instructions for a notice to be put in the paper saying that he had 'conked out'. A euphemism too: but by its sheer surprise-effect in the context, it brought one back from the decent, euphemistic neutrality of the column to something like the reality of death.

Both newspapers and television use euphemisms in another aspect of their existence. This is the way in which they actively present themselves and their material. Here again we come close to the area of advertisers' euphemisms, though what they are trying to do is to obfuscate or joke winningly about short-comings of their own. On television all men appear tall, as one realizes with a shock when one sees some of the short ones in the flesh. You might almost say that on television a big man is a euphemism for a short man. Certainly the 'Big Match' is no bigger than any other—it is merely the one chosen for showing that day. 'Another chance to see' a programme means that you are getting a repeat. 'Of special interest to the disabled' means 'for the disabled, but we hope we can persuade a few able-bodied viewers to watch it too'. 'The news' on radio and television is itself a kind of euphemism—as is brought out by the more precise introduction that Radio 3 announcers sometimes use: 'Here is a summary of the news.'

The people who make television have their own euphemisms for many aspects of their trade. As in other cases, these euphemisms brighten the dullness or give the conscience a short holiday. Sexual euphemisms about boringly non-sexual matters are particularly common. Two-kilowatt television lamps are yellow at the back and known as 'blondes'; the smaller lamps are red at the back and called 'redheads'. The word 'sexy' itself has extended its meaning widely—a tedious news story can be treated in a 'sexy' way by any device that makes it more interesting; a good angle on the story is 'a sexy way of looking at it'.

A particularly good euphemism is the one used for cutaways, which is the technical term for brief shots of faces, inserted in a recorded discussion to give an impression of the give and take of the participants' reactions. (They are usually filmed after the discussion, and slotted in at apt moments.) These are known as 'noddies', a word delightful both for its nursery air and for its sharp observation of the sage nods that participants in television discussions are inclined to give if they think the cameras are on them. An irony is added by the fact that directors prefer not to use actual nodding shots in such circumstances because they are thought to look artificial. Nursery euphemisms crop up in other contexts, often giving some more serious disguise to the nature of what is being said. 'Is it a bang-bang?' means 'Is it a violent shot?'—and therefore, alas, more likely to interest the viewer.

Disasters attract their euphemisms, in the small world of the television studio as much as in the great world of international relations. 'It's falling off the air', used while a programme is being broadcast, means 'It's a failure'. A more technical euphemism for something that has gone wrong is 'Hair in the gate!' This has a literal meaning that is also used—it describes the commonest setback in filming, when a fine sliver of celluloid from the film has got into the aperture (or 'gate') of the camera (you can sometimes see the wiggly trace of such a 'hair' on the screen). But it has evolved into a joky cry, used consolingly when practically anything goes wrong.

Television workers show their greatest detachment from the world they work in, in another phrase: when people are being invited to speak on a subject, the question may come up: 'Are they the usual pundits, hacks etc.? Or are they *real people*?' Here the euphemism or pseudo-euphemism 'real people' is employed not so much to bump up the value of the kind of people it refers to as to devalue their rivals.

We come finally to those euphemisms that are common to media workers in the different fields—all of whom, as we have seen, share the same broad habitat. Drink figures conspicuously in that habitat, and euphemisms for 'drunk' are often required. 'Legless' is well known; 'châteaued' is a more recent one, effective both in its primary meaning and in the punning echo it contains. I read in one advertising magazine that a certain, superior restaurant was 'not your Camembert butty and vin leglesse number'. The results of over-indulging in two London restaurants much used by the media are respectively 'a Bertorelli belly' and 'the Rugantino rumble'.

Self-defence, in the end, is what all euphemisms come back to. So let us end, too, on some of its subtlest personal forms. 'It needs a lot of fine tuning' is often a very satisfactory way of saying 'I've done nothing about it yet.' 'He'll add a new dimension to our discussions' is excellent when you are really thinking 'I can't imagine why we're bringing him in.' 'At the end of the day', as in remarks like 'At the end of the day it all comes down to money', is a phrase with particularly rich applications. It exudes a sort of long-experienced, man of the world matiness, under guise of which the crudest conclusion can be forced on the person you are speaking to.

But one should perhaps avoid being too severe on the euphemism-user in this all-pervasive climate of euphemism. Who among us can hope to be saved? If the reader examines this essay too closely, I am afraid he will find a number of attempts at euphemistic complicity between us, too.

The Law

DAVID PANNICK

(i)

AT 10.30 p.m. on a December evening in 1891, Miss Daisy Hopkins was arrested by the Revd F. Wallis, a Pro-Proctor of the University of Cambridge. She was charged with 'walking with a member of the University'. On conviction before the University court she was ordered by the Vice-Chancellor to be detained for fourteen days in the University gaol.

Miss Hopkins applied to the Queen's Bench Division of the High Court.[1] Her lawyers argued that the charge disclosed no offence known to the common law, statute, or the Charter of the University. It was explained, on behalf of the University, that the charge was in the usual form for such cases and was 'always understood to mean that the woman charged was in company with an undergraduate for an immoral purpose'. The Revd Wallis told the court that he knew Miss Hopkins 'to be a reputed prostitute'.

Lord Coleridge (the Lord Chief Justice) observed that 'nobody would suppose that a person simply walking with a member of the University, who might be that member's mother, or sister, or wife, or friend, was guilty of an offence against the law which would justify the Vice-Chancellor in imprisoning him or her'. Mr Justice Smith similarly had 'not the slightest doubt that this woman was tried upon a charge of immorality; that there was ample evidence to justify that charge of immorality. . . . What is more,' he added, 'she and [her lawyer] knew perfectly well she was being tried upon that.' Nevertheless, the judges concluded, the conviction must be quashed because Miss Hopkins had been charged with something which did not constitute an offence. The Vice-Chancellor, or anyone else, 'could not use a form of words which did not give jurisdiction, and yet give themselves jurisdiction by saying, "Oh, we meant them in a sense which would have given us jurisdiction, and they are words which we have for a long time used, and which we understood to give us jurisdiction".'

Lord Coleridge and Mr Justice Smith stubbornly refused to recognize the validity of the euphemism adopted by the University. It would be an error of interpretation of their decision as disastrous as that made by Miss Hopkins (who, in 1892, sued the Revd Wallis for false imprisonment and failed because he was found to have had reasonable cause for arresting her)[2] to conclude that the euphemism therefore has no place in the law.

(ii)

Lawyers have, as Jonathan Swift observed, 'a peculiar cant and jargon of their own, that no other mortal can understand'. They take care to ensure that all legal business, including the drafting of legislation, is conducted in this language 'so that it will take thirty years to decide whether the field left me by my ancestors for six generations belongs to me or to a stranger three hundred miles off'.[3] This language, condemned by Jeremy Bentham as 'literary garbage', 'lawyers' cant', and 'flash language',[4] serves various purposes, none of them in the public interest. It unites lawyers, distinguishing them from laymen. It makes the law mysterious and incomprehensible to those laymen, thus ensuring a steady supply of work for lawyers who are needed to interpret the language they have invented.[5] The language of the law fosters the illusion that legal problems are remediable only by the application of the medicine of the specialist. Only a lawyer can resolve the complexities of the problem: better see a lawyer; 'don't trust Whatsisname' (as the memorable Law Society advertisement warned consumers). Legal language also enshrouds the law, hiding it from the public it exists to serve. The idiom of the lawyer leads to public ignorance of the content of the law (which paradoxically refuses to recognize that ignorance of the law should be a defence), to uninformed criticism and to unmerited praise. It provokes the indifference of too many laymen towards the law and the contempt of so many litigants for a legal system they do not understand. Legal jargon also helps to make sound acceptable what in plain terms would be seen as outrageous: 'In law, what plea so tainted and corrupt / But being season'd with a gracious voice / Obscures the show of evil?'[6] Sir Edward Coke (the seventeenth-century Lord Chief Justice who was a founder of the modern law) claimed that the ancient Britons wrote their law in Greek 'to the end that their discipline might not be made common among the vulgar'.[7] To avoid the adverse consequences of the legal vernacular, in Thomas More's *Utopia* the populace 'have no lawyers among them, for they consider them as a sort of people whose profession it is to disguise matters'.

The legal tongue is not the only tool of legal mysticism. The separate development of lawyer and layman in a country that contains them both is also aided by the fanciful costumes in which lawyers dress and by their extraordinary ceremonies and procedures, including their practice of bowing before each other. Alexander Herzen, visiting an English court for the first time in 1853, was struck by 'the comicality of the medieval *mise-en-scène*', the climax of which was the appearance of the judge 'wearing a fur coat and something like a woman's dressing-gown'.[8]

It is the speech of the lawyer, though, which holds the charade together. This has been understood by perceptive laymen from Jesus ('Woe unto you lawyers. You have taken away the key of knowledge')[9] to the Marx Brothers ('The party of the first part shall be known in this contract as the party of the first part').[10] In the opening paragraphs of *Bleak House*, Dickens describes how the heart of the London fog rests in the High Court of Chancery. There the lawyers are 'groping knee-deep in technicalities, running their goat-hair and horsehair warded heads against walls of words'. Only on isolated occasions have lawyers recognized that they suffer from this disease. To his credit, Lord Justice Cumming-Bruce acknowledged in a 1980 decision that 'parts of this judgment I am afraid are still drafted in a kind of legal jargon which may later have to be translated into English, and I hope it is intelligible'.[11] It is one thing to spot the symptoms. It is much more difficult to find a cure.

There are several distinguishing characteristics of legal language. First, there is the extraordinary prolixity of legal speech. Lawyers are, as Swift explained, 'a society of men . . . bred up from their youth in the art of proving by words multiplied for the purpose that white is black, and black is white, according as they are paid'.[12] Hence, in Brobdingnag

Gulliver discovers that no law of the country may exceed in words the number of letters in their alphabet, which is twenty-two.[13]

Secondly, there is the frequent reliance on archaic forms, such as *aforesaid, heretofore* and *thenceforth*. Thirdly, there is the common use of Latinisms, from *ab initio* to *ex post facto*, reducing the litigant, *ex parte*, to *in forma pauperis*. Fourthly, legal language delights in unnecessary repetition: *the truth, the whole truth and nothing but the truth . . . to have and to hold . . . his last will and testament . . . null and void*. Fifthly, it revels in clichés that are generally avoided in ordinary speech: *rack and ruin . . . part and parcel . . . safe and sound*. Sixthly, lawyers use language as a protective shell, designed to insulate them from the consequences of their words or actions: *without prejudice . . . in my submission . . . it would seem . . . the alleged . . . if any*.

Seventhly, the language of the law welcomes the euphemism. It uses it for a variety of purposes including ceremony, obfuscation and the avoidance of what might otherwise be distasteful. But it is important to note that the euphemism, while part of the armoury of legal language, is but one linguistic device amongst many others used by lawyers to communicate in a tongue that cannot be fully understood by others. The legal profession is well aware that, in Bentham's words, 'the power of the lawyer is in the uncertainty of the law'.[14] Lawyers willingly embrace the euphemism when it can assist in the furtherance of their objectives. None of this might matter except that, as an American judge, Justice Johnson, once pointed out, the vital interests of a party to legal proceedings 'may depend upon a comma'.[15]

(iii)

The euphemism plays a central part in the daily life of the law. Barristers prefer to be called *counsel*. This suggests that they act as a friend or confidant rather than in a professional capacity. For similar reasons, when appearing in court on behalf of a client (the date and time having been fixed *through the usual channels*, that is by the court telling the barrister's *chambers*—his offices—when the case will be heard), the barrister is paid a fee for the first day and a *refresher* for each subsequent day. The term *refresher* cleverly implies a physical necessity for what is, after all, a mere financial transaction (the negotiation of which barristers leave to their office managers, or *senior clerks* as they like to be known). To explain why they feel obliged to represent rogues and scoundrels, barristers tend to refer to *the cab-rank principle*. This is not merely a peculiar euphemism (barristers usually emphasize that they are a profession, with *clients*, not merely workers, with customers). It is also a serious defamation of the ethics of taxi-drivers.

Once in court, the barrister begins to communicate with the judge in a language full of euphemisms. Barristers *make submissions* rather than present arguments. They introduce these arguments with an obsequious *May it please your Lordship* where 'Hello, good morning Judge' would do. The fictional Sir Cyril Tart QC does not stretch credibility too far when he opens a case with the words, 'If your Lordship pleases—as, may I add, your Lordship habitually does'.[16] The barrister presents his arguments *with respect*, *with great respect* or, on occasions, *with the greatest of respect*. The degree of respect voiced is, of course, in inverse proportion to the willingness indicated by the judge to agree with the arguments being advanced.

A barrister acting for the opposing party is always *my learned friend* (as in *it may be helpful to your Lordship and to my learned friend if I* . . . meaning it will certainly be helpful to me; or *in all fairness to my learned friend* . . . meaning that one is about to put the legal boot in). This is irrespective of the intellectual abilities of one's opponent and whether or not one has just made his acquaintance. This euphemistic legal amity is again reflected in the practice of the court of inviting argument from an *amicus curiae* (friend of the court), usually a barrister briefed by the State.

If the judge shows an argument to be nonsense, a barrister may *resile from* it. A barrister does not withdraw an argument. If a point assists, a barrister may *pray it in aid*. If the judge sees a helpful argument hitherto ignored by the barrister, the latter will tell the former that *your Lordship puts the point far better than I could*. Applying the principle that it is easier to persuade a person of the truth of a proposition if one first leads him to believe that he has already expressed it, the phrase *it's your Lordship's point* is a euphemism expressed whenever the judge has shown the slightest understanding of the argument being developed. It is only to the trained observer of the law courts that Sir Ethelred Rutt KC reveals himself as a figment of A. P. Herbert's imagination when he responds to a comment from the judge with the words, 'Your Lordship is extraordinarily handsome and good.'[17]

Applications are dismissed and appeals are rejected, often because the *most careful note of the evidence taken by my pupil* is revealed to be totally unreliable. Barristers do not leave the court without a farewell. But they never wave the judge a cheery or a disappointed goodbye. Rather they depart with a misleading *I'm obliged my Lord*, or, if they have dismally failed to obtain what they requested from the judge, *I'm much obliged*. On occasions the case will not proceed to a judgment from the judge. What has seemed an unacceptable offer from the other side on the first morning of a trial will, after one's witnesses have *failed to come up to proof* (meaning that they told one a pack of lies before the trial), be grabbed as a *good settlement*, or, if that is too implausible, be accepted as a *moral victory*.

The language used by the judiciary is replete with euphemisms. Their preference for the euphemistic is indicated by their wish to be known as *my Lord* or *your Honour* or *your Worship* (the last of these being an anachronistic but revealing indication of the vanity that can afflict adjudicators in minor courts and tribunals). To depersonalize the law, judges refer to themselves as *the bench*. To encourage a belief in their unity and amity they sit as *brethren* (a euphemism that gives a not wholly misleading indication of the frequency with which women are appointed as judges). It was, no doubt, an intentional piece of irony that the book which claimed to reveal the professional jealousies afflicting US Supreme Court judges was entitled *The Brethren*. To avoid expressing the absurd rules that govern a barrister's dress in court, a judge annoyed at a barrister who is not wearing a waistcoat (or who is guilty of some similar heinous offence) will say to him *I cannot see you* (or *hear you*) *Mr X*.

The judgment of the court depends on euphemisms. Sometimes this is designed to avoid inflicting unnecessary pain. *While it is not for one moment suggested that Mr X is deliberately seeking to mislead the court, it is apparent to me that his memory, like that of many others, has grown hazy with the passage of time*, sounds so much more acceptable than a conclusion that Mr X is a liar. (See similarly, *when the evidence given by the Plaintiff conflicted with that given by the Defendant, I preferred the evidence of the Plaintiff, having heard and seen their demeanour in the witness box*.) For a judge to begin his judgment with a statement that he *has every sympathy for the Defendant* is fatal to the cause of that party.

It is not only the feelings of litigants and witnesses that are spared. Judges and barristers depend upon each other for satisfactory working conditions. Hence, when a barrister hears a judge say in his judgment that *the Plaintiff's counsel presented an argument of the utmost ingenuity* or that he *made powerful and helpful submissions* or, worst of all, *said everything that could be said on behalf of his client*, he knows that his client has lost. Part of the beauty of the *Misleading Cases* of A. P. Herbert is that the judges ignore these conventions. Only in fiction could Lord Merrymind, President of the Probate, Divorce and Admiralty Division of the High Court, refer in his judgment to 'the many errors in Sir Robin's laborious and, if he will forgive me, rather laughable argument'.[18]

Judges do not state or accept the obvious: for example, that Paris is the capital of France or that Monday is the day after Sunday. They *take judicial notice* of such facts. It does sometimes seem as if the Lord Chancellor organizes an annual competition with a prize for the judge who takes judicial notice of the most obvious fact. A likely winner in any year would be Mr Justice Woolf who, in 1980, mentioned 'the programme, principles and policy of the Labour Party which for the purposes of this judgment I will accept are inconsistent with the programme, principles and policy of the Conservative Party'.[19] It is the phrase 'for the purposes of this judgment' which gives this statement its classic quality as a piece of judicial irony. A judge does not directly tell a barrister that the latter has failed to convince the former with an argument and that it is time to move on to another point. Rather, the judge will inform the barrister that *I hear what you say*. The barrister, familiar with this code, acknowledges the judge's statement with the reply *I will not improve my submission by repetition; you have the point*.

There is a range of handy euphemisms employed by judges as

part of their reasoning in deciding a case. The *doctrine of precedent* applies 'a maxim among these lawyers, that whatever has been done before may legally be done again: and therefore they take special care to record all the decisions formerly made against common justice and the general reason of mankind'.[20] This raises a problem for judges. What part of a previous decision is binding in this way? Lawyers have invented the concepts of *ratio decidendi* to indicate the central, binding element of a previous decision and *obiter dictum* to represent the peripheral part of the previous case which was not essential to the judgment and so is not binding on later judges. But how do we distinguish one from the other? The spurious scholarship of legal philosophers is blown away by the explanation given by Lord Justice Asquith: 'the rule is quite simple: if you agree with the other bloke, you say it's part of the *ratio*; if you don't, you say it's *obiter dictum* with the implication that he is a con-genital idiot'.[21] Where the essence of a previous decision with which a judge disagrees cannot so easily be dismissed as *obiter dictum*, the judge may, as a last resort, categorize the previous decision as *per incuriam* (an acceptable legal euphemism for a judgment which was obviously wrong). It may be that the earlier judgment was *per incuriam* because *the court did not have the benefit of full argument*—that is, neither the barristers nor the judge saw the crucial point.

Appellate judges are especially adept in the use of euphem-isms when explaining why appeals fail. *Whereas this court would not necessarily have exercised its discretion in the same way as the trial judge* means that the court does not agree with the trial judge but does not propose to do anything about his decision. Similarly, as soon as one hears an appeal court refer to the *special knowledge and experience of the lay members of the industrial tribunal* or to the fact that *it is only in the very rarest of cases that this court will interfere with a finding of fact by a trial judge*, one knows that an appeal has failed. The equivalent euphemism in the Judicial Committee of the Privy Council hearing appeals from Commonwealth countries is to refer to the *expert knowledge of local circumstances and conditions pos-sessed by the trial judge*. The Criminal Division of the Court of Appeal can be expected to refer to *the trenchant summing-up* of the trial judge. In other words, he directed the jury to convict.

This is to be distinguished from what the Criminal Division of the Court of Appeal call *a careful but trenchant summing-up*—that is a direction to the jury to convict, but with a passing reference to the burden and the standard of proof on the prosecution. That court may decide *to apply the proviso*, a reference to section 2(1) of the Criminal Appeal Act 1968 which requires the Court to allow an appeal against a conviction, for example if the trial judge made an error of law, 'provided that the Court may, notwithstanding that they are of opinion that the point raised in the appeal might be decided in favour of the appellant, dismiss the appeal if they consider that no miscarriage of justice has actually occurred'. In other words, the Court of Appeal think the appellant committed the crime, so they are not going to let him get away with it.

When reaching conclusions that lack common sense judges like to refer to *the balance of convenience* (irrespective of the inconvenience caused by the judgment) or to *the dangers of opening the floodgates* (without explaining why having to do justice in other cases should be an argument against doing justice in the present case). In judicial language, *clearly* signifies a logical fallacy or a factual statement of doubtful accuracy (as in 'the parties, an illiterate Taiwanese fisherman and a Turkish sardine exporter, clearly intended this contract to be governed by English law').

The work of the Parliamentary draftsman often leaves the courts with the task of interpreting the incomprehensible. A judge rarely says that a statute is gibberish. He may refer to *an anomaly*. He may even comment, if provoked, that *the language of the draftsman is not easy to comprehend*. Note the difference between this and the phrase *at first sight the language of the draftsman is not entirely easy to comprehend*. The latter is a euphemism for the judge condemning the statute as gibberish but indicating his intention to do a bit of legislating himself. If judges are not averse to making law, they state that they are merely exercising the discretion given to them by *the doctrines of equity*, for example the doctrine that the court will not assist someone who comes to court *without clean hands*. Or they may assert that they are only applying *the common law*. This is a splendid euphemism, suggesting a body of principles, indexed and labelled, known to and belonging to all the people.

In fact, as Jeremy Bentham explained, the common law is 'dog-law' made by the judges. He asked: 'Do you know how they make it? Just as a man makes laws for his dog. When your dog does anything you want to break him of, you wait till he does it, and then beat him for it. This is the way you make laws for your dog: and this is the way the judges make law for you and me.'[22] A different perspective was taken by the Lord Chancellor in one of A. P. Herbert's *Misleading Cases*: 'The pity is that there is not more judge-made law. For most of His Majesty's judges are much better fitted for the making of laws than the queer and cowardly rabble who are elected to Parliament for that purpose by the fantastic machinery of universal suffrage.'[23]

If, on the other hand, judges are reluctant to extend the frontiers of the law, they will refer to the dangers of applying *palm-tree justice* (not to be confused with poetic justice) or of measuring the law by *the length of the Chancellor's foot*.

(iv)

The substance of the law mirrors the practice of the law in its fondness for euphemisms. Here one can see the reluctance of the law to call a spade a spade. Language, and the euphemisms it employs, evolves with the spirit of the times. The Usury laws, repealed in 1854, returned as the Moneylenders Acts 1900 and 1927. The relevant legal provisions are now contained in the Consumer Credit Act 1974 which talks of an 'extortionate credit bargain'. The Mental Health Act 1959 repealed the Lunacy and Mental Treatment Acts 1890 to 1930 and the Mental Deficiency Acts 1913 to 1938. In Queensland, Australia, the Intellectually Handicapped Citizens Bill 1983 was brought forward to replace the Backward Persons Act 1938.

Sex is treated euphemistically in the law, as elsewhere. Until 1857, a cuckolded husband could sue the other man for *criminal conversation* with his wife. Judges, alone amongst educated people (or any other people), refer to couples partaking in *marital relations* or having *carnal knowledge* or, even, agreeing to 'enjoy conjugal felicity'.[24] A *common law marriage* is not a legal marriage at all. It may, however, be of interest to social security inspectors who want to know whether an unmarried couple are *cohabiting*. The common law marriage is not to be confused with the *marriage of convenience*, which is a marriage entered into to gain some legal advantage, for example under immigration law. But does anyone choose to get married where it is inconvenient to do so (unless there is a *shotgun-wedding*)?

Rape used to be known as a *criminal assault* and a *criminal operation* was a euphemism for an abortion. Rape of a minor is a *statutory rape*. To *interfere with* someone is sexually to assault them. In this oppressive climate of sexual innuendo, Mr Justice Ashworth, for the Divisional Court, was a brave man to comment in 1972 on the 'Victorian gentility which prevented people calling a penis a penis'. He was considering section 4 of the Vagrancy Act 1824 which made it an offence for someone to be caught 'wilfully, openly, lewdly and obscenely exposing his person . . . with intent to insult any female'. Mr Justice Ashworth had no doubt that 'at any rate today, and indeed by 1824, the word "person" in connection with sexual matters had acquired a meaning of its own; a meaning which made it a synonym for "penis" '.[25]

When a judge is unsure whether to use a euphemism in the sexual context (perhaps because none is readily available), he may compromise and refer, for example, to 'a so-called "sex-change operation" ' involving 'a so-called "artificial vagina" '.[26] On occasions a judge may mix euphemisms with direct language in this context for no apparent reason. In a 1976 decision, Lord Denning explained that Mr Hook, a market trader, 'had an urgent call of nature'. All the 'lavatories or "toilets" as they are now called' were closed. So Mr Hook 'went into a side street near the market and there made water, or "urinated" as it is now said'. On being reprimanded by a security officer, 'Mr Hook made an appropriate reply. Again we are not told the actual words, but it is not difficult to guess. I expect it was an emphatic version of "You be off" '.[27] How very different from the law reports of an earlier age: in 1663, Sir Charles Sidley was fined 'for shewing himself naked in a balcony, and throwing down bottles (pist in) . . . among the people in Convent Garden . . .'.[28]

Commercial matters also provide fertile ground for the breeding of legal euphemisms. The plain speaking of Lord Macnaghten, 'Income tax, if I may be pardoned for saying so, is a tax on income',[29] is misleading in this respect. The world of bond washing and reverse annuities is quite prepared to adopt euphemisms if it means tax liabilities can more easily be avoided (not *evaded*, as tax practitioners will emphasize). *Tax planning* is a very acceptable term for what is not always a laudable pursuit. It suggests constructive activities where usually what one finds is 'another circular game in which the taxpayer and a few hired performers act out a play; nothing happens save that the Houdini taxpayer appears to escape from the manacles of tax'.[30] *Golden handshake* and *black economy* are similarly anodyne phrases for practices which do not necessarily satisfy moral or legal principles. To *pierce the corporate veil* is to make legally liable the shyster behind a company which has limited liability.

An *agreement subject to contract* is no legal agreement at all. Its cousin is the *gentlemen's agreement*, reported to have been defined by Vaisey J. as 'an agreement which is not an agreement, made between two persons, neither of whom is a gentleman, whereby each expects the other to be strictly bound without himself being bound at all'.[31] An *ex gratia payment* is made to settle a claim without conceding legal liability. One knows when lawyers really have identified a binding agreement because they will refer to the parties having reached a *meeting of minds* and having given *consideration*, which implies neither concern for the other party nor the provision of fair value for the promise given by that other party. If the parties have not expressly agreed all the relevant terms of the contract, the court may imply terms for them. It will do so by applying the euphemistic device of *the officious bystander*, whose function it is to conceal the fact that the judge is making up the contractual terms for the parties. To this annoying individual is attributed the habit of asking the parties, when they are in the process of agreeing the contract, whether a particular term is part of their agreement. If they would reply to such a question, 'Of course' (a more likely and reasonable answer being 'Mind your own business'), then the term is said to be implied into the agreement.

The officious bystander must be the brother of that experienced legal euphemism *the reasonable man*, also known as *the man on the top of the Clapham omnibus*. The hopes of many litigants have been destroyed by judges comparing their conduct unfavourably with that attributed to the reasonable man. He is so remote from the imperfection of human beings that his appearances in the law reports suggest that he is 'devoid . . . of any human weakness, with not one single saving vice'.[32]

No area of the law is immune from infection by the euphemism. In family law, a *non-accidental injury* is harm to a child thought to have been inflicted by its parents. In immigration law, immigrants from the *New Commonwealth* are blacks. *Affirmative action* means discrimination in favour of blacks or women (sometimes erroneously called *minorities*). An employee who acts outside the course of his employment, with the consequence that the employer is not liable for any acts of negligence, is *on a frolic of his own*. Workers on strike are *taking industrial action*. To have *constructive notice* of an event means that one had no notice of it, but should have done. (Similarly, lawyers refer to *constructive fraud*.) The dignity and solemnity of the phrase *eminent domain* make almost acceptable the concept it signifies: the right of the State to take private property for public purposes on paying reasonable compensation. *Internment* is imprisonment without any, or any adequate, trial. The entire legal system centres on the devotion of certain politicians to *law and order*, an overworked euphemism (especially at Conservative party conferences) for the State telling people what to do and locking them up in unpleasant circumstances for long periods of time if they do not do it.

The criminal law fosters euphemisms almost to the same extent as it is enriched by underworld slang. The process is by no means a modern development. *The Duke of Exeter's daughter* was a fifteenth-century instrument of torture resembling the rack. Nowadays, suspected criminals who are *helping the police with their inquiries* (as in the old joke about the proud mothers boasting of their sons' achievements: after various mothers have told how their sons are lawyers, doctors or accountants, one lady exclaims, 'Yes, but my son is only eighteen and already he is helping the police with their inquiries') are not subjected to such devices. But a suspect may, if he refuses to co-operate, perhaps by *turning Queen's evidence* or becoming a *supergrass*, find that he *has the book thrown at him*, or as American prosecutors say, be subjected to *felony augmentation*. The court may hear evidence from an *agent provocateur*, 'an official spy who causes an offence to secure a conviction. . . . There is no other phrase, and for a very good reason; the idea is so repugnant to British notions of fair play and decency that it has never found expression in our language.'[33] On conviction, the criminal may be given a *life sentence*, which may well mean he serves less than ten years in prison. He may be *detained during Her Majesty's pleasure*, in other words for an indeterminate period. If he is fortunate, the criminal will serve his *custodial sentence* in an *open prison*.

A *juvenile delinquent* (that is, a young criminal) who has not been a success at an *approved school* used to be sent for *borstal training*. That sentence has now been replaced, presumably as part of a policy of attempting to deter crime by tough talk, by a non-euphemistic sentence of youth custody. In the USA, prisons are *correctional facilities* and prison wardens are *institutional superintendents*.[34] The rehabilitative purpose of imprisonment, though long since revealed as an expensive illusion by criminologists, lives on in the United Kingdom by virtue of section 4 of the Vagrancy Act 1824. This deems certain persons to be 'rogues and vagabonds' whom it is lawful to commit 'to the house of correction'. If and when we copy Idi Amin, the infamous tyrant of Uganda, and call our secret police the *State Research Bureau*, then we really shall have cause for concern.

(v)

A study of this sort could not legitimately ignore reverse legal euphemisms. The layman has taken some revenge for the inaccessibility and absurdity of legal language by using the law as source material for euphemisms of his own. *The Solicitor General* is, according to the experts,[35] a euphemism for the penis. To be *in chancery* is a pugilistic term meaning to have one's head under an opponent's arm while he hits you with the fist of his stronger arm.[36] Furthermore, *legal fiction* 'is used colloquially as a facetious euphemism for an untruth'.[37]

Each generation of laymen has mocked the lawyer in this respect because it has well understood that in the language of the law 'care has been taken that each particle of sense shall be drowned in a deluge of words'.[38] There could be no other explanation for the existence of section 72 of the Housing Act 1980, described by Lord Roskill, a distinguished Law Lord, as 'the worst piece of Parliamentary drafting for 1980'.[39] Section 72(1) provides that 'rent tribunals . . . are hereby abolished'. Section 72(2) adds that 'the functions [previously]. . . conferred on rent tribunals shall be carried out by rent assessment committees'. So far so good. But section 72(3) takes us back where we started by announcing that a 'rent assessment committee shall . . . be known as a rent tribunal'. To prove that Parliament is not solely responsible for the excesses and the absurdities in the language of the law, and that judges fully play their part, one needs only to look at the headnote to a case decided by three judges in the High Court in 1916. After hearing and considering legal argument, the court decided that 'ice-cream is not "meat" within section 3 of the Sunday Observance Act 1677'.[40] If Parliament and the courts do not improve their language, someone will have to *read them the Riot Act*.

NOTES

I am very grateful to many friends and colleagues who, consciously or unconsciously, provided me with material for this essay.

1. *Ex parte Daisy Hopkins* 61, Law Journal Queen's Bench 240 (1891)
2. Ibid. p. 250 n.
3. *Gulliver's Travels: A Voyage to the Houyhnhnms*, ch. 5
4. *The Works of Jeremy Bentham* (ed. John Bowring, 1843) vol. 3, p. 260 and vol. 7, p. 282
5. Ibid. vol. 7, pp. 280–2 and see H. L. A. Hart, 'The Demystification of the Law' in *Essays on Bentham: Jurisprudence and Political Theory* (1982), pp. 29–30
6. *The Merchant of Venice*, III. ii. 75–7
7. Quoted in David Mellinkoff, *The Language of the Law* (1963), p. 37
8. *My Past and Thoughts: The Memoirs of Alexander Herzen* (trans. Constance Garnett 1968) vol. 3, pp. 1095–6
9. Luke 11: 52
10. *A Night at the Opera*
11. *O'Brien* v. *Sim-Chem Ltd.* [1980] 1 Weekly Law Reports 734, 737
12. *Supra* n. 3
13. *A Voyage to Brobdingnag*, ch. 7
14. *Supra* n. 4, vol. 10, p. 429

15. *US* v. *Palmer* 3 Wheaton's Reports 610, 636 (1818) cited by Jerome Frank, *Courts on Trial* (1949), ch. 21

16. A. P. Herbert, *More Uncommon Law* (1982), p. 279

17. *Uncommon Law* (1977), p. 9

18. *Supra* n. 16, p. 253

19. *Parkin* v. *ASTMS* [1980] Industrial Cases Reports 662, 669

20. *Supra* n. 3

21. 'Some Aspects of the Work of the Court of Appeal' (1950), *Journal of the Society of Public Teachers of Law* 350, 359

22. *Supra* n. 4, vol. 5, p. 235

23. *Supra* n. 17, p. 156

24. *Paterson* v. *Paterson* 1938 Session Cases 251, 259 cited in R. E. Megarry, *A Second Miscellany-at-Law* (1973), p. 161

25. *Evans* v. *Ewels* [1972] 1 Weekly Law Reports 671, 674

26. *Corbett* v. *Corbett* [1971] Probate 83, 90

27. *R.* v. *Barnsley LBC ex parte Hook* [1976] 3 All England Reports 452, 454–5

28. 83 English Reports 1146 (1663). The story is also told in *The Diary of Samuel Pepys* (ed. Robert Latham and William Matthews, 1971) vol. 4, pp. 209–10

29. *LCC* v. *Attorney General* [1901] Appeal Cases 26, 35

30. *W. T. Ramsay Ltd.* v. *IRC* [1979] 1 Weekly Law Reports 974, 979 per Templeman LJ.

31. R. E. Megarry *supra* n. 24, p. 326

32. *Supra* n. 17, p. 4

33. Ibid p. 79

34. Jessica Mitford, *The American Prison Business* (1974), ch. 1

35. Judith S. Neaman and Carole G. Silver, *A Dictionary of Euphemisms* (1983), p. 34

36. See, for example, John Lord Campbell, *Lives of the Lord Chancellors* (5th edn., 1868) vol. 10, p. 290 n.

37. J. E. S. Simon, 'English Idioms from the Law' 76, *Law Quarterly Review* 283, 304 (1960)

38. *Supra* n. 4, vol. 7, p. 281

39. 125 *Solicitors' Journal* 232 (1981) cited in Francis Bennion, *Statute Law* (1983), p. 124

40. *Slater* v. *Evans* [1916] 2 King's Bench 403. Cited in Glanville Williams, 'Language and the Law II' 61 *Law Quarterly Review* 179, 189 (1945)

Do Doctors Mean What They Say?

DIANE JOHNSON and JOHN F. MURRAY

WE had supposed that doctors, involved as they are with the ultimate facts of existence, might also be involved in some intimate way with the creation of linguistic stratagems to palliate these facts and soften what cannot finally be softened. We had thought that doctors might prove an interesting contrast to priests, whose otherworldly preoccupations permit plain speaking on matters of this world. We had hoped doctors would speak in a language richly euphemistic on the subject of human imperfection, poetic, firmly encouraging in its counsels of defiance and struggle.

But it is not so. Doctors, perhaps with a certain cruelty, refuse euphemisms to their patients, depending for effect instead on the awesome and often terrifying proper names of diseases: you have bronchial asthma or bronchiectasis when you thought you only had a little wheeze. If it is not cruelty in the doctor to tell you what you really have, then it is prudence and good psychology. The patient who is told to his horror that he has *pityriasis rosea* will take better care of it than of a harmless rash; on the other hand it would not do to tell someone he has a little touch of Hansen's disease when some friend will know that this is leprosy. The doctor must decide. There is a sense, of course, in which the real, solemn, Latin name of something (put there by doctors) confers upon a disease, or on its sufferer, an importance which may be a kind of comfort. This is the name, at any rate, which the sufferer will repeat to his friends; he will tell them he has *pityriasis rosea*.

Apart from using the euphemisms for dying that are a part of common speech, doctors seem less inclined than other people to use medical euphemism, while other people are more apt to use euphemism about medical than about many other matters; this creates, presumably, a little communication gap which causes people inevitably to complain of not being able to talk to their doctors. 'Little', by the way, is a euphemistic adjective frequently, if not constantly employed to diminish the seriousness of matters and it is a favourite of both doctors and patients.

It is natural that patients and sufferers should have recourse to euphemism, wan gambit that it is. It is hope and faith (though these days a fast-fading faith) in technology, which makes us name our bodies in images that suggest mechanical reliability and dependable regularity: the heart is a 'ticker' or a 'pump', we have plumbing—passages, pipes, and tubes—and our nervous system is our wiring. Some day, alas, we all have to 'wear out'. The verbs we use to describe the process of getting ill are themselves euphemistic, and are revealing of the underlying psychological significance of various ills. You fall ill, for one thing, and falling is an accidental event. But by certain illnesses —the grippe, for one—you are seized, which implies a hostile intention on the part of fortune towards you. On the other hand, you catch a cold—and catching implies a degree of co-operation from you. We catch things, therefore, in ways which are our own fault; we blame ourselves—we should have worn galoshes, and should not have sat in a draught. We do not blame ourselves, though, for ailments which could have been avoided by prudence and less of human frailty—hangover or indigestion, for example. These things do not strike us, nor do we catch them; we have them, is all.

Sometimes a delicate evasion—verb, noun, an eloquent ellipsis—conveys what we mean about common human afflictions too tiresome, embarrassing or revolting to be named at all. 'It' stands for a number of unspoken things. So do forms of the verb 'to be', as in the note from Willie's mother: 'Willie can't come to school because he hasn't been. I've given him something to make him go, and when he's been, he'll come.' Evasions are usually connected with the bowels or sex, and dictated by reticence or the conventions of speech of a given community. 'How are things down there?' one informant reports being asked by her doctor. 'And how are the waterworks?' This patient is not sure whether this is the doctor's prudery or what he imagines to be hers. One wonders whether Queen Victoria's gynaecologist spoke plainly to her, and what plain speaking meant in the nineteenth century.

Nineteenth-century names of diseases, and indeed their

names since earliest times, were euphemistic, touchingly so, testifying to the hope, mystification, and resignation felt by patient and physician alike. 'Consumption', above all, described itself euphemistically, rendering gradual and painless, and perhaps not inevitable, the work of the ugly tubercle bacillus (*mycobacterium tuberculosis*), whose depredations would surely be accomplished with the Latin precision of the name it received soon after its discovery in 1882. No doubt it was better to get the 'king's evil' than scrofula, and 'dropsy' described a lethargic but not tormented end. 'St Vitus's dance' sounds more jolly than potentially fatal, 'shingles' suggests merely a neatly fitted armour of scales, and 'piles' hardly conveys the suffering reported by those afflicted with haemorrhoids, whose numbers, to judge from American television advertising, are legion, but whose characters are stoical and language euphemistical.

When ailments are serious and have some metaphoric significance involving judgement or justice, as if they have been sent by God or otherwise visited upon someone, these ailments are apt to be called by their own names or by superstitious abbreviations: arthritis, emphysema, cancer (or The Big C). If an ailment is trivial or humanly manageable, it gets a nickname: a sniffle, the clap. No ailments are voluntary, of course, but some do seem to strike in such a way as to augment a person, to swell him up or make him larger, and these are treated with more verbal seriousness than those which, when they strike, diminish the sufferer and force him to give something up—nausea, diarrhoea, even menstruation. These invite ridicule. The more humiliating and repulsive, if at the same time not dangerous an affliction, the more likely it is to receive a light, dismissive name—the erps or barfs, the trots, the flu, 'la tourista', or, in the words of President Jimmy Carter's gaffe to the President of Mexico, 'Montezuma's revenge'.

Euphemisms for the menstrual period are an interesting study in themselves. Quite familiar to all women are the terms which designate this biological function as unwelcome: 'the curse'. But among free-spirited unmarried women, or married women with enough children to suit them, 'the visitor' is always welcome; sometimes he is simply called 'my friend', as in 'I am having a visit from my friend'. The visitor is always a he, and sometimes he is called Harvey or by some other man's name.

His appearances are sometimes also called 'appearances', or merely something you see, as in the famous example of a woman who was sent to the ophthalmology clinic because she told the doctor: 'I ain't seen nothin' in three months.' Men use euphemisms for menstruation involving rough humour or regret. So-and-so is 'on the rag'. Among servicemen during the Second World War a woman might be said to be 'flying baker', an all-red signal flag.

The process by which members of one sex impute to parts of their bodies, or disorders thereof, the opposite sex is also euphemistic, awarding to the beard or testicle or womb a measure of autonomy and mystery which puts it a little out of its possessor's control: *la barbe, les bourses* and *les couilles* (testicles, both feminine nouns), *l'uterus* (masculine). It is not necessary to take responsibility for this mysterious Other. An exception might be the penis, which men do not appear to think of as 'she', though they do objectify it as 'he' or 'it' or call it by the name of an intrusive and randy animal, such as a cock, but rarely as 'me'.

In the matter of speaking euphemistically to patients, British and American doctors differ, often to the dismay of the transatlantic patient. The British doctor uses euphemism more, the legacy, perhaps, of a time when the educational status or social class of the doctor was almost certainly higher than that of his patient, unless he had an aristocratic practice, when, being of lower social status, the doctor would be even more certain to avoid the unpleasant fate of the messenger. Whatever the history, it still appears to be true that British doctors employ figures of speech which they imagine will be more intelligible and acceptable to their patients, whom they suppose to be less well-educated than themselves. These assumptions are not made by American and French physicians (or so they claim), who oblige the patient to pretend he understands the sober and actual name of his condition even if he does not. This in turn gives the American doctor, at least, a certain reputation for pompousness, but pompousness is better tolerated than condescension. Perhaps this is an effect of revolutions. M. de Tocqueville noted something of the kind.

One obviously has to be careful in using euphemisms derived from one set or nationality when talking to a person in another context, or at least one must be aware that simple words change meanings elaborately. Asking an elderly Jamaican for the history of his operations, the doctor was mystified to learn that he had one each morning after breakfast. A patient reports being bewildered, in an Irish hospital, at what to respond to the nurse who would ask her each morning whether she had a 'tick for the book'.

The best way for a doctor to address his patients is a matter of debate in modern medical schools. Young American doctors are advised not to call their patients by their first names unless they are prepared to be spoken to with similar familiarity: 'And how are we today, Sally?' 'I don't know about you, Dave, but I have a pain in my stomach.' 'We', the royal 'we' doctors are criticized for using, is probably euphemistic in intention, arising less from delusions of grandeur than from the hope of reassuring the patient that the doctor's opinions would be backed up by droves of colleagues if they were called in on the case. Alternatively, the 'we' means the doctor and the patient, with the doctor hoping to convince the patient that the two of them are alike, a stratagem which always fails to inculcate the identification and trust intended. Instead of 'we', the doctor may also sometimes say 'medical science', another euphemism for this very *ad hoc* and disorganized art.

There was a time when all physicians used euphemisms. They had to, and it was part of their training. Back in the days when medical students and The Professor met in front of The Patient, in the clinic or at the bedside, the students took turns presenting and then discussing the patients they had been assigned to evaluate in a highly formalized teaching exercise. You could not call the patient an old drunk to his face, so he became an 'ethanol abuser' instead. The dreaded word cancer was not permitted, because The Patient might not know that he or she had it, so The Professor was told about 'mitotic disease'. The Patient may have had a history of 'lues' (syphilis) or 'acid-fast disease' (tuberculosis), both extremely common problems at the time. Blood was always 'heme' and so on. An elaborate system of euphemistic substitutions evolved for the express purpose of allowing medical teaching to take place with The Patient, on whom the discussion centred, present.

Now, all that has changed. Medical students still present

their cases, not to The Professor but to An Attending Physician, a euphemism for a member of the medical school faculty whose turn it is to be the legal physician of record so that a bill can be sent. To be a Professor of Medicine a few decades ago was acknowledgement of clinical wizardry and unusual patient-related expertise. Today's professor is seldom seen in the wards or clinics any more and, if he is not out of town, will most likely be found in his laboratory or at a committee meeting. Moreover, today's case presentation no longer requires The Patient, who may not even be visited during the teaching session of which he is the focus; 'patient' is itself a euphemism. Along with the disappearance of The Professor, The Patient, and the teaching formality went medical euphemisms constructed for the sake of tact, and in their stead came an equally elaborate system of communication in jocular descriptions, verbal short cuts and, above all, acronyms.

Some acronyms are inappropriately, or inadvertently, euphemistic, as in the case of the dreadful new disease AIDS, which stands for Acquired Immune Deficiency Syndrome. 'AIDS', with its cheerful, helpful ring, is also the name of a well-established brand of diet candy, which carries on, notwithstanding, advertising itself on American television. It is said that in the Bible belt the disease is referred to as WOGS, or Wrath of God Syndrome. This refers to the high incidence of AIDS among homosexuals and drug abusers. Elsewhere still, the victims of AIDS, most of whom belong to one of a few well-defined high-risk populations, are referred to as members of the 4-H club (heroin users, Haitians, homosexuals and haemophiliacs). The 4-H clubs are also organizations of wholesome young American future farmers. These jokes, in bad taste even by the low standards of doctors, illustrate a tendency of medical language generally to develop under- or overtones of the sardonic, directly destructive of euphemism. In some cases, though, euphemisms are abandoned because of their lack of irony. Doctors used to speak of 'sacrificing' an animal in an experiment, implying an almost religious faith in science which even they no longer hold or expect in others.

American doctors report that they are careful not to use euphemisms, and are concerned instead to provide a clear and carefully worded scientific explanation of a patient's condition as a precaution against being sued, in which case they have to show that they have explained the medical significance or the risks of the treatment they have provided. Patients for their part are given releases to sign in which they acknowledge that they have understood the potential benefits and hazards of the treatment they will be undergoing. In the tense atmosphere of possible litigation that increasingly pervades American medical practice, the humane and cheerful properties of understatement, 'we'll have to go in and take a little look', are lost for good.

Doctors do not of course use euphemisms among themselves to mitigate or deny the sad facts of disease, dying, death. They seem rather to pride themselves on speaking casually of it, with the familiar bravado of comrades in a dire situation, no one wishing to usurp for himself an undue measure of the collective dismay over these grim facts which has presumably brought them alike into this 'helping' profession (or, to use another current American euphemism, 'caring' profession, which includes nurses, social workers, orderlies and counsellors—all wishing, presumably, to distinguish themselves from the implied 'uncaring' professions). Young physicians and medical students have a language all their own that fills the wards, corridors, classrooms and elevators in hospitals throughout the world and sounds as uncaring as possible.

Perhaps T. S. Eliot set it in motion when he had a patient 'etherized upon a table'. Now virtually every medical noun has been turned into a verb. A desperately ill patient admitted to an intensive care unit is 'lined up', which means that several lines and tubes are put into parts of his body to provide for and to monitor vital functions such as breathing, blood pressure and the like. Depending on his condition, he will either be 'tanked up' (given fluids) or 'pruned out' (given diuretics for dehydration). On ward rounds, the fact that the patient has been receiving supplementary oxygen at a flow rate of two litres per minute through two little prongs that fit inside the nostrils is described as 'we gave him two litres of nasal prongs'. Such talk has a euphemistic value for the physician, by putting some emotional distance between him and the extremely ill or dying people he meets in such numbers. Unkempt, usually poor, alcoholic, often bad-smelling patients are 'grumes' (from the medical term 'grumous'), or 'crocks', or 'old birds'—not, that is, people, because the idea of people in that condition is distressing and would affect a doctor's judgement. Doctors appear to need, as much as patients do, the protective ministrations of language if they are to be of any use to the patients who trustfully consult them.

The Religious Speak-Easy

PETER MULLEN

THERE is a sense in which euphemism is the opposite of poetry: poetry is the attempt to provide vivid images of the world in language that is sincere because it has been thoroughly cleansed. This is the ceaseless task which Eliot referred to when he spoke of the need 'to purify the dialect of the tribe'. Religion, too, has its rites of purification. So it might be expected to contain very few euphemisms in its scripture and liturgy—those texts which are the poetic representation of both this world and the world to come. The eternal verities demand language to match, language that itself embodies the certainties to which it refers, honest, confident language of great strength and power. If we speak of God in any but the most exalted terms, then that must mean we are reserving those terms for someone or something else; and that is to break the First Commandment: 'Thou shalt have no other gods before me.' To invent a religious language that is weak and vacillating, circumlocutionary, vague or euphemistic is to steer perilously close to idolatry. Recently I received a kind of confirmation of this assessment from a most unexpected quarter: I had been criticizing new translations of the Bible and new liturgical forms when the Chairman of the Liturgical Commission himself complained that I was using 'strong language'.

But it is not only new translations and new liturgies that contain weak language—though it must be said that they do so to the extent of raising attenuation to a theological principle; even the Authorized Version of the Bible knows how to be mealy-mouthed when circumstances or manners require it. There is, for instance, the wonderful story of King Eglon's murder by the treacherous, left-handed Ehud. To be sure, the AV is not squeamish about gory details:

And Ehud put forth his left hand, and took the dagger from his right thigh, and thrust it into his belly: and the haft also went in after the blade; and the fat closed upon the blade, so that he could not draw the dagger out of his belly; and the dirt came out.   (Judges 3: 21–2)

But when it comes to telling us what Eglon was doing when he was struck by sinister misfortune, the translators take refuge in an ambiguity in the Hebrew and say, 'he covereth his feet in his summer chamber' (3: 24). And it is left to the New English Bible to tell us the truth: 'He must be relieving himself in the closet.' The squeamishness of the AV here is difficult to account for, except on the grounds of simple misunderstanding, for the old Bible does not usually go in for undue delicacy when describing bodily parts and functions: 'they may eat their own dung and drink their own piss with you' (2 Kings 18: 27). This is too much for the NEB which turns 'piss' into 'urine'. That word 'urine' does not fit because it has modern clinical-medical connotations —we think of taking 'samples' of urine in little bottles to the doctor's surgery; but piss-drinking is unmistakably unpleasant.

However, there are occasions when what looks like a euphemism, a typical piece of the NEB's daintiness, renders the ancient tongue with greater accuracy. The translators of the AV mistook the Hebrew idiom in 1 Samuel 25: 22 for a straight-forward literalism and so came up with 'any that pisseth against the wall'. The original means to suggest simply 'anyone'. So, for once, the NEB shows more imagination in translating the Hebrew figure of speech into 'a single mother's son'. But this inspiration must have evaporated three verses further on when 'good-for-nothing' is substituted for the AV's 'man of Belial' (i.e. the Devil). The characterization of evil has indeed suffered the debilitating effect of the friendly euphemism if the Devil's son is only a good-for-nothing—like a truant from the Fourth Form who has been stealing apples from the Housemaster's orchard.

The Psalms are written in language that must have done much to purify the dialect of the tribes of Israel, and both the AV and Coverdale translations preserve that original stark and turbulent picture of the tempestuous Lord rumbling around Sinai, threatening the heathen with hailstones and coals of fire and affronting even kings in his righteousness. But new transla-tions, even when they do not exchange strong words for weak ones, so often remove the theatre of God's activity to an altogether more urbane and humanly manageable plane. 'Let the people tremble' says the AV in Psalm 99. 'The peoples are perturbed' is the NEB's rendering of the same verse. What, the Lord reigns between the cherubims and the whole earth is moved and yet the people are only 'perturbed'! But the word 'perturbed' hardly belongs in the same language as 'tremble'. Who is likely to be perturbed?—that Housemaster perhaps, as he confides to the Head his worries about the academic progress of the Lower Sixth.

The image of the public school occurs often when one looks into modern Psalters. The rumbustious, violent and unpredictable God is tamed, turned into a kindly visitor, perhaps one of those aged or even deceased benefactors to whom we are urged to show gratitude on Open Day. 'Lord, Thou hast searched me out and known me' says the AV at the beginning of Psalm 139. But the scriptural translation of which Roman Catholics are most proud (the Jerusalem Bible) says instead 'Yahweh, you examine me'. (Yes, you, Yahweh, you have been my Hebrew tutor for the last two terms: you—and not some other teacher—you examine me in the oral!) The thoroughness, the ruthlessness and the painfulness of being searched-out and known has vanished to be replaced by something that is arrogant, a challenge to the Almighty: Go on, examine me then—just see if you can find any fault!

This Old Testament God can be capricious but it is also possible to appeal to him to answer 'in thy faithfulness' (Psalm 143: 1). The NEB translates this as 'Be true to thyself', which is unspeakable insubordination or else it is back to the public school and Speech Day again, where that aged benefactor emerges from his accustomed limbo to misapply Shakespeare to moralizing at small boys: 'To thine own self be true.' That same kindly old visitor might also have said what the NEB says in place of 'The fear of the Lord is the beginning of wisdom' (Proverbs 9: 10)—'The first step to find wisdom' etc. This is mere programmed-learning, religion by numbers and, like painting by numbers, it will never make anyone into an artist. It is a pity to use such a drab technique in religion since here we are concerned with the art of the soul. 'Beginning' ('In my end is my beginning') offers a perspective which is not offered by 'the first step'. What, we wonder, is the second step? 'Well, today, children, we have taken our first step and tomorrow on "Blue Peter" we shall turn over the page and take our second step.'

The Jerusalem Bible, in its obsession with literal-mindedness (as if heaven were all a matter of street plans and diagrams), is forever anxious to show off its technical proficiency and by so doing it avoids both euphemism and anti-euphemism because it eschews the English language altogether. It does not matter that for nearly five hundred years people have begun Psalm 23 with the words 'The Lord is my shepherd'; the JB would not have us ignorantly suppose that those were King David's words. No, he said 'Yahweh is my shepherd.' And so we must say that too. Sometimes this pedantry, this pseudo-scholarly fascination with all that is merely foreign and obscure, is just silly, as in 'You, Yahweh, examine me'; occasionally it is mindlessly unpoetic and banal, as in the substitution of 'Acclaim Yahweh' for 'Make a joyful noise unto the Lord' (Psalm 100: 1); but in one case (Psalm 91: 1–2) the meaning is rendered impenetrable:

He that dwelleth in the secret place of the most high shall abide under the shadow of the Almighty. I will say of the Lord . . .   (AV)

becomes

If you live in the shelter of Elyon and make your home in the shadow of Shaddai, you can say to Yahweh . . .   (JB)

This sort of thing almost rivals the Revised Standard Version in the business of parading the translators' acquaintance with the slightest nuance in the ancient languages but also their ignorance of what will go into ordinary English. The RSV renders the 'giants' of Genesis as 'nephilim' and the 'two pence' which the Good Samaritan gave to the innkeeper as 'two denarii'—lest we should imagine that the currency of the Roman Empire was the same as that of Britain, pre-decimalization. This is a particularly perverse sort of obscurantism and self-contradiction in texts which were always meant to make plain what was cloudy in the original English Bible. In the same way (in case we should think of Sydney Smith's trumpets and *pâtés de foie gras* or brass bands in the park), St Paul's 'sounding brass and tinkling cymbal' (1 Corinthians 13: 1) is given as 'noisy gong or a clanging cymbal'. Notice how the literalism, this busybodying and tinkering with what has always been understood, utterly spoils the effect because it destroys the picture. The RSV makes a habit of iconoclasm, as for instance in its destruction of that very familiar phrase from St Mark 2: 12: 'Arise, take up thy bed and walk.' The drama, the imagery and therefore all the immediacy of this command is absent from the RSV's version, 'Take up your pallet and go home.' Because we must on no account be allowed to imagine (whoever did?) that the poor paralytic slunk off carrying his four-poster, we have forced upon us the literalism 'pallet': and the result sounds like advice to a sloppy painter.

When Tim Rice and Andrew Lloyd Webber can produce a smash-hit musical called 'Joseph and his Technicolour Dreamcoat', we have proof that the 'coat of many colours' of Genesis 37 (AV) is an item of clothing known by all. There is no need for those phantoms of the lapidary style who produced the RSV to tell us that the original Hebrew means' a long robe with sleeves'. More colourlessness. And why, when the AV gives us 'compassed about' (Hebrews 12: 1) 'with so great a cloud of witnesses' does the RSV remove the Dantesque imagery and offer instead the word 'surrounded', which has none of the comforting, sustaining, mystical power of the original, but suggests only old black and white movies where the wagon-train is besieged by Red Indians? The NEB, also, cannot tell the difference between speech that is poetic and metaphoric and speech that is literal and descriptive. That is why for 'wolves in sheep's clothing' (Matthew 7: 15) we are given instead the pantomime howler 'men dressed up as sheep'. We recall perhaps Ulysses' escape from the Cyclops or else that pejorative phrase 'mutton dressed up as lamb'.

Euphemisms are a sign of a retreat from what is solid, tangible and everyday to something like misplaced reticence and the indirectness which separates man and the world. In the world (and in the AV) the dead Lazarus 'stinketh', but in the RSV we have the delicate avoidance of anything so corporeal in the substituted phrase 'there will be an odour'. Similarly, in the AV men are 'at meat' or they 'sup'; but the RSV mentions a Pharisee who 'asked [Jesus] to dine'. And the NEB will not allow its governessy St Paul to address the unbeliever as 'Thou fool' (1 Corinthians 15: 36); he is permitted only the oblique comment 'How foolish!'—so that instead of repudiating those who ask

'How are the dead raised up? and with what body do they come?'
he might be commenting behind his hand on the behaviour of
those who venture out without their mackintoshes on a rainy
day. This is the same diluted and shockable St Paul who speaks
softly to the citizens of Corinth—the most sinful city since
Sodom—saying, 'I actually hear reports of sexual immorality
among you.' Gosh! we think. 'Actually'? Golly!—whatever
next? The AV does not beat about the bush: 'It is reported
commonly that there is fornication' (1 Corinthians 5: 1).

There is a great deal of this polite drawing-room chat in most
new translations of the Bible, as if sin were not bad but only bad
form. 'Be perfect'—Paul's uncompromising injunction to those
same Corinthians—comes out as 'mend your ways'; Christ's
white-hot condemnation of the Pharisees in the words 'Ye fools
and blind' (Matthew 23: 18) is cooled into the impersonal
abstraction 'What blindness'; and his rebuke to the disciples on
the road to Emmaus 'O fools and slow of heart' (Luke 24: 25) is
weakened to become 'How dull you are.' How dull indeed.

Sometimes the enervation of scripture seems to occur for no
other reason than that the translators are afraid of strong
language, as if a powerful presence were the last thing they
wanted to associate with Almighty God. And so the AV's 'pearl
of great price' (Matthew 13: 46) is exhibited in more of that
patronizing 'Blue Peter' language as 'a pearl of very special
value'. And sometimes even the end of the world is described as
if it were only an exceptionally hot afternoon at Goodwood:

My dear friends [that is the NEB's urbane, housetrained St Peter] do not
be bewildered by the fiery ordeal that is coming upon you, as though it
were something extraordinary.   (2 Peter 4: 12)

At other times euphemism is the unmistakable sign that there
has been a failure of nerve, as for instance in the JB's translation
of *Makarioi* (blessed) in the Sermon on the Mount as 'happy'.
Reward in heaven is being played down here, one suspects, in
deference to modern man's famous doubts about the reality of
the world to come. But those beatitudes speak of a more
enduring benediction than anything conveyed by the word
'happy'; you can be as happy as Jeremy Bentham by consulting
the utilitarian calculus; you can be happy at Butlin's holiday
camp ('Are we happy?' 'Yes, we are!')—but to be truly blessed

has nothing to do with the moth-eaten treasures of this world. They are so bland, these translators. Everything must be inoffensive, bland. The bland lead the bland and they both fall into the kitsch.

It is only fair to record that, when it comes to details of a sexual nature, the AV can be as euphemistical as anyone else. Frequently the words used to describe the sex act are 'uncover nakedness' (another example of the literal transcription of a Hebrew metaphor); but I wonder if the NEB's 'had intercourse with' is much better. It is so much like the indulgent, sleazy puritanism of some Sunday newspapers which say the same and also talk of someone 'being intimate with' someone (or notoriously saying 'intimacy took place') when nothing could be further from the truth. But worse than all the rest is the JB's 'sleep with' which brings to mind the jargon of 'Espresso Bongo' or, worse still, 'do your duty', which suggests that sex was the invention of Lord Kitchener. The AV often says 'knew' as in 'Adam knew his wife' and we know what this means, honest, non-cerebral, carnal knowledge of the type approved of by D. H. Lawrence. And perhaps the expression 'go into' (AV) is, as it were, the most straightforward of the lot—except that as a description of the kinds of activities going on in Corinth it might seem rather limited.

There is a sort of discreet charm about the AV's rendering of Genesis 18: 11 'It ceased to be with Sarah after the manner of women.' This seems to 'reach up the underclothes of words', as that other great admirer of biblical prose, Dylan Thomas, said. When I first read those words as a pubescent confirmation candidate I recognized the sexual mystery in them right enough; but the JB was written in the era of sex education, so it can confidently come straight out with 'ceased to have her monthly periods', which is a plain anti-euphemism in the ordinary sense, but which, because it abolishes the mysteriousness of the manner of women, is reductive, banal. And 'the great whore of Babylon' (AV) seems to lose what is left of her character when the JB refers to her as 'the famous prostitute'. Who? Eskimo Nell, who else?

There is a rare example in the NEB of a euphemism that is even more gratuitously offensive than the original which it sought to replace. In the story of the Prodigal Son, the AV tells how he 'devoured his living with harlots' (Luke 15: 30), but, in a phrase to rouse the wrath of the liberated sisterhood, the NEB has the lad 'running through your money with his women'. Perhaps it would be only flippant to suggest a compromise, such as 'running through his harlots with your money'. When it comes to that certain condition in which ladies sometimes find themselves before it has ceased to be with them after the manner of women, we find that most modern versions are prepared to say 'became pregnant' in the case of ordinary lasses, such as Lot's daughter, but that the special case of the Blessed Virgin Mary required the accurate and evocative (but somehow less blunt) expression 'with child'.

The infelicities and desecrations of modern translations of the Bible are not as intrusive as those to be found in revised liturgies. We can always sit quietly at home and read the AV; but it is becoming increasingly difficult to find an Anglican church which still uses the traditional services of the Book of Common Prayer, except here and there for Evensong and for early morning (said not sung) celebrations of Holy Communion.

The liturgy of the Church of England most widely in use, the Alternative Service Book, is itself a kind of long-running—very long, over a thousand pages—euphemism for the real Prayer Book. The Occasional Offices come off worst. Take 'The Marriage Service' for instance, which title is itself something like a euphemism for 'The Solemnization of Matrimony' (BCP). Don't they believe that marriages are solemn any longer, or what? 'The Marriage Service' is like that other creation of the liturgical revolution, 'Family Services'—it is the language of the advertising industry, as if the parson is all the time saying 'Don't miss this special offer!' The new rite is only a pale copy of the original wherein the earthy sections which mention 'sin', 'fornication' and 'men's carnal lusts and appetites' are noticeable only by their omission. Happy Families has replaced 'this holy estate' and all is euphemistically suffused in the costless, happy glow of the bourgeoisie praying to its kindly God. Just look at the Introduction, where it used to say:

. . . which holy estate Christ adorned and beautified with his presence and first miracle that he wrought in Cana of Galilee.　　　　(BCP)

Now, in the ASB, gone is the holiness, gone the adorning and beautifying and, of course, gone is the miracle, and we are simply told that Christ 'was himself a guest at a wedding'. Not even *the* guest, mind you! Was there ever a clearer case of wine into water? Very frequently liturgical revisers attack their critics for complaining about 'mere words'. This is a strange cry coming from those who have made it their business these twenty-five years to weigh words as carefully as possible. It also shows a more serious misunderstanding; for there can never be anything 'mere' about words. The choice of words is always crucial because they are the stuff of meaning. Philosophers know this and so do poets; so did T. S. Eliot, who wrote of 'the intolerable wrestle with words and meanings'. Why should liturgical scholars, who by their own profession deal with the issues of ultimate significance, imagine that they will be exempted from the responsibility of saying what they mean? And we can, in the absence of occult perception, tell what they mean only from what they say. No other method is available to the critic.

Thus, when from 'The Marriage Service' all those stern but reassuring words about matrimony as 'a remedy against sin and to avoid fornication' are omitted, we can only assume that the Church no longer condemns sin (though not, of course, the sinner) and that what has been for centuries regarded as essential Christian doctrine is now, in this inoffensive, sugary rite, repealed, revoked, and cast aside. And if morality be overturned, can theology survive? Hardly. For a little further down the page we discover that where, in the Book of Common Prayer, matrimony was an estate to be entered into 'reverently, discreetly, advisedly, soberly and in the fear of God', nothing of the kind applies any longer. For what does the new book know of reverence, of discretion and sober advice? It says only 'responsibly and after serious thought'. So 'serious thought' will now do for what was once 'the fear of God'! This is atheism by stealth if not quite (or yet) atheism by decree.

The BCP contains that stern warning to the couple:

I require and charge you both as ye will answer at the dreadful day of judgement when the secrets of all hearts shall be disclosed . . .

It is, among other things, a caution against bigamous and unlawful marriage. That the new book omits all reference to the day of judgement should come as no surprise—scholars who can abolish 'sin' and 'the fear of God' will have no trouble with the prophecies of Christ about the end of the world and the certainty of God's judgement. But the form of the caution has been changed in such a way that it no longer has any force at all: 'I am required to ask . . .' (ASB). Notice the weakness of that passive voice: 'I require' (BCP) is a challenge; 'I am required' could be a notice from the Rate Office or HM Inspector of Taxes. It conjures up the image of the officiating priest as pretending that the responsibility for the asking—and there is a world of difference between asking and requiring and charging—is not his, and that he is only doing it because some tedious and unseen legal bureaucracy insists.

When it comes to the giving and receiving of a ring and the joining of hands, the ASB reveals its utter lack of understanding of what is going on. The BCP says simply, 'with this ring I thee wed'. Six words each of one syllable. Words which, as a vicar, I know fit exactly the movement, the drama, the liturgy at that moment. But they have been dropped and replaced in the ASB by 'I give you this ring as a sign of our marriage'. Nearly twice the number of words. Was this done, as we are told so many of the revisions have been done, because we do not understand the original? What is misunderstood here is not just the properties of drama but the nature of symbolism itself: a grievous fault in a liturgiologist. 'With this ring I thee wed' makes the symbolism clear; at that moment the man puts the ring on the woman's finger. 'I give you this ring as a sign of our marriage' is wordy, ugly, and redundant. She *knows* that the ring is a sign. To have to *say* that it is a sign means that the sign does not work. Moreover, the bride does not want to hear a lecture on symbolism on her wedding day.

The ad-man has also been at 'The Burial of the Dead', which is now called 'Funeral Services'—almost excusable I suppose in the era of cremation; but why not 'The Burial or Cremation of the Dead'? Certainly the revisers have not shown themselves in other places to be averse to parentheses or alternatives. But the ambience that produced the ASB does not like to dwell much on too solid flesh—as we saw in 'The Marriage Service'—on corpses and on death; so we should expect that liturgiologists who have so little time for corporeality even when it is

animated will have even less to do with it when it is deceased.
Take that proud, confident statement which the minister used
to pronounce as he led the coffin down the aisle: 'I know that my
Redeemer liveth' (BCP). These are words of faith made more
faithful by the music of Handel, words and a tune known by
almost everyone. Surely it is the business of liturgy to fasten
upon and use perceptions and images like this one which go
deep? So why leave it out? The reason soon becomes clear: those
words are followed by 'though after my skin worms destroy this
body'. And a book that will not mention 'fornication' and
'carnal lusts' will hardly bring itself to a remembrance of
'worms'. (Incidentally, northerners have never been squeamish
about this issue: compare the later verses of 'On Ilkla Moor Baht
'At'.) But the forfeiting of the line about worms means that the
profound faith of the next and final line must be given up as well.
So the ASB cannot say (as the BCP says), 'yet in my flesh shall I
see God'. The omission reveals a loss of nerve which in turn reveals something much more serious: the loss of faith. Does the
Church no longer believe in the resurrection of the dead? At this
crucial stage in the burial service, it must at least remain in doubt.

That long speech of St Paul from 1 Corinthians 15 has been
nicked and cut so that in the ASB the relentless build-up, the
theological crescendo of hope has been ruined. The empty-
headed translation does not help. Where in the BCP Paul
repudiates those who doubt the resurrection with the words
'Thou fool', the new rite substitutes 'these questions do not
make sense'. This is weak beyond measure; it is the governessy
St Paul again (whom we first met in the NEB) telling the girls to
stop asking silly questions. And in true euphemistic style, this
St Paul will not utter the word 'corruptible' with its connotation
of 'decay' and so he has to say 'perishable' instead, which
reminds us not so much of mortal flesh as of rubber boots left to
dry by the radiator.

None the less, this bland modern thing the ASB, which dare
not mention worms, does contrive to render the lesson from I
Thessalonians in a way which, in the middle of all that lack of
affirmation, scarcely-veiled disbelief and dousing of faith's holy
fire, is utterly unbelievable:

Those who have died in Christ will be the first to rise; then those of us

who are left alive shall join them, caught up in the clouds to meet the
Lord in the air.   (1 Thessalonians 4: 13–18)

What are we to make of that? We can make nothing of it in the
context of a rite which has so studiously avoided earthly realities. If they dare not tell us earthly things, how shall we believe
them when they try to speak to us of heaven?

If there is a phrase better recalled than 'I know that my
Redeemer liveth', it is 'earth to earth, ashes to ashes, dust to
dust'. The ASB again speaks softly. It says 'In appropriate cases
these words may be omitted.' When? What would constitute an
appropriate case? Those words make equal sense in the
crematorium and at the graveside. The immediately following
words in the BCP, 'who shall change our vile body', are also left
out, of course. Vile bodies have no place in these obsequious
obsequies. What, corpses at burial services?—whatever next?
But the BCP mentions 'our vile body' so that in the very next
line it can contrast this with the undying hope 'that it may be
like unto his glorious body'. And because the ASB omits the
vileness, it must also omit the glory. Once again, the cause of
euphemism has entirely emasculated the great Christian belief
that dying we live. Because there is no death in ASB 'Funeral
Services' there can be no resurrection either. Faced with such
disingenuousness and dissimulation, won't people soon begin
to refuse the ministrations of the Church altogether and opt for
the dignified affirmation of secular humanism: 'He lived and
now he is dead. Let us honour his memory'? For that is where
the nothingness of ASB funerals is pointing them—or else to
wordless disposal.

The Litany has been rejigged so that it manages to include
petitions for causes which are dear to the hearts of all
ecclesiastical politicians: church unity, for example: 'Give it
[the Church] that unity which is your will.' This is a euphemism
of truly 'open-texture', the complete euphemism which succeeds in saying absolutely nothing, so that it can be construed to
mean absolutely anything. Something so unspecific is not a
prayer at all of course. It is only included so that rival politicians,
all with different ideas about unity, can make one holy noise
under the same roof—and then be blameless when things do not
work out the way they had hoped. It is also a sure sign that the

prayer for deliverance from hypocrisy (further up the page) is not expected to work.

I will go quickly through 'Holy Baptism', from which is omitted all mention of the fact that 'all men are conceived and born in sin' (BCP), as well as those other telling phrases 'the Old Adam', 'crucify the old man' and 'the devil and all his works'. In what the ASB calls 'the rejection of all that is evil', the devil is not so much as mentioned, let alone renounced. All reference to the Ten Commandments is left out. The revisers do not see that by playing down the idea of sin, they make the doctrine of regeneration of little effect and so 'Holy Baptism'—but the word 'Holy' is not used, of course—is in the ASB no longer beautiful, awe-inspiring—the place of holy water in the mystical washing away of sin—but only pretty, a sentimental prelude to the booze-up and the cake, an opportunity for photographs: photographs that will evidence *what*?

Evening Prayer in the ASB has been much softened, so that there is no reference in the Confession to 'miserable offenders'—but we *are* 'miserable' when we offend; that is Christian doctrine—or to the fact that we have 'erred and strayed like lost sheep'. I can understand that the compilers of the ASB do not relish the comparison with sheep, but by omitting this reference, the rite's link with scripture, with the parable of the Lost Sheep, is severed. I know the way their reasoning went: modern man—that much-vaunted creature for whom this catalogue of sanctimonious euphemisms was con- cocted in the first place—cannot, in his industrial alienation, make much of stories about sheep; so mention of sheep will not be made. But the sheep are still there in the heart of St Luke's gospel and even modern translations of the Bible are content to leave them alone. Is it the purpose of the ASB then to deny the symbolism of God's word upon which all liturgy has always been based? The Magnificat in the ASB is certainly less than magnificent, but what are we to make of a version of the Nunc Dimittis which renders the line, 'Now, Lord, lettest thou thy servant depart in peace' as 'Lord, now you let your servant go'? It evokes the image of a schoolboy in distress of bladder, rather than of spirit. Can you imagine the new version said by a congregation of forty in a country church? Can you imagine what it sounds like sung in a Gothic cathedral?

The BCP service of Holy Communion opens with the words of the prayer which Our Lord taught us. The ASB rite 'A' begins with:

'The Lord be with you'
'And also with you.'

This is the modern replacement for 'The Lord be with you: and with thy spirit.' (I have heard it said that the 'also' was added because the first and unusually thoroughgoing alternative which occurred to the revisers, 'And with you', was thought likely to demand and receive the addition of an extra word —certainly balance would demand it—and that this might even sound rude!—'And with you *too.*') The ASB version of the Nicene Creed speaks of Christ not as 'the only begotten Son of the Father', but as one who is 'eternally begotten'. Is this piece of sham antique to be understood, I wonder, by couples who have difficulty (or so it is alleged) with 'with this ring I thee wed'? And in the Gloria and the Creed 'sitteth' has been changed to 'seated'—that pin-striped, committee-meeting word as in 'Please be seated, gentlemen.' Where? A little to the left of the Liturgical Commission's filing cabinet, perhaps.

The most serious omissions in the Holy Communion (ASB) concern the invitation to Confession and the Confession itself. That old invitation in the BCP is full of images which actually move us and encourage us to make confession of our sins. It is about a real man doing something, 'following', 'walking', 'taking', being 'in love and charity with [our] neighbours'. The new invitation is drab and bland—as if it assumes that we shall want to confess our sins *naturally*. But they have spent enough time denying or ignoring our fallen nature already in the poor revision of Holy Baptism. We no longer 'acknowledge and bewail our manifold sins and wickedness'; we have no longer sinned 'in thought, word and deed'; there is no mention of God's 'wrath and indignation' (hence all reference to his pardon is worthless); and we do not say of our sins 'the remembrance of them is grievous unto us: the burden of them is intolerable'. All these things are now regarded as far too gloomy to mention. But is the age which has produced the concentration camps and Hiroshima any less sinful than Cranmer's? Doesn't an age taught by Freud know that 'the remembrance of them is grievous unto us: the burden of them is intolerable'—because our sins and the guilt which corrupts us will not go away but will fester in the unconscious parts from which it will burst forth in 'wrath and indignation', in the form of all kinds of neurosis and mental disturbance, and that the only cure is by acknowledging and bewailing?

There is more shallowness and shoddiness in the mutilated Prayer of Humble Access, in the effete substitution of 'It is indeed' for 'It is very' before the Sanctus and in the omission of 'tender mercy' at the beginning of the Prayer of Consecration. But we can understand why a committee which defends itself from all genuine feeling, expressed in language which is at once plain and direct, would shy away from the real thing in a word like 'tender' applied to God.

The world of contemporary religion is beset by euphemism because those who were appointed and ordained to defend and proclaim the truth of religion—teachers, parsons, bishops and so on—have lost their nerve. There is no longer any 'Religious Instruction' in schools and the reason is that no one believes any longer that he has authority to instruct. It has all become a matter which requires pupils to 'make up their own minds'. But make them up on the basis of *what*?—a smattering of 'world religions', 'reverence for life' or the technological-Benthamite Babel of irresponsibility which has replaced civilization. And then, of course, there is always the telly to be our comforter in the valley of the shadow of death.

Bishops will talk about everything from amateur politics to even more amateur economics rather than teach the faith; parsons will do anything except say 'Let us pray'—the alternatives are hilariously evasive: 'Let's pray', so that he is seen to be with it at the Youth Club; 'a moment of quiet', but *he* is about to talk for five minutes; 'bow our heads', instead of kneeling here where prayer has been valid, and so on. But there is one new publication which perfectly sums up the present vacillating, enervated, forsworn Church in England. It is called 'Hymns for Today's Church'. (Note the excitement: '*Today*'s Church'! Wow!) In one of the many forgettable verses therein to be found, there is the suppressed hope that God will be with me 'in my depression'. The people of God depressed? That is the final loss of faith. Depression in a Church tranquillized by euphemisms. That hymn should be retitled, 'Who Would True Valium See'.

Politics

SIMON HOGGART

EUPHEMISMS occur less in British politics than one might imagine. Abuse of the language is, of course, as common at Westminster as it is in any other national legislature, but more often it takes the form of hyperbole, evasion, vagueness and plain untruth. The principal reason for this is the adversarial nature of British politics. Every time someone tries to slide a euphemism into the language, his opponents promptly match it with the corresponding dysphemism.

Take the phrase 'unilateral nuclear disarmament'. This has been in common use in Britain for twenty-five years or so. In the early 1980s, however, people on both sides of the argument decided it would no longer serve. Someone in the Labour Party, aware that it had gained a patina of disagreeable overtones, coined the term 'non-nuclear defence'. This was eagerly seized upon by the party's then leader Michael Foot who lost no opportunity to use it in speeches and broadcasts. The new soubriquet had two advantages: it contained a positive word, 'defence', which countered the pacifist feel of 'disarmament', and it cashed in on the general suspicion of all things nuclear. Of course it begged the important question asked by its opponents, which was whether there could be a 'non-nuclear' defence against a nuclear threat.

Naturally the Conservatives had to reply to this shift in the linguistic struggle, and came up with 'one-sided disarmament'. 'One-sided' brought suggestions of unfairness and bias as well as of defencelessness. It too begged the opposition's main question. Many people might, incidentally, regard the term 'peace movement' as another unacceptable euphemism for unilateral disarmament.

Though 'one-sided' is just the English version of the Latinate 'unilateral', the phrase never really caught on except in speeches by Conservative politicians. Possibly it was too obviously propagandist, which in turn made broadcasters wary of it. For a political euphemism, or dysphemism, to do its intended job of influencing public opinion by stealth, it must be acceptable to the middle ground, to the great majority of people who do not feel politically committed.

Take this short extract from Hansard. A Labour MP, Jeff Rooker, is debating various changes in the social security rules with the Conservative minister responsible, Norman Fowler:

Mr Rooker: '. . . are the Government still looking to see where in the system they can make the cuts? Will the Rt. Hon. Gentleman spell it out for us?'

Mr Fowler: 'We are examining a number of areas inside the social security system to see if savings can be made.'

The words 'cuts' and 'savings' mean here exactly the same thing—reductions in public expenditure—and the two opponents each use the word appropriate to their side of the political fence without even appearing to notice the switch. Labour is using the dysphemism 'cuts' with its overtones of physical violence, and the Tories use 'savings', a euphemism which suggests thrift and responsibility. In this case the Labour Party won the public verbal battle, since 'cuts' passed into the language of ordinary people. Obviously one can't imagine a protest banner labelled 'Stop These Savage Savings', but equally 'cuts' was used in homes and workplaces, as well as in the press, on radio and on television.

The euphemisms which take root fastest are those which serve an equal purpose for both sides of the argument—in other words, where it is in nobody's interest to circulate a contradictory dysphemism. For any politician to talk about 'the poor countries of the world' might offend those countries, therefore they became 'the emergent nations' or the 'developing nations', whether or not they were actually developing. Like most euphemisms, this soon took on the original unwanted overtones, and so a further euphemism was required—in this case 'Third World'. Sometimes the same countries are referred to simply as 'The South', as in the 'North–South divide'. The corresponding dysphemism used by some right-wing politicians and ideologues is 'debtor nations', which implies the reckless waste of other people's money, though of course every country in the world is a debtor in one form or other. The term has not entered general circulation.

Almost all politicians dislike displeasing almost all groups of people if they can avoid it, and therefore are usually willing to agree on euphemistic terms for them. This often strikes me as offensive in itself; the fact that a euphemism is thought necessary implies that the original term is, in some degree, abusive. Thus 'Jews' is thought too harsh and even anti-Semitic. Politicians prefer to say 'members of the Jewish community'. 'Community' is no doubt supposed to soften the blunt 'Jew' and implies an identity of political and social interest which might not always exist. For instance, politicians commonly talk about 'our Asian community', though the diverse collection of Indians, Bengalis, Sikhs, and Pakistanis who live in Britain probably have less in common, including language, than a Highland crofter and a Cornish fisherman.

In a similar way 'ethnic' has arrived from the US as a euphemism for 'black and brown'. Oddly enough, the phrase 'ethnic group' is tautological unless it is being used as a euphemism —though the *OED* suggests that in the fifteenth century 'ethnic' meant 'pagan', which is certainly not the effect intended today. Possibly these complicated circumlocutions are meant to act as a counterbalance for the many insulting dysphemistic words often used for coloured people: the neutral terms 'black' or 'Pakistani' are not sufficient, and the tortuous 'members of our Caribbean ethnic community' is necessary to balance 'wog'.

Nobody in Britain is 'poor' any longer, at least not in political speeches. 'Poor' was replaced by the euphemistic 'deprived', 'underprivileged', and 'disadvantaged'. It is now returning as a dysphemism, as in the headline 'Thatcher's New Poor' which appeared over an article attacking Tory economic policies. The word evokes politically useful memories of the poorhouse and the Poor Laws.

The new Left occasionally turns up an extraordinary form of euphemism of which a good example, recently coined, is 'heterosexism'. This means 'being prejudiced against homosexuals', a state of mind which of course is opposed by almost all members of the new Left. The use of the long-winded neologism (instead of 'hating gays' for example) gives status not to the prejudice, but to those who attack it. The word also makes their opposition easier. Instead of saying 'the trouble with you is that you're prejudiced against homosexuals', which is merely a critical observation, you can spit 'heterosexist!', an instant condemnation. Thus the word is simultaneously euphemism and dysphemism.

Another curiosity is the Left's use of 'kids' instead of 'children', which was presumably thought insulting since it implied, well, childishness. In some left-wing literature it is quite common to see 'kids' used not as affectionate slang but as the technical term for persons under the age of about fourteen. The fringe Left uses 'youth' instead of 'young people' to create a slightly different effect. 'Basingstoke youth sent a raspberry to Mrs Thatcher' suggests all the young people of Basingstoke, rather than the half-dozen members of the Workers Revolutionary Party actually being referred to.

The running battle over state control of the economy has seen the corpses of many euphemisms carried from the field. 'Nationalization' for 'compulsory purchase by the state' is roughly 100 years old. Various failings, real or imaginary, in state-run undertakings created the need for fresh euphemism, and 'public ownership' was promptly produced. The Right, meanwhile, came up with 'free enterprise' which, by combining two attractive words with popular overtones, made a first-rate euphemism for 'untrammelled capitalism'. 'Free enterprise' had some success, and while it was never used by Labour politicians, it was sometimes employed by normal members of the public speaking normal English. The Left, therefore, varied 'public ownership' with 'public enterprise'. This brought rousing suggestions of mercantile buccaneers at the head of British Rail or the National Coal Board.

'Private', however, has remained a vogue word, and so the act of 'selling off state-owned assets' acquired the euphemism 'privatization'. But the ugliness of the new word, and the fact that the Government has woefully mishandled some recent sales, suggest that another new euphemism will shortly be required. 'Economic liberation' might do, though oddly enough 'liberty' is a word used principally by the Left in this country. The right-wing term is 'freedom'; hence the leftish 'National Council for Civil Liberties' and the extreme right-wing 'Freedom Association'. It's pleasant to note that this was originally the 'National Association for Freedom', which dropped its 'NAFF' acronym shortly after 'naff off' became a royal euphemism for 'fuck off'.

British politicians are not as eager as Americans to embrace long Latinisms. They are keener on 'endings' than on 'terminations', happier with 'tax cuts' than with 'fiscal adjustments'. A phrase such as 'motorized transportation module' for 'school bus' would sound simply absurd in British parlance. However, they have been much keener on adopting modern US military jargon, possibly feeling that the mystique of terms such as 'preemptive strike' and 'theatre weapons' confers a needed degree of authority upon their speeches. However, I think it unlikely that an American word such as 'pacification' would be used here in place of 'military conquest'.

Indeed, the notorious Saturday debate on the Argentine invasion of the Falkland Islands on 3 April 1982 is remarkable for the shortage of euphemism—though one might single out stock phrases such as 'established military control' for 'took by force', 'inflicted casualties' for 'killed and wounded' and 'take appropriate action' for 'kill as many people as necessary'. These, however, are so common as to have lost their euphemistic qualities.

A certain amount of jargon was used in the debate, especially by warfare experts such as the Defence Secretary, Sir John Nott. He spoke about the absence of a 'trip-wire force' and said of a ship that it would retain 'out-of-area capability'. However, the main function of the debate was to put the country into a warlike mood, and therefore the language was not euphemistic but hyperbolic, aimed at raising the temperature. Thus, the Argentine invasion was 'unprovoked' and 'bellicose', 'naked, unqualified aggression', 'shameful and disreputable', 'delinquency'. One Tory MP, Mr Ray Whitney, suggested that negotiations should not be abandoned, so his colleague Sir John Biggs-Davison demanded to know whether 'defeatism is to be spoken'. The archaic nature of the phrase was no doubt intended (perhaps subconsciously) to evoke memories of Munich and 'appeasement'—itself a good example of a euphemism becoming a dysphemism through the failure of the strategy which it described.

Often British politicians prefer a fake homeliness where an

American might choose a long-winded construction. A US politician on the stump will grow misty-eyed when he speaks of 'our senior citizens', whereas a Briton would talk about 'our old folk', or simply 'pensioners'. It's worth comparing this with the anguished way in which British advertisers will avoid saying 'old'—a clothes advert offers dresses for 'the mature woman', an insurance scheme suggests 'preparation for the golden years'.

Sometimes what appears to be a euphemism is simply clumsy expression. Harold Wilson, describing the effect of devaluation in a 1967 broadcast, said: 'It does not mean, of course, that the pound here in Britain in your pocket or purse or in your bank has been devalued.' What he wished to say, of course, was that devaluation did not mean people would be able to buy 14.3 per cent fewer groceries next day or that their rent would cost 14.3 per cent more. He appeared, however, to be claiming that the pound had not lost any of its domestic spending power. The phrase was seen as a failed attempt at euphemism and clung to him for the rest of his career.

Similarly Harold Macmillan's famous attempt to belittle the resignation of his entire Treasury team of ministers in 1958 was not so much a euphemism as a deliberate political statement. By dismissing the event as a 'little local difficulty' he was actually demeaning the political significance of the three men concerned. The full sentence ran: 'I thought the best thing to do was to settle up these little local difficulties and then turn to the wider vision of the Commonwealth.' As it happens, constant reference to foreign affairs can have a euphemistic effect; domestic events are supposed to appear trivial compared to the mighty deeds transacted on the world stage. Again, opposition politicians almost always make sure that the attempt fails: witness the persecution of James Callaghan in 1979 after he returned from the Guadeloupe summit of world leaders in the midst of the 'Winter of Discontent' and observed: 'I see no signs of mounting crisis.'

Each department of government has its own jargon, and this can also have a euphemistic effect. Sir Anthony Eden, when Prime Minister, said on one celebrated occasion: 'We are not at war with Egypt. We are in a state of armed conflict.' To a diplomat, the term 'at war' has a precise technical meaning and implies that there has been a formal declaration of war; to the layman, however, the term is virtually synonymous with 'armed conflict'.

In fact, diplomacy has its own range of euphemisms, most of which have now been used too often to achieve the desired softening. 'Cordial' talks are not positively acrimonious; 'wide-ranging talks' cover several topics of which many are irrelevant to the problems in hand. 'Full and frank discussion' or a 'full and frank exchange of views' imply some degree of ill-feeling. 'Both positions were stated clearly' means there was no agreement; 'some progress towards agreement' means that minuscule concessions were made on either side. Such phrases observe the diplomatic niceties, but fool none of the professionals, whether politicians, diplomats or journalists.

One of the rare examples of the niceties not being observed came in February 1984 when British Labour leader Neil Kinnock had an argumentative conversation with Mr George Schultz, the US Secretary of State. A State Department spokesman said afterwards that there had been 'clear differences of viewpoints'; Kinnock said that Schultz had 'got out of his pram'. This is a dysphemistic slang term for 'lost his temper'.

Economics produces a phenomenal amount of jargon, and some of this can at least appear to have a euphemistic effect. Sir Geoffrey Howe, when Chancellor of the Exchequer, memorably spoke of 'growth going backwards' when he meant 'recession'. This appallingly clumsy figure of speech was roundly derided at the time, and rightly so, though it seems unlikely that Sir Geoffrey was trying to deceive people into believing that 'growth going backwards' meant the same as 'expansion'. Rather, he was using 'growth' as a reference to a particular statistical scale. To an economist it is no more ridiculous to talk about 'negative growth' than for a physicist to discuss the 'heat' of an ice-cube.

'Recession' was, incidentally, an American euphemism of the 1920s, and was used as a more soothing word for 'crisis'. Originally it meant a milder, short-term version of a 'depression'. Now it seems to have become a euphemism for a real depression, as in 'the present world recession has proved deeper and longer lasting than had been predicted'.

Economists' jargon is often used by politicians to give some respectability to their mistakes: 'shortfall' sounds better than 'failure', 're-adjustment of our estimates' better than 'switching from our wildly mistaken guesswork'.

Northern Ireland and the events there (called by some people 'civil war', by the Government 'civil disorder', and by the Irish themselves 'the troubles', a splendid euphemism) have produced a large crop of euphemisms. Few politicians, Irish or British, wish to acknowledge the fairly obvious truth that the dividing line between the two tribes in the province is primarily religious. Therefore Roman Catholics are called 'the minority community' by the Government, and also by the Protestants who wish to establish in the public mind the fact that they themselves are in a majority. Catholics tend to term themselves 'Republicans'. Protestants call the province 'Ulster' even though it includes only six of the original nine counties which constituted Ulster. Similarly Catholics often call it 'the six counties' to stress that it is a mere fragment, and not the administrative and political unity implied by 'Ulster'.

Government has coined several euphemisms to help—as much as anything—with the difficult task of accustoming its voters at home to an undeclared civil war. People imprisoned without trial were known as 'detainees'. Bombs became 'devices'. Fatal shootings were 'incidents' (also a London Transport formulation for 'body on the line'). Riots were 'disturbances'. The army was on the streets of Northern Ireland 'in aid of the civil power', which meant, more accurately, 'to cope with the complete breakdown of public order'. 'Detainees' were jailed at a prison ten miles from Belfast called 'Long Kesh'. When this name came to imply repression, it was changed to 'HM Prison, The Maze'. The IRA (or 'the Republican Movement' as it prefers to term itself) retaliated by renaming the place 'Long Kesh Concentration Camp'.

The IRA and the various other para-military groups (in itself a euphemism for 'terrorists' quite as insidious as 'freedom fighters') improved their status in their own eyes by adopting formal military ranks and terminology. Thus the head of a cell would be called 'Officer Commanding "B" Company, Belfast Brigade'. A small group of bombers would be an 'active service unit'. The authorities responded with various dysphemisms; IRA attacks were invariably 'cowardly', though in fact membership of the IRA is a risky business involving a rather greater chance of death than, say, chartered accountancy. It may be wicked to shoot at soldiers, but it isn't cowardly.

One might have expected the names of ministries to drift into euphemism, especially as it is in the interests of both sides for this to happen. Yet the obvious switch from 'War Office' to 'Ministry of Defence' is the only one I can detect. There is much heavy irony about 'Ministry of Ill Health' and so on, but verbal swindles seem fairly rare. The Employment Secretary is occasionally called the 'Minister for Unemployment' but both terms are misnomers; in fact, he is the minister for labour relations rather than for creating jobs.

Political journalists have their own euphemisms, though such is the deviousness of the press that what appears to be euphemistic may actually be the reverse. 'Friends of Mr X', for instance, was once a ciphered way of saying 'Mr X', a means of quoting him without nailing him with the responsibility for his words. Just as often it can mean 'someone authorized to speak on his behalf' or even, literally, 'a friend of Mr X'. However, as the phrase became generally known, it swerved wildly in purport between 'Mr X himself' and 'someone who has met him once or twice and claims to know what is in his mind'.

'Downing Street sources' means 'the Prime Minister's professional press spokesmen, talking off the record'; on the record quotes are generally signalled 'a Downing Street spokesman said . . .'. Phrases like 'the signs are' or 'it now seems likely that' generally mean 'my hunch is', or 'if forced to guess by my editor . . .'. Sometimes they indicate that someone has given the journalist a heavy hint that something will happen, but the reporter is unwilling to chance his arm by asserting it strongly.

Usually, of course, journalists are under pressure to raise the temperature, to make ordinary quotidian political discourse sound more exciting than it really is. So a routine disagreement is known by the dysphemism 'major row' or 'massive split'. 'Criticized' becomes 'slammed', 'lashed out at' or 'launched a vicious attack on'. Years ago, when I worked on the *Guardian*, I described a perfectly ordinary argument between Patrick Jenkin and Tony Benn about coal stocks; the copy was returned with a request to 'put some blood into the first paragraph'. The temptation to make things sound worse than they are is even greater for writers on popular newspapers, where space is short and it is assumed that readers are easily bored by politics.

But the pressure on journalists to dramatize events is no worse than the pressure on politicians—especially those in opposition. For one thing, opposition politicians inevitably attract less attention than ministers in Government. Most of them soon discover an identity of interest with the press: the more colourful their criticism, the more willing the newspapers are to print it. A front-bench spokesman who said, 'We have some reservations about these new measures, though by and large think them fair and workable', would certainly find himself out of the press and probably out of a job as well. Hence the use of dysphemism in politics on a scale probably greater than in any other field of human activity.

For example, 'obscene' (largely left-wing) stands for 'unjust', as in 'the obscene poverty of our inner cities', or 'the obscene decision to spend millions on nuclear weapons while our children go without milk'. Some people have argued that the word is being ridiculously misused since it refers specifically to sexual grossness; in fact *Chambers* dictionary offers both 'disgusting' and 'repellent' which seem to fit the intended meaning fairly neatly.

'Byzantine' is now a catch-all word for anything at all complicated or even different from the status quo; such a system inevitably results in 'total chaos', which generally indicates 'some misunderstandings'. 'Bankrupt', as in 'this bankrupt government', generally means 'run out of new ideas for the time being'; 'morally bankrupt' means the same plus 'and we disagree with what it has done already'. 'Hijack' has come in over the past few years, and usually implies making changes which the speaker does not favour to some institution or other: 'this Government has hijacked the Health Service/education system/North Sea Oil . . .'.

A 'scandal' is generally nothing of the sort, being merely a policy the speaker doesn't like, as in 'the monstrous scandal of agricultural support prices'. 'Appalled' means 'displeased', 'shocked' equals 'mildly surprised', 'nauseated' much the same. Compromises are invariably 'shabby', deals always 'sordid' and often 'little' as well. Allies and acquaintances are 'cronies', as in 'The Chancellor's cronies in the City will be celebrating this

Budget . . .'. A decision is never a mere mistake but a 'bizarre folly' or a 'grotesque misjudgement'.

And so forth. Against this Grand Guignol vocabulary, a Government's attempts at soothing euphemism scarcely have a chance. 'Offsetting measures' to mean 'tax increases in one area to compensate for decreases in another' is dull and flat compared to 'a savage attack on the living standards of every family in this country'. 'A monstrous assault on working-class people' is always going to blot out 'modifications', an occasional euphemism for 'unpopular changes in the regulations'. When Governments promulgate policies which lead to factories being closed down, they like to term it 'rationalization', but they can't for long, because the opposition immediately calls it 'tossing another 500 workers on to the human scrap-heap'. If the Government takes a decision in private, it has acted 'in squalid secrecy'. If it does the same publicly, then its behaviour is 'blatant'.

Given the terrible battering (political dysphemism for 'slight financial loss') suffered by the poor euphemism, it seems appropriate that the most famous political euphemism of them all was actually nothing of the sort. In 1906, when a minister in the Colonial Office, Winston Churchill defended the Chinese labour contract in the Commons. He described the details and concluded that it might not be a desirable contract, 'but it cannot in the opinion of His Majesty's Government be classified as slavery in the extreme acceptance of the word without some risk of terminological inexactitude'. The context makes it clear that he didn't mean what everybody has always assumed he meant—'a lie'.

The State

ROBERT NISBET

WHAT we call political philosophy is so overladen in the West with euphemism, panegyric, and idealization that anyone might be forgiven for occasionally failing to remember just what this philosophy's true subject is: the political State, unique among major institutions in its claim of absolute power over human lives. For so long in Western history have euphemisms drawn from kinship, religion, nature, reason, mechanics, biology, the people, and other essentially non-political sources been ascendant that it is downright difficult to keep in mind that the State's origin and essential function is, as Hume pointed out, in and of force, above all, military force. What procreation is to kinship and propitiation of gods is to religion, monopolization of power is to the State.

There is no political order known to us in history, from ancient Egypt to contemporary Israel, that has not originated in war, its claimed sovereignty but an extension and ramification of what the Romans called the *imperium*, absolute military command. The seed of the State in history is anything but the family; it is the war chief and his band. If we desire an image of some archetypal revolt against the patriarch, it is better to go back to some young war leader eager for battle than to sons lustful of their mother. War is the origin of the State, and, in Randolph Bourne's familiar phrasing, is the health of the State. Modern war, grounded as it usually is in the kinds of political and moral ideals, or claimed ideals, which can justify almost limitless expansion of the State at the expense of society, is very healthful indeed to any form of State.

The essence of the State, then, is its unique possession of sovereignty—the absolute, unconditional and imprescriptible power over all individuals and their associations and possessions within a given area. And at the basis of the State's sovereignty is the contingent power to use the military to compel obedience to its rule. This is as true of democratic as despotic States. We properly distinguish among governments of States; there are indeed differences between monarchies and oligarchies, between republics and democracies, and between social democratic and totalitarian political orders. The absoluteness of the State underlies each of these governments.

The most democratic of contemporary States claims a monopoly of power within its borders, exclusive possession of and control over the military and police, the right to declare war and peace, to conscript life and appropriate income and property, to levy taxes, to supervise the family, even, when necessary, the Church, to grant selective entitlements, administer justice, and to define crime and set punishment. The political State is the only association whose freedom to act cannot be limited by the State. With all respect to differences among types of government, there is not, in strict theory, any difference between the powers available to the democratic and to the totalitarian State. We may pride ourselves in the democracies on Bills or other expressions of individual rights against the State, but in fact they are rights against a given government and can be obliterated or sharply diminished when it is deemed necessary, as in the United States and other Western-democratic powers in the two World Wars. Philosophers may appeal to 'natural' and 'inalienable' rights, but these fall in the province of the ideal, not the historic and practical. Such 'rights' exist by tolerance and are as nothing against constituted majorities, even, indeed, unconstituted majorities.

It is not strange, then, that the history of the State should be accompanied by the rich embroidery of euphemism. Any institution born of war, that thrives in war, and that claims unique absoluteness of power over all individuals within its borders requires all the symbolic assistance it can get. Such assistance has for a very long time been the offering of the political clerisy. Like the Church, the State must have its defenders, rationalizers, justifiers, and its scribes and prophets. Also like the Church, the State must have its dogmas and rituals, its feast days, its saints and martyrs, and its sacred objects. If pre-political spirits and essences are invoked in the name of the State, well and good, for from the beginning the

process of politicization of ancient belief and custom has been a
marked characteristic of the State, especially in the West.

Family. The oldest of euphemisms for the State's distinctive
military power is drawn from the realm of kinship, which is
natural, given the age and universality of family, clan, and
kindred in mankind's history. Although the *patria potestas* of
kinship has always been in deadly conflict with the *imperium* of
the warrior-king, it was but sound policy for the latter to take on
some of the coloration of the former. Thus early kings or chiefs
might claim themselves patriarchs. Recurrently in history,
kings have been rulers of *peoples* rather than territories; they
were this in the early Middle Ages. *King* is a derivation of Old
English *cyng*, meaning kinship.

The patriarchal image of the State was nourished by a good
deal of theology during the Middle Ages, and feudalism itself, as
we find it at its height, was an ingenious fusion of military
substance and kinship symbol. Patriarchalism survived the
decline of medieval society to become invigorated in the seventeenth century by Robert Filmer in *Patriarcha*, a work that
deserves a good deal better than to be known chiefly today as the
target of Locke's and Sidney's natural law thrusts. The truth is,
Filmer's book has a good deal of solid learning in it, however
false in historical terms his patriarchal thesis may be—though
no more false to history than natural law theory—and to this
learning he added an impressive insight into popular psychology
in politics. The Tory Party is the result in considerable measure
of Filmer's political views.

The enduring appeal of patriarchal euphemism is well
illustrated in the modern world by the popularity everywhere of
such words and phrases as *fatherland, mother country, sister-
nations*, and the like. It was with a keen sense of the antiquity of
kinship metaphors in politics that George Orwell chose to give
his horrifying totalitarian government the label of Big Brother.
In the United States, in July 1984, Governor Cuomo of New
York, in a single national political address, likened the State
some two dozen times to a family, albeit without designation of
either Big Daddy or Big Brother. But in many ways the most
telling example of the power of a euphemism in thought is the
argument in political and social philosophy—extending from

Aristotle to modern political ethnology—that the State is but the natural development through time of kinship. It assuredly is not, but the myth appears to be ineradicable by now.

Religion. Religion is second only to family in its fecundity of euphemism for the war-born State. Pre-political man was as saturated by religious as by kinship influences upon his thinking. Almost as hoary as the patriarch is the prophet in mankind's annals. How better to give root to a military conqueror's acceptance by the conquered than to sanctify, even deify him, to make him at worst an indispensable voice of the gods, at best one of the gods himself. Egyptian kings were addressed in rescript and inscription as Aton, Horus, Re, and so on in order to give expression to their claimed identities as sun-gods. The speed with which passage from the human to the divine could occur, and much later than the age of Egyptian pharaohs, is well illustrated by the careers of Alexander in the Hellenistic world and of Octavian, conqueror of Mark Antony at Actium, in the Roman. The latter was obliged by still-respected republican tradition to be more subtle than had been Alexander, but even so not a great deal of time passed before Octavian became officially *Imperator Caesar divi filius Augustus*, a title that artfully fused the military, the divine, and kinship.

Christianity was born in a setting of emperor-worship, and from the beginning its teachers and missionaries sought to nullify as far as possible the influence of the imperial religion upon Christian minds. But taking the long history of Christianity into account, it is impossible to overlook the readiness with which Christian faith and dogma could include acceptance of the sacredness of royal office if not personage. The crowning of Charlemagne by the Pope as *Holy* Roman Emperor suggests first the claim of suzerainty by Church over State, including power of investiture of kings, but second the allowance by Church of sacred character to the kingship. Even the most powerful and assertive of popes in the Middle Ages did not deny to kingships their holy, if derivative, status. It was, however, in the Reformation that the unqualified divinity of kings was once again proclaimed in the West. As Luther, Calvin and others saw the matter, elevation of kings to divine status in their rule, that is, directly divine status, unmediated by Church, was as powerful a blow as could be struck at the hated and feared papacy. We tend to associate James I of England most prominently with the Divine Right of Kings because of his early-manifest fascination with the theology of the subject. It was under Charles I, though, in 1640, that what must be the all-time high in English belief in royal divinity was expressed to represent the great majority of the clergy. The statement begins: 'The most high and sacred order of kings is of Divine Right, being the ordinance of God Himself, founded in the Prime laws of nature, and clearly established by express texts both of the Old and New Testaments.'

Despite the numerous rationalist criticisms to which the divine right panegyric was subjected in the next two centuries, it survived healthily. It was the influential Hegel who declared the State—with the Prussian state foremost in mind—'the march of God on earth'. And even when the German political idealists chose to retreat God to the background, obvious surrogates for God abounded: Dialectic, World-Spirit, and so on. Moreover, as I shall shortly maintain, a new type of religious contemplation of the State arose in the late eighteenth century, to spread riotously in the following century; one that would attract vastly greater numbers of followers than the original Divine Right theory ever did.

(ii)

Political euphemisms have by no means been confined to patriarchal or religious views of the State. The kind of rationalism that began to flourish in the seventeenth century and continued in ever more encompassing degree through the succeeding centuries is rich in euphemisms. Some of the more influential are: *machine, organism, general will, popular sovereignty, community,* and *welfare.* We shall look at each of these in the remainder of this essay.

Machine and Organism. To liken anything to either machine or organism was a favourite occupation of seventeenth- and eighteenth-century philosophers, and it would have been extraordinary had the political clerisy not seized upon both of these euphemisms as means to advance understanding and

acceptance of the political State. The organic could be illuminated by analogy to one or other of the mechanical pumps which
dotted the landscape in the seventeenth century, especially in
England, and the social and political could be explained by the
organic or the mechanical, or both, as in the case of Hobbes.

In his *Leviathan*, Hobbes first abjures the use of metaphor in
scientific writing (what he refers to as 'demonstration'), but his
own ears were deaf to his warning. Metaphor abounds in Hobbes's political writings. In the original edition of *Leviathan*
there is a frontispiece of a giant human being, his body made up
of minuscule human beings. Hobbes was of course laying the
ground dramatically for his demonstrations throughout the
book that the State is at once organism and machine. The
principles of statics and dynamics, so highly visible in the
natural philosophy of the age, are seized upon with avidity by
Hobbes in his explanation of political process. The State is, just
like the machine, an artificial body, one governed by its inherent
statics and dynamics. There is an 'artificial soul' that gives 'life
and motion to the body'. Human ingenuity has created 'engines
that move themselves as doth a watch'. What is the heart but 'a
spring; and the nerves but so many strings; and the joints but so
many wheels, giving motion to the whole body'. The State, like
the human body, can suffer malfunctions as the consequence of
foreign substances introduced. Thus, for Hobbes such corporate
bodies as the corporations of his day are likened to 'worms in the
entrails of natural man'. Intermediate groups are for the most
part declared to be 'little worms which the physicians call
ascarides'. Undue conflict in government can induce a 'pleurisy'
that breeds 'stiches' and other pains. Hobbes's special form of
naturalism scored on both his physical and organic com-
parisons; and in his mind the physical and organic were really
one, for what was the organism but a divinely constructed
machine?

In Locke too the impress of the physical sciences is very
evident. The State is at bottom 'one body politic' with the
capacity to move as one body under the direction of a 'soul' that
gives life to human society. When the Legislative (the political
government) is 'dissolved', 'dissolution and death' must follow.
From Locke there is a straight line to the writings of the
philosophes in France, so many of whom employed the figures

of machine and organism to underscore belief that almost identical processes are found in the State and the human body. On such analogies and implicit laudations, modern political science was founded.

Social Compact. The metaphor of a contract or compact among individuals as source and rationalization of the political State was not born in the seventeenth century, but it reached its maximum expression then in the history of ideas. The idea of contract had been made a popular one by the revival of Roman Law where contract is given prominent place in civil codes, and the general spread of economic enterprise from the sixteenth century on could only popularize among thinkers the notion of a vindicating role played by contract applied to almost any relationship. For philosophers and political intellectuals alike, the effect of the idea of contract was mesmerizing. The ugly reality of political-military power in dominance over multitudes could be transmuted into a relationship among individuals that, like any bona fide economic agreement, was simply a free contractual relationship among assenting, willing, individuals. It really did not matter whether the social contract was believed to have historical reality at some remote time in the past or whether it was more of a spirit, tacit but pervasive, in a political population. All that mattered was that pure reason devise a justification for the absolute State that could render the divine right or patriarchal theory obsolete.

Natural law was a perfect host for the maturation of the euphemism of contract. In the seventeenth century, substances were deemed of greater reality than relationships. Man was the primary substance; his social relationships with others represented by traditional institutions were insubstantial, shadowy, mere reflections cast by individuals. For reality one must begin with the individual, his drives, passions and his reason. One must also postulate, as physical scientists did, some beginning void, some condition of nature in which nothing but man, solid man, existed. No matter how different the views of the nature and implication of contract might be, ranging from Hobbes to Locke to Rousseau, there was no doubt that everything began with a state of nature inhabited by atom-like individuals living without institutions, without culture, without morality. For Hobbes this state of nature was dreadful, a place of unceasing war, with life 'solitary, poor, nasty, brutish, and short'. He pointed to the Indians of North America as contemporary instance of what all mankind had once known. This is amusing, for the Indians Hobbes specifically referred to were those of the Atlantic coastal area, most of them in the great Iroquois League, well used to political institutions and to frequent war. However nasty and poor their lives may have been, it would have made more sense to charge this to the political State, not to any pre-political condition of nature. It doesn't matter. The social contract for Hobbes is the *vis creatrix* by which the absolute State, Leviathan, came into being. Awful as its power is, life within it is vastly to be preferred to the even more awful state of nature. Every civil war, every rebellion, even every criminal individual act, is, Hobbes tells us, an eruption, and dreadful reminder of the natural condition of man. It was by contract that Leviathan was brought into existence, and it is by contract that under no circumstances may its absolute power ever be challenged.

This was too much for other natural law philosophers of the century, Locke foremost among them. Yes, an original state of nature in which men had freedoms, and yes, a contract by which natural freedoms were incorporated in the State, but not with the result that such freedoms would be destroyed; only that the natural freedoms would be converted into civil freedoms, and remain essentially intact after the contract had been made, indeed crucial elements *of the contract*. The contract, Locke declared (years before the Revolution of 1688 which so often is still mistakenly thought to have been Locke's prime inspiration), holds the sovereign as well as the subjects accountable, and if the day comes when the sovereign fails to protect individuals' lawful rights, especially the right of property, popular revolt is justified. In fact, it is not really revolt by the people, for whatever there had been to revolt against was destroyed by the sovereign, by the sovereign's prior flouting of the terms of the contract, thus unilaterally ending it and thereby opening the way to the establishment of a new and once again legitimate contract.

We think usually of the metaphor of contract as simply a conceit of the seventeenth and eighteenth centuries, a plaything

that was dropped by philosophers at the end of the Enlightenment. But it is too beguiling a figure for intellectuals not to reach
surface from time to time. The much-lauded work of a decade
ago by John Rawls, Professor of Philosophy at Harvard, *A Theory
of Justice*, is sufficient evidence of that statement. Rawls pur-
ports to deal objectively with equality—that is, equality of
economic, social, and moral circumstances, complete
equality—by virtue of what he plainly regards as a geometrically
rigorous chain of deductions. Rawls dismisses the pertinence of
historical and scientific data to his implicit question and
chooses to revive the fiction of an original state of nature. What
Rawls calls *his* state of nature is 'the original position' within
which imaginary individuals exist behind 'the veil of silence'.
Our minds are directed to a hypothetical group of human beings
so anterior to culture (with all its inbuilt prejudices) that they
are ignorant of name, origin, social status, knowledge of good
and evil, or even intelligence and temperament. Such beings
exist, for Rawls's purposes, in an 'original position' that is for all
the world like a seventeenth-century state of nature. Just as
Hobbes, Pufendorf, Locke, and many others fashioned states of
nature to accord with their respective preferences for government, so does Professor Rawls fashion his 'original condition'
and his 'veil of ignorance' to accord with his unambiguous
desire to see equality of condition the law of the land.

(iii)

The People, Yes. Very probably the most fateful concept of the
late eighteenth century in politics was 'the people'. Not the
numerical aggregate of all who lived within a given set of
boundaries, for this could include rabble on the one hand and
tyrants and exploiters on the other. Rather, those individuals
who could free their minds of sectarian prejudices and loyalties,
who could in rational way make their individual ways to
comprehension of the general good, and who acted virtuously in
political matters—these were the people properly understood. If
government were based in the people—properly understood—it
would be inherently incapable of tyranny, for the people would
never tyrannize itself. Rousseau's momentous idea of the
general will epitomized perfectly this vision of the people in

contrast to a mere multitude. But the vision went well beyond Rousseau, and it has made its way uninterruptedly through nineteenth-century ideas of plebiscitary dictatorship to twentieth-century totalitarianisms. None of the latter would use 'totalitarian' as a label. For that matter even 'communism' tends to be eschewed in favour of, say, 'People's Democratic Republic'.

The social contract myth had lulled philosophers' minds into acceptance of a popular basis of the State. Even Hobbes, with his unbearable state of nature and his harsh Leviathan made some kind of compact among human beings the basis for political power. As we have seen, Locke carried the contract-myth to the point where apparent derelictions on the part of the government with respect to property and other natural rights could be interpreted by the people as failure to uphold the contract and justification therefore for revolution with the object of establishing yet another contract.

Rousseau went even further. *The Social Contract*, published more than a century after Hobbes's *Leviathan*, presented contract in a new light. It was nothing in the dim past, nor was it to be construed as tacit in any existing State. It was the means whereby, for the first time in history, the true, the only legitimate, State *could* be brought into being. What is required, Rousseau argued, is a contract among individuals whereby 'each of us puts his person and all his power in common under the supreme direction of the general will'. Once entered into, the contract is irrevocable and the newly established general will absolute in power. Rousseau had only contempt for Lockean notions of natural or other rights persisting after the formation of the State. The contract demands the total surrender, alienation, of 'each associate, together with all his rights, to the whole community'.

Such an alienation of rights does not, however, connote despotism. Since all members of the newly-formed State are equal—in loss of natural rights and in acquisition of equality of membership in the political community—it will never be to one man's advantage to seek to tyrannize his associates. As soon as the State is formed, it becomes automatically impossible to hurt one member without hurting the entire political body, with all members affected. Similarly, 'the sovereign power need give no guarantee to its subjects because it is impossible for the body to wish to hurt all its members'. The general will alone is sovereign, and whoever 'refuses to obey the general will shall be compelled to do so by the whole body. This means nothing less than that he will be forced to be free.'

But what is the general will? Rousseau indulges in no nonsense about majorities or even unanimities necessarily being the substance of this will. For, he points out, there is the 'will of all', and although this *may* be identical with the general will in a given situation, there is nothing mandatory about it. The general will appears only when a people has first banished from its collective mind all thoughts of individual or partisan interest. Rousseau has in full measure the Enlightenment's general hatred of such intermediate groups as kindred, Church and guild, and he insists therefore it is 'essential, if the general will is to be able to express itself, that there should be no partial society within the State'. The frontispiece that Hobbes used for his *Leviathan*—a human giant whose body is composed of a mass of tiny human bodies—would have served Rousseau's own purposes admirably. There is identical insistence upon the danger that is posed by intermediate groups and associations within the political population. Between individual and sovereign there can be nothing that is not of the sovereign's making and under the sovereign's power.

Rousseau's genius, and the basis of his multiform appeal in the centuries following, lies in the care with which he enclothes his sovereign's monolithic power in such words as 'people', 'public interest' and, above all of course, the 'general will'. As I have already noted, the last is so far from being synonymous with the expressed wish of a majority of the citizens that it must be explicitly distinguished from mere numbers. What makes the will general 'is less the number of voters than the common interest uniting them'. But how, we ask, is this common interest to be ascertained, to be recognized when it exists? Not, Rousseau tells us clearly in his *Discourse on Political Economy*, through any assembling of the people. It is by no means certain that any decision of the assembly would reflect the general will, such a method would be 'impracticable' in a large nation, and, most important, such assembly 'is hardly ever needed where the government is well-intentioned: for the rulers well know that the general will is always on the side which is most favourable to the public interest . . . so that it is needful only to act justly to be certain of following the general will'. Needless to say, there have been few governments in history which have not considered their rule, however harsh, as just.

Rousseau believed the religious impulse in man to be fixed and ineradicable. What was necessary, therefore, was to unite religion and the State. This Rousseau did through what he called the 'civil religion'. Christianity will not do as religion for it reminds its communicants too often that salvation lies only in the next world, in the supernatural. Moreover when war breaks out Christians 'know better how to die than how to conquer. What does it matter whether they win or lose? Does not providence know better than they what is meet for them?' To speak of a 'Christian republic' is a contradiction in terms, Rousseau argues, for the devout Christian's mind is by its essence conditioned against the special obligations and sacrifices necessary to good government.

'There is therefore a purely civil profession of faith of which the Sovereign should fix the articles, not exactly as religious dogmas, but as social sentiments without which a man cannot be a good citizen or a faithful subject.' The tenets of this religion will concern the State and its members 'only' so far as they have reference to morality and to the duties requisite to the State's welfare. Rousseau speaks with all the force of Dostoevsky's Grand Inquisitor about the dogmas of *la religion civile*. 'While it can compel no one to believe them, it can banish from the state whoever does not believe them . . . as an anti-social being, incapable of truly loving the laws and justice, and of sacrificing at need his life to his duty.' Beyond this, if anyone, after publicly professing belief in these articles, behaves 'as if he does not believe them, let him be punished by death'.

Vox Populi, Vox Dei. Although Rousseau's *Contrat Social* seems to have been one of the least read of his books during the decade leading to the outbreak of the French Revolution, it became one of the best read of books during the Revolution. A contemporary writes of knots of people to be seen at almost every street corner excitedly discussing, often with sacred text in hand, Rousseau's classic. Robespierre claimed that he read passages from the book every morning with breakfast. He was far from the only Jacobin leader to revere the book. The reason is not far to seek. No one else had so glorified the people—the population, that is, freed of its dissenters, criminals, traitors, bigoted, and otherwise wicked—and so convincingly demonstrated that government could reach any height of repressiveness so long as it was anchored in the people.

It is no wonder, then, that the French Revolution brought the ideas of people and nation to a white heat that would tend to melt all other loyalties. From Mother Russia in the east across the Continent and the Atlantic to the United States, the nation became almost literally the Voice of God. Once the sacred State had been premised upon belief that the ruler was a god; now it was the people, conceived as nation, to which holy attributes were given. Only in more or less millennialist religious congregations had anything comparable to the spirit of nationalism in the nineteenth century ever been seen. But the god of nationalism lay within, not outside and above. National anthems or hymns proliferated. So did pledges of civil allegiance, political saints' days, national feasts, commemorations of the departed, tributes to political martyrs, affirmations of the providential nature of one's State and its needs.

The United States serves very well as example of the power of civil religion—down at least through the Great War. Americanism vied with Christianity as the religion of true believers. Americanism had its proper calendar of saints' days for Washington, Jefferson, Jackson, Lincoln, and others. It had its Torah or Pentateuch in the Declaration of Independence and the Constitution. Medallions, scapularies, banners, epigrams, paintings, statues, and other essentially religious objects abounded. Its Nativity was of course the Fourth of July, down until perhaps a half century ago observed by Americans more fervently than any of the Christian holidays. From the time of the Revolution, America was regarded by its citizens—immigrants from all parts of the Old World included—as possessed of the same kind of luminosity that the founding Puritans had professed to see in what John Winthrop had referred to as 'a city as upon a hill'. For the early Puritans their New World colony was to be the part of the earth where Christ would first appear in the Millennium and begin his thousand-year rule. For many millions of Americans in the nineteenth century there was quite literally an American religion, and basic to it was the belief in the redemptive mission of the United States in the world. More than anything else it was this belief that governed the mind of Woodrow Wilson during his tragic presidency. For Wilson, both before and after American participation in the Great War, the sacred obligation of America was, in his words, 'to teach other peoples how to elect good men'. To 'make the world safe for democracy' meant, of course, American-style democracy. If he and other worshippers at the national altar needed anything to quicken faith, to bring belief to a white-hot intensity, it was the almost transfiguring experience of 1917–18. Never perhaps in history had a large people known religious conversion so quickly and powerfully. From a nation of neutrals, of fastidious rejection of European wars, Americans became, with only a few exceptions, crusaders, as avid to carry the religion of Americanism to the old world as their medieval forerunners were in their Christian mission. Americanism quite literally swamped Christianity, or perhaps better subjugated it. It was a rare Sunday sermon that gave God the attention that America the Beautiful got. After all, nearly 200,000 volunteer speakers, the so-called Four-Minute Men, patrolled the land under Wilsonian orders to make certain that the American cause was properly recognized at every assemblage, and to ignore or oppose them was almost instant ground for popular indictment as heretic. The Kaiser and all Germans were necessarily infidels, worse, minions of hell, disciples of the devil. To be charged with pro-Germanism could be as deadly an experience as being charged with witchcraft in the seventeenth century. When President Wilson chose to go to Europe immediately after the Armistice, with the clear intent of reaching the peoples of Europe over the heads of their rulers, the massed street crowds in every capital were ample evidence to Americans that the religion of Americanism would ultimately prevail everywhere.

I am not suggesting though that the religion of nation-state was limited to America, no matter at what intensity. Throughout most of the nineteenth century, down through the early years of the Great War, nationalism could be as ecstatic and mystical a thing for Europeans as for Americans. Intellectuals, today overwhelmingly dismissive of anything smacking of patriotism, were then prime movers in the new religion. France and Germany ran hot competition in the published works of historians and philosophers to establish the sacredness and the appointed mission of their respective nations. Not since the Reformation had Europe known the enthusiasm that now permeated nations rather than cults.

The Great War brought all of this to fulfilment—and then near-disappearance. It is difficult today to summon up, much less explain, the states of mind which were a commonplace all over Europe on matters of devotion, sacrifice, and martyrdom in behalf of nation. During at least the first two years of the War the young, those who faced almost certain death or injury in the trenches, were as religiously caught up as any of their elders. To give one's blood for England or France was like the medieval Crusader's gift of blood for Christ. All the primordial militarism of the first States in history was nakedly displayed in the Great War, but few saw nakedness; only robes of divinity. Rousseau's civil religion, at the zenith of its nineteenth-century ascendance, saw to that.

Social Welfare. During the twentieth century yet another euphemism for political power has made its way into popular usage: the social welfare state. If the horrors of the Great War together with some of the disclosures of revisionist history afterwards had dulled appreciation in the West for the sacred nation, then the image of economic and social provider might be substituted for nation. The provider-State reached a considerable popularity in Western Europe early in the century, and even in the still-individualist United States the ideas of Theodore Roosevelt and, separately, of Herbert Croly gained favour among intellectuals. But it was the Great Depression that provided fertile soil for the dissemination of the conception of the State as social welfare worker.

It is one of history's ironies that the word 'social' should have been so easily appropriated by the political clerisy. When this word achieved popularity in the West in the early nineteenth century, the context was overwhelmingly the *non-political* spheres of society—family, neighbourhood, local community, and voluntary co-operative association foremost. To French sociologists and radical anarchists alike, the State and the political were in bad odour after the totalitarianism of the Revolution. Auguste Comte, founder of sociology, led the way in seeking to repudiate the political and to exalt the social as the only feasible alternative. Alas for Comte's hopes, the political clerisy was already at work before he died in seizing upon the 'social'.

It is not difficult to understand the attractiveness of the 'social' in place of the 'political', for the latter had inevitably become somewhat stained in the public imagination. There were too many citizens for whom the State was still a reminder of war and taxes, and, in any event, there were simply limits to what could be done with the word 'political'. Such neologisms as 'politicization' and, worse, 'politicalization' didn't recommend themselves when reference was being made to the political State's ownership and control of increasingly large areas of economy and society. Such words may have told the truth, but it is the function of language to be able to conceal, as well as reveal, the truth.

Social was made to order as a beguiling prefix. 'Social reform', 'social security', 'social budget', and 'social value' were so much better as labels for what governments were actually doing than would have been any of these with the word 'political' used instead of 'social'. Similarly, for those who could dream of an ever more State-dominated future, socialism was much to be preferred to politicism. And who is to say the clerisy is wrong? How, for instance, could the now mammoth and always near-bankrupting 'social security' system in the United States have ever reached its eminence and load of close to 40 million people if it had been called in the beginning 'political security' or something so mercilessly exact as 'State charity'.

Big euphemisms in politics spawn small ones. Thus 'civil rights', once a precise term for individual rights within the governing process, now stands mostly for group entitlements, Social Security and Medicare being only the biggest. 'Affirmative Action' is the euphemism used for a widening complex of highly negative actions by the State against individual liberties. The phrase is obviously more felicitous to political sensibilities than 'quota system' which is in fact the substance of 'affirmative action' by the government. It is politics alone that has generated the race to euphemism by the various 'public interest' groups concerned with enlarging the number of government grants. Thus the once-honoured 'elderly' and 'aged' have been retired for good in favour of 'senior citizens'. Similarly, 'cripple' has become a veritable obscenity out on the hustings and in legislative halls. Its place is taken for the present by 'the disadvantaged', with 'the disabled' coming up fast. The blind and the deaf have given way to the 'sight-impaired' and the 'hearing-impaired'. The feeble-minded are gone, succeeded by 'the exceptional' in all public laws. And, finally, through political legerdemain, the poor and needy have been at last banished, replaced by 'the underprivileged'.

Soulcraft. Recently a resurgence of the moral and the sacred has taken place in American political thought and action. George Will, political columnist, has given benediction to this resurgence in his book *Statecraft as Soulcraft*. The time has passed, Will declares, when the governing machinery can properly limit itself to the actual behaviour of individuals and 'to concern itself with soybeans but not virtue'. He is contemptuous of the late Supreme Court Justice Frankfurter's insistence that government consider behaviour, not 'the inner mind', of those it rules. No longer may moral matters such as abortion, birth deformations, and school prayers be left where they have been for millenniums, chiefly in the hands of the family and the Church, and in our day the medical profession. But, writes George Will, none of this is to be regarded as 'compelling persons to act against their settled convictions; it is not a collision of wills. . . . Rather it is a slow, steady, gentle, educative, and persuasive enterprise.' That it is also an enterprise in which police, prosecuting attorneys, courts, and prisons quickly and necessarily enter seems not to matter to the self-styled Moral Majority and its prophets.

George Will and his allies believe that this assignment of virtue to the political state has Edmund Burke for its ancestor. In truth, it is not Burke, who abominated centralization of political power, and especially in the moral realm, but Jean-Jacques Rousseau who gave birth to the philosophy of political manufacture of virtue and of virtuous minds. Early in his life, Rousseau tells us in the *Confessions*, he had come to the realization that people's moral lives are shaped by political

government. It was thus easy for Rousseau to reach the conclusion in *The Social Contract* that when government coerces, it is
only 'forcing men to be free', and of course virtuous. Government must penetrate 'into man's inmost being', Rousseau
declares, if it is to progress from merely ruling men to 'making
men as they should be'. It is the sacred task of government,
Rousseau concludes, to change human nature, to transform
'each individual, who is by himself a complete and solitary
whole, into part of a greater whole from which he . . . receives his
life and being'. Rightly do we perceive the Rousseauian State as
a form of permanent moral terror.

It is doubtless cruel, but it is necessary to remind the Moral
Majority in America that behind the totalitarian States of the
twentieth century lie, without exception, vast schemes of
attainment of virtue in the citizenry through limitless uses of
political force. Lenin, Stalin, Hitler, Mao, and Pol Pot have not
been by nature sadists and carnage-mongers. They have been,
though we shrink from the word, *idealists*, so certain of being
morally right in a world of evil that they believed themselves
justified in the use of political power ranging from simple decree
to what the Nazis in a triumph of political euphemism called
the Final Solution. From Marx, Lenin drew a picture in his head
of the perfect socialist man, and in the interest of creating this
being, no limit to the use of the force necessary could properly
be regarded as virtuous. Again it is cruel but necessary to see
Leninism in its several forms as nothing less than Soulcraft.

Afterword. It is almost too much to bear. More than two
thousand years of political euphemism and panegyric, and with
what result? The State, born of war and nourished by war, has
become, all euphemism notwithstanding, more powerful, more
inquisitorial in human lives, than at any time in its history. It is
as if Mars, god of war, were exacting tribute from us for having
sought for thousands of years to conceal with euphemism the
union of war and State. For in our century the State has reached a
pinnacle of force never before known in history, and warfare has
taken more lives in devastation, killing, and mutilation than in
all previous centuries put together.

Intimations of Mortality

JOHN GROSS

(i)

MANY writers in recent years have argued that we find it much harder than earlier generations did to look death full in the face. According to Arnold Toynbee, for instance, writing in 1968, 'the word "death" itself has become almost unmentionable in the West', while in *The Hour of Our Death* Philippe Ariès cites the contemporary French philosopher Vladimir Jankélévitch: 'Is not the taboo word *death* above all others the unpronounceable, unnameable, unspeakable monosyllable that the average man, conditioned to compromise, is obliged to shroud modestly in proper and respectable circumlocutions?' Death, we are frequently told, has replaced sex as the great forbidden subject: hence we have developed, in Geoffrey Gorer's famous phrase, a 'pornography of death', and, more recently, a science of thanatology, an attempt to let in the light in the same spirit as that of the sexology of old.

Whether or not we go along with this whole line of thinking, one thing seems obvious: statements like those of Toynbee and Jankélévitch can scarcely be meant to be taken literally. There is no real embargo in our society on any of the common words for death, and no comparison between people's reactions to them and the effect that would have been produced in a Victorian drawing-room by any of the common words for sex. Still less is there any question of a taboo in the sense in which an anthropologist might use the term. In many primitive societies, for example, it is strictly forbidden to pronounce the name of someone who has died, since to do so would be to summon him from the shades, with dangerous consequences. If he has to be mentioned, a conventional term is substituted: some Australian tribes speak of him as 'that one', the Nandi of East Africa refer to him as 'the deceased' or 'rubbish' (which in this context presumably counts as a euphemism). Quite apart from our very different attitude towards preserving the names of the dead, there is plainly nothing in our experience which corresponds to this kind of verbal restriction.

There are times, admittedly, when more or less everyone would agree that direct talk of death ought to be carefully avoided. A mother whose child has just been killed in an accident, a patient learning for the first time that he has only a few weeks to live—it would be peculiarly brutal not to acknowledge that the wound is still raw, or not to do one's best to soften the blow. But a set euphemism, at such moments, would defeat its own purpose. What are needed are words which blur or stave off, if only for an instant, the dreadful finality of the facts. So we fall back on the most effective forms of euphemistic talk, reticence and vagueness: 'I'm afraid it's bad news', 'I was terribly sorry to hear what happened'. Quite often a gesture or an expression—pursed lips, lowered eyes—will be enough to convey the essential message. (A set gesture, if we had one, might be acceptable where a set euphemism is not—something like the traditional Chinese way of referring to death by clenching the hands and throwing the head slightly back.) And this reluctance to spell things out is not necessarily just a question of tact. It can also imply that words are inadequate, and that the very notion of death is an outrage. What is (momentarily) unmentionable is also unspeakable.

Unless one has strong religious beliefs (and even then), a particularly difficult problem can be deciding how to break the news of somebody's death to a child. Geoffrey Gorer, in 1963, found that of a group of parents with children under sixteen who were questioned in this connection, rather more than half had used some form of euphemism. The commonest were religious ones—'gone to Heaven', 'gone to Jesus' and the like—used by people with no real religious convictions and no belief in an afterlife. Set down in cold print this may seem mawkish, and no doubt in some cases it would have been better if the parents had simply told the truth as they saw it; but so much depends on age, temperament, circumstances, on what kind of questions the children asked, on whether the religious phraseology was offered as a substitute for the facts or as an explanatory gloss. My own preference, if a euphemism has to be used, would certainly be for the analogy with sleep, but I think this is the last subject on which anyone ought to issue a general prescription.

Except when dealing with children, and except at times of great stress, we could probably dispense with euphemisms for death completely without ever being forced to violate the minimal decencies. But many people, perhaps most, still feel the need for a more conventional type of euphemism, to be used either on formal occasions or (when it seems appropriate) as a means of making death sound just a little less deathly. Any number of common terms have been pressed into service for this purpose—to *depart*, to be *called home*, a hundred others—but over the years it is *pass away* which has established itself as the clear favourite.

Not without growing opposition, however. Anyone who thinks of 'passing away' as an innocuous, take-it-or-leave-it locution will be suprised at the amount of hostility it can arouse. Arnold Toynbee denounced it (along with *pass on*) as a symptom of Western man's loss of belief in human dignity. Hugh Rawson, in *A Dictionary of Euphemisms* (1981), jeers at it as a phrase 'which flowered in the fertile soil of pre-Victorian prudery', as part of a general 'prettying up' of death.

One's first reaction to such comments is that it can make a good deal of difference exactly how and when a particular expression is used. 'My husband passed away six weeks ago' would strike many of us as somewhat more defensible than 'My grandfather passed away in 1927'. But two general points are also worth considering. First, if substituting a milder term for death is a sign of weakness, it is a weakness which we share with our ancestors: there is nothing new about it, nothing specifically modern or decadent. In Anglo-Saxon times, for instance, when a king died the chroniclers generally preferred to describe him as 'departing' or 'faring forth'. And secondly, as the Anglo-Saxon example suggests, euphemisms of this type are often primarily intended as a mark of respect for the dead, a slightly (but not absurdly) loftier way of putting things. The idea that they are invariably inspired by squeamishness is a caricature, if that.

As for *pass away* itself, it deserves its success. It was first used as a euphemism in the Middle Ages, but it has remained free from any taint of archaism; it is unpretentious, but there is a touch of poetry lurking in it as well. (The simple word 'away' can be made to reverberate with powerful suggestions of yearning, dissolving, desolation—as it does, for instance, in the 'Ode to a Nightingale' or in Hopkins's 'dearest him who lives alas! away'.) At the same time, unlike *pass on* or *pass over*, *pass away* works equally well for believers and non-believers, since it holds out no promise one way or another about a future existence. Death might turn out to be nothing more than a melting back into the universe, although this is at least made to sound an undemanding process. There are no death throes, no final wrench: the dying person fades away like an old soldier, and passes mildly away like the virtuous men in Donne's poem. (The more abrupt term *pass out* is reserved for mere fainting.) It is in fact the intimations of tranquillity which give *pass away* its strongest appeal, since a quiet ending is what we all hope for: in death announcements in the press, for instance, the commonest adverb—the verb itself is increasingly omitted—must almost certainly be 'peacefully'. (You also quite often come across the rather disconcerting combination 'peacefully and suddenly'. This seems to be saying that a speedy peaceful departure is even better than an ordinary peaceful departure, but in most cases the main purpose of 'suddenly' is probably to signal a heart attack.)

Of the direct synonyms in English for death, *decease* and *demise* are words which keep their distance. *Decease*, although it started out as a euphemism, was gradually taken over by the lawyers, until it became the standard technical term for death considered in its legal aspects; it still remains available outside the courtroom for euphemistic use, in a diminished and rather colourless way. The same is true of *demise*, which was a legal term from the beginning, originally denoting the transfer of an estate and then the transfer of sovereignty at the end of a reign. *Defunct* seems to me more resonant—and so, undoubtedly, does Shakespeare's (and Eliot's) 'defunctive music'—but as a term applied to human beings it is now obsolete. So, for serious purposes, is *expire*, with one or two minor exceptions (it is apparently still used as a routine expression in some hospitals). While it remained in general circulation, expiring offered a somewhat more decorous alternative to dying, but it could also be used with greater force in its more precise original sense of

breathing one's last. There was nothing particularly euphemistic about Dr Johnson's 'groan of expiration'. In the course of
the nineteenth century, however, its secondary meanings took
over; it became a word for licences and season tickets, and as a
term for dying it declined into burlesque—as in Mrs Leo Hun-
ter's expiring frog, or the wretched child who expires in Belloc's
Cautionary Tales.

Perish has a more distinguished history. It is the only standard
English word for meeting an untimely death, as opposed to
dying in general; it also has strong biblical associations, and in a
religious context it often signifies moral or spiritual ruin. (Cow-
per's comparison of himself to the castaway—'We perish'd, each
alone'—rubs in the double meaning.) *To perish* can carry the
threat of coming to nothing, of utter extinction; conversely, it is
sometimes used in a very generalized sense —'truths that wake,
to perish never'—where it is felt that death would be untimely
whenever it occurred. It is a big word, a word for heroic and
tragic occasions—and a word that we are no longer quite
comfortable with. To some extent, I think, it was one of the
verbal casualties of the First World War. There is a feeling that
its grandeur has been debased to the point where it is often
merely grandiose, or at any rate too literary. Or perhaps too
journalistic: disaster victims still perish with some regularity in
the newspapers, particularly when a longer word than 'die' is
needed to fill out a headline.

Mortal is an interesting case of a word which has retained all
its strength as an adjective but lost much of it as a noun. While
'mortal' in the sense of 'subject to death' means exactly what it
says, the main point of describing men and women as mortals is
to indicate a fairly cheerful acceptance of human limitations.
Mortal in this sense is also a term with distinct egalitarian
undertones: we may all be doomed, but at least we are all in the
same boat. Hence 'ordinary mortal', 'fellow mortal', 'mere
mortal', and a drift towards the jocularity of 'thirsty mortal' and
the like. (The man who is a mere mortal, incidentally, was
almost certainly once a little perisher.)

Yet however much we learn to live with it, sooner or later
most of us need to be consoled for the miserable fact of our
mortality. When we do, we tend to resort to a limited range of
images and figures for describing death. In eighteenth-century

France, for instance, according to John McManners, 'even those who refused to accept the possibility of an afterlife talked of a "journey", 'voyage", "sleep", of the "harbour", the "door", and the "refuge" '. Most of these examples can also be found among the common 'alleviations of death' listed by Richmond Lattimore in his study of Greek and Latin epitaphs, along with the idea of death as a home, as an inn, and as a means of repaying a debt. And a number of other metaphors are almost equally familiar: nightfall, the onset of winter, a leave-taking, an actor making his exit.

Three main images run through this repertory of consolation. Many of the images keep open at least the possibility of an afterlife—by way of reassurance for believers, as a satisfying fiction for non-believers, as a vague hope for the waverers and doubters in between. They achieve this, as McManners says, through their ambiguous implications of progress towards a further goal: the inn may be only a temporary residence, the sleeper may wake up in a better world. But sleep can also be thought of simply as longed-for repose, as the 'sleep after toil' in the famous couplet by Spenser:

> Sleep after toil, port after stormy seas,
> Ease after war, death after life does greatly please.

A second large group of consolatory metaphors are variations on this basic idea. They cover a wide range of feeling, and if the emphasis falls too heavily on pain or *taedium vitae* they can begin to sound too bitter to offer much comfort. But they can also shade into the third great department of consolation, the idea of death as something profoundly natural—as natural as breathing. It may be sad, but it feels right.

Most of these images have been in use for thousands of years, and in themselves they are inevitably shop-worn and trite. As such, it seems reasonable to classify them as euphemisms. But they also provide the root metaphors of much of the most notable writing about death, of poetry in particular, and given enough poetic power and wit they can still perform the same service as effectively as ever. If one of the functions of literature is to breathe life back into clichés, another is to redeem euphemisms from blandness.

Some of the traditional analogues of death find a sardonic

echo in slang. To *go west* is to follow the setting sun; the daisies in *pushing up the daisies* are poor relations of all the flowers that spring up from corpses in ancient myth and legend. Both these expressions are fairly genial, partly because they are so familiar, but modernizing an old phrase can also be one way of showing that you mean business. A final leave-taking and eternal rest sound a lot less drastic than *the long goodbye* and *the big sleep*.

Most slang terms for death, as you would expect, tend to diminish its significance, and some of them are openly callous. But light-hearted is not necessarily the same thing as hard-hearted, even in this context. To say that someone has popped off or pegged out may be no more than a rueful acknowledgement that death is an everyday occurrence, and that we must not allow the fact to depress us unduly. Once again, a great deal depends on circumstance, on time and place and tone of voice. 'I saw Miss Gee this evening, and she's a goner I fear.' For a doctor to talk like this to his wife at dinner seems to me perfectly natural, and does not indicate any particular lack of sympathy. For him to have told Miss Gee to her face that she was 'a goner' would have been professional misconduct.

Tough talk is not always as tough as it seems, and it can mellow with age. A striking example of this, if some philologists are to be believed, is the ever-popular *kick the bucket*. The origins of the phrase are obscure, but the *Oxford English Dictionary* lists it under 'bucket', an old word meaning a yoke or beam, and suggests that it may refer to the practice of hanging up a slaughtered pig by its heels (hence the kick). If this is in fact the case, the original unflattering comparison has long since been lost sight of. Nor does the phrase carry any connotation of suicide, although an alternative theory is that it refers to the bucket on which someone is standing in order to hang himself. Most people probably never think about its origins at all, and have a rather indistinct image of a bucket being kicked over for some indeterminate reason. A vigorous image, at all events: it might be a kick of protest.

And what does it mean when X tells Y that their casual acquaintance Z has kicked the bucket? The main feeling is surely that solemnity ought to be avoided. Not out of positive disrespect, or as a sign of ill will: even allowing for an element of self-assertion (unlike poor Z, they are still jaunting along), the chances are that they regret what has happened. But they are men who, in E. M. Forster's phrase, have 'invested their emotions elsewhere', and under the circumstances anything too muted or melancholy would ring hollow. And yet at the same time they prefer not to mention death by name. It might strike a chill, and most of us—most mortals—sometimes feel the need for cheerful euphemisms as well as respectful ones.

(ii)

'Christians', says Sir Thomas Browne, 'have handsomely glossed the deformity of death, by careful consideration of the body, and civil rites which take off brutal terminations.' The time for formal solemnity is above all at funerals and burials, and to speak of euphemisms in this connection is generally to speak of solemnities which have gone wrong. And in the modern world they can go wrong to an unprecedented degree, with America, notoriously, setting the pace.

The two classic texts here are of course *The Loved One* and Jessica Mitford's *The American Way of Death*. Both books record a riot of euphemisms, and in the nature of the case many of them are variations on old themes. The language of the American funeral industry is less novel than it initially appears; as Philippe Ariès says, it derives directly from nineteenth-century consolation literature, with funeral directors taking over where the ministers of those days left off. But industrialization has also brought with it a new brand of sales-talk. The specimens collected by Jessica Mitford confirm how little Evelyn Waugh exaggerated: a last look at the corpse is a *memory picture*, the death certificate has become a *vital statistics form*, if you have had the foresight to purchase a *pre-need memorial estate* you will be ferried to it in a *professional car* (formerly known as a hearse). Everything possible is done to avoid mentioning death and its associations, although a few of Miss Mitford's examples also hint at the kind of colloquialisms which professionals tend to use among themselves by way of relief from the restraints they are forced to observe in public. 'We do not "haul" a dead person,' Victor Landig warns the aspiring mortician in *Basic Principles of Funeral Service*, 'we transfer or remove him.' 'Haul' is not quite in the same class as Hamlet lugging the guts into the neighbour room, but if we could eavesdrop on funeral practitioners for any length of time we would no doubt hear a number of outright dysphemisms. One of the embalmers at Whispering Glades, in *The Loved One*, talks cheerily of 'the meat', until Mr Joyboy puts a stop to it; in her book *Design for Death* Barbara Jones reports that within the space of ten minutes, while visiting a crematorium, she heard ' "fry" to the staff, "cremate" to me and "commit" to the customer'.

'The loved one' itself owes much of its unpleasantness as a phrase to its slick commercial overtones. It has a certain precedent in *the dear departed* of Victorian times, which may have been acceptable at a funeral, but must often have sounded unbearably unctuous in ordinary conversation. (In France, incidentally, Waugh's novel is known as *Le Cher Disparu*.) But at least 'the dear departed' was never taken up and exploited by the marketing department. What is particularly objectionable about 'the loved one' is its presumptuousness, as of an insurance salesman telling you that you owe it to your loved ones to take out one of his policies.

In recent years a number of streamlined funeral terms have been imported from America into Britain, and we have managed to come up with a few equivalents of our own, such as 'positioning' for 'laying out'. But the Americans have been at it for much longer. The American funeral industry was roaring ahead by the late nineteenth century, and some of the euphemisms it sponsored were concerned not so much with sparing the customer's feelings as with raising the industry's social status. The most famous example is *mortician*, which began to replace 'undertaker' in the 1890s. 'Undertaker' itself had once been something of a euphemism—it originally meant a contractor of almost any kind—but in the course of the eighteenth century its funereal associations came to predominate. They were probably reinforced by the suggestion in the word of someone who shovels you under; more to the point, an undertaker is a tradesman, and 'mortician', formed on the model of 'physician', was a bid for full professional standing. The term flourished during the Babbitt era—'a mortician', according to a joke current in the 1920s, 'is the man who buries a realtor'—but it was subsequently

somewhat devalued by the appearance on the scene of beauti-
cians and cosmeticians. American funerals are now generally
supervised by neutral-sounding 'funeral directors', although
there are alternative terms available to emphasize that funeral-
directing is one of the caring professions—*grief therapist*, for
instance, and *bereavement counselor*.

Edmund Wilson, writing as a staunch rationalist, was
prepared to put in a good word for Whispering Glades. Its
patrons, he thought, were 'more sensible and less absurd than
the priest-guided Evelyn Waugh': while they were merely trying
to gloss over the physical consequences of death, for a Catholic,
sustained by the fantasy of another world, the fact of death was
not to be faced at all. To a non-believer, indeed, it must often
seem as though the flight from death, as Miguel de Unamuno
said, is at the heart of all religion. But if religious rites are a
charade, and charades are to be avoided, where does that leave
the non-believer who still feels the need for some form of ritual
or ceremony to mark his passing? It is possible, we would all
agree, to devise obsequies which are in better taste than those
practised at Whispering Glades, but good taste offers only
limited guidance in such matters. The few well-chosen words at
the crematorium can sound sadly inadequate, and attempts to
construct a secular liturgy seem doomed to fall flat—the more
high-toned the attempt, on the whole, the more prosaic the
result. Think of Comte and the Positivists, with their sacra-
ments of *transformation* (at the time of death) and *incorpora-
tion* (removal to an honorary burial ground seven years later if
the candidate was judged worthy). Even the most devout
Positivist may sometimes have asked himself whether the
prospect of being incorporated was not a little unexciting in
comparison, say, with that of being posthumously *promoted to
glory* in the Salvation Army. And as for the traditional faiths,
what rationalistic ritual could hope to compete with their
linguistic riches, and their immense resources of precedent and
continuity? It is easy enough to understand why, in the presence
of death, even hardened free-thinkers often edge back towards
the language of the Bible and the Prayer Book. Edmund Wilson
himself asked for a psalm and a chapter of Ecclesiastes to be read
at his funeral, and had an Old Testament phrase—in
Hebrew—inscribed on his grave.

In a secular society people tend to be buried in cemeteries rather than churchyards, and 'cemetery' is another word which nowadays causes a fair amount of disquiet. It comes from the Greek *koimētērion*, meaning 'a dormitory', which was originally taken over as a term for burial ground by the early Christians. During the Middle Ages its use was confined to church Latin, but by the seventeenth century, according to Philippe Ariès, *cimetière* had replaced *charnier* in spoken French as the everyday word for a graveyard. In English, on the other hand, it was not until the nineteenth century that 'cemetery' passed into general use—and the difference shows. Roughly speaking, it is the difference between Valéry's *cimetière marin*, the graveyard by the sea, and Philip Larkin's 'Cemetery Road'. Whatever the euphemistic intention behind the word may once have been, the predominant associations of 'cemetery' today are municipal, impersonal, and bleak. It is more comfortable (and, in America at least, increasingly common) to talk of a *memorial park* or a *garden of remembrance*.

Not that this shift of emphasis is insincere. If perpetuating the memory of the dead is the only kind of immortality we can believe in, it is bound to assume even more importance than it had in the past. Loved ones who have passed away are *always in our thoughts* (though not literally, needless to say—we would be in a psychiatric ward if they were). The memorial service and the memorial meeting flourish as never before, in response to social needs which a funeral by itself can no longer fulfil. (It is quite common, in my experience, to refer to memorial meetings as services even when they are purely secular in content.) And if epitaph-writing is a lost art, the simple inscription—a name, dates, at most a brief text—speaks all the more strongly for the irreducible will to survive. 'Some there be, who are perished, as though they had never been'—and our last hope, when all else fails, is not to be numbered among them.

In the days when epitaphs were florid and elaborate, there was abundant scope for euphemism. A thorough search through graveyards would no doubt reveal a good many misers who are praised for their thrift, and domestic tyrants whose piety has been commemorated by their victims. But then, even an epitaph which tells nothing but the truth is not expected to tell the whole truth. Dr Johnson, who believed that the best epitaphs were those which set virtue in the strongest light, laid down what seems an obviously sound first principle. It was no part of an epitaph-writer's job, he maintained, to attempt an impartial summing-up: 'On the tomb of Maecenas his luxury is not to be mentioned with his munificence, nor is the proscription to find a place on the monument of Augustus.' And in spite of some picturesque exceptions, most people would surely agree: an epitaph is generally assumed to be laudatory by its very nature. So is a funeral speech or a memorial address, although not quite to the same extent, since in the modern world (it may have been different in the past) it is hard to sustain a note of unqualified praise for any length of time without provoking a few sceptical thoughts in the audience. A full-scale encomium is usually more persuasive when an imperfection or two can be at least lightly hinted at—lightly, and if need be euphemistically: but euphemisms are so much in order at such moments that unless they are exceptionally clumsy they scarcely call for comment.

In an obituary, on the other hand, the art of euphemizing can often be seen at its most piquant. A good obituary is poised midway between a tribute and an objective assessment: in some respects it is meant to anticipate the verdict of history, but at the same time the injunction not to speak ill of the dead is still felt to be very much in force. Hence the fascination of trying to decode an obituarist's guarded phrases and fine distinctions. 'He did not suffer fools gladly'—or, alternatively, 'he was not always patient of minds slower than his own': a difficult man to work with, it is clear, but are we meant to conclude that he was a perfectionist, or a martinet, or a complete and utter swine? What exactly are we to make of 'sometimes disconcerting frankness', 'an occasional capriciousness', 'an endless fund of good stories'? And whom would you rather have found yourself sitting next to at dinner—the industrialist who was 'of strong and all but wilful personality' or the diplomat who 'did not invariably practise the art of pleasing', the civil servant who 'concealed a warm humanity behind a somewhat stern demeanour' or the eminent scientist who was 'a shy man: this quality at times gave him an appearance of aloofness, perhaps even of rudeness'.

All these examples are taken from the obituary columns of *The Times*, which have been known to provide roughly the same kind of pleasure as the crossword puzzle. And not only do obituaries often have an element of the guessing-game about them: there can be added savour in the thought that they are usually written while the subject is still alive. In America, incidentally, an obituary held in reserve for future use is itself sometimes referred to by a less forthright name and described as a *prepared biography*.

(iii)

There are many more terms for killing listed in *Roget's Thesaurus* than there are for dying, and at first it may seem as though there ought to be many more euphemisms. The taking of life, after all, is far more likely to be accompanied by feelings of guilt and shame, to say nothing of the need for concealment, than death through natural causes. But then it is equally likely to excite abhorrence and condemnation and the plainest of plain speaking; while as for the perpetrator, if he is ready to talk openly about what he has done he is probably either confessing or boasting. One way and another the synonyms for killing are seldom calculated to make it sound less reprehensible—unless, that is (and it is a huge and sinister exception) it is killing carried out in the name of the State or some equivalent higher authority.

Far from slurring over the enormity of murder, most variants on the verb 'to kill'—to kill deliberately—are meant to make it more vivid. This is obviously the case where the methods employed are specified, but with one or two exceptions it is no less true where they are left vague. *To dispatch*, which sounds brisk and relatively painless, is, I think, a genuine euphemism, and *to do in*, which has semi-jocular possibilities, might just be reckoned to qualify. But 'to do away with', 'to make short work of', 'to finish off' are terms which effectively convey the brutality of the deed, while 'to put down' (like a dog) sounds particularly malevolent. It would be a mistake, in fact, to follow the Fowlers too closely when they define a euphemism in *The King's English* as 'the substitution of a vague or mild expression for a harsh or blunt one'. Vagueness is not necessarily the same thing as mildness: it can be menacing, or contemptuously off-hand, or it can leave the full horror to our imagination.

So too with slang. Most slang terms for killing (or anything else) aim at added pungency: where they are euphemistic—*to bump off, to take for a ride*—it is only for sardonic effect. But it is the vaguest words which carry the deadliest message, words of all work like 'get' and 'fix'. In one of her essays Mary McCarthy recalls how a colleague at the college where she was teaching broke the news of Gandhi's assassination: 'Have you heard? They got the Mahatma!' Almost any colloquialism would have jarred at such a time, doubly so in conjunction with the honorific 'Mahatma', but what makes 'got' particularly offensive is that it is so casual, that it reduces the event to a commonplace.

Since Gandhi's day political assassins have learned the trick of referring to their killings as 'executions'. This is perhaps not a true euphemism, since its purpose is essentially to imply that legitimacy rests with the terrorist (or freedom-fighting) movement rather than with the government it is trying to subvert. But *execution* itself, which in the abstract could signify carrying out any number of different tasks—the kind of tasks performed by executives and executants and executors as well as by executioners—was originally, in its death-dealing sense, a euphemism. So was *capital punishment*, which thanks to the generally favourable associations of 'capital' still manages to retain a certain blandness in comparison with 'death penalty'. (*Decapitation*, on the other hand, has a severely technical ring to it.) Among slang terms for inflicting a death sentence there are some nice examples of black humour, such as *shock* for 'electrocute'; once again, however, it is the imprecise expressions which tend to have the ugliest overtones. *Turning off* a condemned man may come to the same thing as *stringing him up*, but it sounds even nastier.

Military euphemisms constitute a subject in themselves, and attempts to glamorize death or to soften its impact inevitably loom large among them. Traditionally this has been accomplished through symbolism, through a heavy reliance on abstract ideals ('honour', 'valour', 'one crowded hour of glorious life'—which culminates in getting yourself killed), and through the use of heightened and semi-archaic language—

> He lay like a warrior taking his rest,
> With his martial cloak around him.

All these devices were pressed into duty on an unprecedented scale in 1914, and frequently given a new twist as well. Soldiers have *fallen in battle*, for instance, for centuries, but *the fallen* (or better still *the Fallen*) as a collective noun for the war dead is a First World War usage which only found its way into the *Oxford Dictionary* in the post-war *Supplement*. The same war also produced, in time, a revulsion against traditional rhetoric, against 'the old Lie: Dulce et decorum est pro patria mori'. But as one kind of euphemistic language faded, another took its place—the jargon of the official spokesman and the modern military communiqué.

The whole story is admirably recounted by Paul Fussell in *The Great War and Modern Memory*, a book which abounds in illuminating examples of chivalric 'high diction', of the humorous and stoical understatement favoured by the men in the trenches themselves, and of the smoke-screens thrown up by officialese ('a brisk engagement' was a way of admitting that around fifty per cent of a company had been killed or wounded in a raid; the parents of soldiers executed by a firing squad were sent a telegram informing them simply that their sons had 'died of wounds'). Mr Fussell also claims—and on the whole I think he is right—that 'there is a sense in which public euphemism as the special rhetorical sound of life in the latter part of the twentieth century can be said to originate in the years 1914–18'.

In many respects, it is true, the principles of public doubletalk remain what they have always been. The basic idea behind *pacification*, for instance, would have been perfectly familiar to Tacitus (*Solitudinem faciunt pacem appellant*—'they make a wilderness and call it peace'). But 'pacification' also suggests a complex and highly organized process, the wholesale application of a scientific technique. Improved methods of killing have left their mark on language as well as on life, chiefly in the form of bureaucratic abstractions and disembodied metaphors which look down from a great height (sometimes almost literally) on the events they describe—*preventive initiatives*, *strategic bombing*, *mopping-up operations*, *surgical strikes*. Since slaughter will out, these coexist with more explicit terms such as 'zapping' and 'fragging' and 'wasting', while war can still give rise to euphemisms of a more traditional cast: *taking out* a town or village, which is roughly the equivalent of wiping it off the map, is a particularly chilling example. But it is the tech-nocratic jargon which is the distinctively modern contribution.

The other great twentieth-century innovation has been mass-murder in the name of this or that ideology, with a manipula-tion of language to match. Here again there are partial pre-cedents: the Inquisition, for instance, with its *auto-da-fé*, the 'act of faith' in which prisoners who had been 'abandoned' to the secular authorities were publicly burned alive. But in com-parison with a Hitler, a Stalin, a Mao, even the most accom-plished tyrannies of the past have come to seem relatively amateurish. Nothing from earlier centuries can really equal modern totalitarianism either for wholesale terror or for sys-tematic mendacity.

A totalitarian regime lives by lies, and at its most malign it can still have recourse to euphemisms—not only (though most obviously) in order to deceive the outside world, but for a whole range of other purposes as well. When the Nazis first began talking of the *Final Solution* they were keeping their options open, but they seem to have been reluctant to admit to them-selves—to start with—just how far they were willing to go, just how final 'final' might turn out to be. When they drew up instructions about *actions* and *resettlements* or created purposefully vague 'special units' and the like, they were confer-ring the illusion of legitimacy on evil, you might almost say of sanity on madness. On the other hand no one can read very far in the literature of concentration camps without realizing how frequently euphemisms were used by the guards as a form of torment, applied with sadistic gloating to unspeakable situa-tions. *Concentration camp* is itself a notorious euphemism —doubly so, in the view of some writers, since it fails to preserve the distinction between 'ordinary' camps (something less than death camps, although they were murderous enough by any normal standards) and those camps whose whole purpose was extermination. But then even 'death camp' seems an inadequate term for conveying all the cruelties that were inflic-ted in such places before death.

In a police state there is always liable to be a thin line dividing euphemisms for murder from euphemisms for other major forms of oppression. Under Stalin, people who were *liquidated* stayed liquidated, as capitalism itself was doomed to be (the metaphor comes from closing down a business). A compulsory course of *political re-education*, on the other hand, held out the promise of survival (or did it?). If you heard of someone being *repressed*, it might or might not mean that he had been shot, as opposed to merely being sentenced to slave labour; if you heard that a prisoner had been *deprived of the right to correspond*, it was wise to assume the worst. And examples could easily be multiplied. A particularly flagrant case is the way in which Western correspondents were steered by the Soviet censorship (some of them, like Walter Duranty of the *New York Times*, all too willingly) into concealing the facts about the terrible famine which ravaged the Ukraine in 1933 as the direct result of Stalin's policies. One independent observer who tried to get the truth across at the time, a Welshman called Gareth Jones, complained bitterly of being frustrated by journalists who had been turned by censorship 'into masters of euphemism and understatement. Hence they give "famine" the polite name of "food shortage" and "starving to death" is softened down to read as "widespread mortality from diseases due to malnutrition".' The censors and their accomplices did their work well, and even today the full enormity of what happened in the Ukraine is very imperfectly appreciated.

In one area, alas, democracies have shown themselves to be every bit as adept as dictatorships at producing truly chilling euphemisms. With the development of nuclear arms we have moved further and further into a world of inhuman abstractions, of 'capacities' and 'capabilities', and the occasional metaphor which peeps through offers little by way of reassurance. A *clean bomb* is a very unclean thing indeed (it kills people but leaves buildings standing), and no more hygienic for also being known as an *enhanced radiation weapon* (an Americanism which, it is to be feared, probably carries an echo of 'life-enhancing'). Nor is it much of a consolation to learn that anything less than a nuclear exchange is now regarded as mere *conventional war*, all in a day's work.

But then the human need for euphemisms is ineradicable. If we do succeed in blowing ourselves up it will come as no surprise if Armageddon is launched under some such code-name as Operation Liberty or Operation Equality, and if the last big bang of all is officially designated Operation Whimper.

NOTES ON CONTRIBUTORS

ROBERT M. ADAMS has recently retired after forty years of college teaching, latterly at the University of California, Los Angeles. His books include *Bad Mouth* and *The Land and Literature of England*, and he is currently collaborating on a new translation, with commentary, of More's *Utopia*.

PATRICIA BEER was born in Devon, where she now lives. After teaching at the University of Padua and London University, she became a full-time writer and has published seven volumes of poetry and two books of criticism.

ROBERT BURCHFIELD is Chief Editor of the Oxford English dictionaries and Editor of *A Supplement to the Oxford English Dictionary* (three volumes, the fourth and last forthcoming). He has also written *The Spoken Word: A BBC Guide* (1981).

RICHARD COBB has recently retired as Professor of Modern History at the University of Oxford. Among his many publications are *Death in Paris* (1978), *Promenades* (1980), and *Still Life* (1983), an autobiographical boyhood portrait of Tunbridge Wells.

D. J. ENRIGHT has taught literature, largely in the Far East, and worked in publishing. He edited *The Oxford Book of Death* (1983), and published his *Collected Poems* in 1981 and *A Mania for Sentences*, essays on language and literature, in 1983.

JOSEPH EPSTEIN is editor of *The American Scholar* and teaches literature at Northwestern University in Evanston, Illinois. His most recent book is a collection of familiar essays, *The Middle of My Tether*.

JASPER GRIFFIN is a Fellow and Classical Tutor at Balliol College, Oxford. He is the compiler of *Snobs* (Small Oxford Books, 1982) and author of *Homer* in the Past Masters series (OUP, 1980), and *Homer on Life and Death* (OUP, 1980). He is at work on a book on the Latin Poets and Roman Society.

JOHN GROSS has taught at London University and Cambridge, worked in publishing, and edited *The Times Literary Supplement*. He has published *The Rise and Fall of the Man of Letters* and edited *The Oxford Book of Aphorisms* (1983).

SIMON HOGGART writes on politics for *The Observer*. Two collections of his *Punch* column 'On The House' have been published, and he is co-author, with Alistair Michie, of *The Pact: Inside Story of the Lib–Lab Government, 1977–8* (1978) and, with David Leigh, of *Michael Foot: A Portrait* (1981).

DIANE JOHNSON is a novelist and Professor of English at the University of California, Davis. She has published two biographies, the most recent being *The Life of Dashiell Hammett*. She is married to JOHN F. MURRAY, who is Professor of Medicine at the University of California, San Francisco.

JEREMY LEWIS is a director of Chatto & Windus/The Hogarth Press. He contributes regularly to the *New Statesman* and the *Spectator*, and was for some time a book reviewer for *The Times* and the *Sunday Telegraph*. He has recently introduced *Mr Facey Romford's Hounds* by R. S. Surtees for the World's Classics series (OUP).

DERWENT MAY is Literary Editor of *The Listener*. His novels include *The Laughter in Djakarta* (1973) and *A Revenger's Comedy* (1979). He is also the author of a study of *Proust* in the Past Masters series (OUP) and of *The Times Nature Diary*, both published in 1983.

PETER MULLEN is Vicar of Tockwith and Bilton with Bickerton in the diocese of York, and editor of *Faith and Heritage*, the journal of the Prayer Book Society. He writes for the *Guardian*, and has recently published a volume of short stories, *Rural Rites*.

ROBERT NISBET is Adjunct Scholar at the American Enterprise Institute in Washington DC. He is the author of many books including *The Quest for Community*, *History of the Idea of Progress*, and most recently *Prejudices: A Philosophical Dictionary*.

DAVID PANNICK is a barrister and a Fellow of All Souls College, Oxford. He is the author of *Judicial Review of the Death Penalty* (1982) and of a forthcoming book on Sex Discrimination Law, and he contributes regularly to the *Guardian* and *The Listener* on legal topics.

CATHERINE STORR qualified in medicine in 1944 and practised as a psychotherapist at the Middlesex Hospital. Most of her writing has been for children, but she has also published six adult novels and a number of articles in the *Guardian*, *Nova*, and other journals.

OXFORD

MORE OXFORD PAPERBACKS

Details of a selection of other books follow. A complete list of Oxford Paperbacks, including The World's Classics, Twentieth-Century Classics, OPUS, Past Masters, Oxford Authors, Oxford Shakespeare, and Oxford Paperback Reference, is available in the UK from the General Publicity Department, Oxford University Press (JH), Walton Street, Oxford OX2 6DP.

In the USA, complete lists are available from the Paperbacks Marketing Manager, Oxford University Press, 200 Madison Avenue, New York, NY 10016.

Oxford Paperbacks are available from all good bookshops. In case of difficulty, customers in the UK can order direct from Oxford University Press Bookshop, 116 High Street, Oxford, Freepost, OX1 4BR, enclosing full payment. Please add 10 per cent of published price for postage and packing.

INSTANT CHRONICLES

A Life

D. J. Enright

Instant Chronicles would be unbearably sad were it not unbearably funny. And no doubt the other way round.

'This is one of Enright's best.' Martin Dodsworth, *Guardian*

'these "Chronicles" have their own quiet authority, which many readers will be glad, in Enright's own word, to "share" with him' Laurence Couple, *British Book News*

'Like D. J. Enright's earlier books, *Instant Chronicles* confers instant pleasures through wit and wordplay ... D. J. Enright's poems are never dull and he is an excellent raconteur with a sparkling stream of anecdotes.' Dennis O'Driscoll, *Poetry Review*

'Enright is a major poet who quietly but insistently reminds us that civilization still matters.' John Russell Taylor, *The Times*

THE OXFORD BOOK OF CONTEMPORARY VERSE, 1945–1980

Compiled by D. J. Enright

This anthology offers substantial selections from the work of forty British, American, and Commonwealth poets who have emerged and confirmed their talents since 1945.

'There is more pithy and Johnsonian good sense in his short introduction than in all the many books that have been written about modern poetry ... one of the best personal anthologies I have come across.' John Bayley *Listener*

THE ENGLISH LANGUAGE

Robert Burchfield

'It would be hard to conceive of a brief tour of the English language that combined expedition with illumination in proportions more attractive than Dr Burchfield's book.' *Listener*

'must surely take its place among the best three or four books ever written about our language' *Birmingham Post*

'Burchfield's brilliant book on the English Language is both scholarly and human. It is the best brief survey I have ever read of the development of English . . . it conveys an authentic sense of the great mystery of language. It instructs, but it also compels wonder.' Anthony Burgess

An OPUS book

THE CONCISE OXFORD DICTIONARY OF ENGLISH LITERATURE

Second Edition

Revised by Dorothy Eagle

This handy and authoritative reference book is essential for anyone who reads and enjoys English literature. It contains concise yet informative entries on English writers from the *Beowulf* poet to Samuel Beckett and W. H. Auden, defines literary movements and genres, and refers the reader to sources for more than a thousand characters from books and plays. It also includes a host of sources of influence on English literary achievement such as foreign books and writers, art, and major historical events.

The Concise Oxford Dictionary of English Literature is an abridgement of Paul Harvey's classic *Oxford Companion to English Literature*.

Oxford Paperback Reference

LINGUISTIC CRITICISM

Roger Fowler

A fruitful recent development in literary studies has been the application of ideas drawn from linguistics. Precise analytic methods help the practical criticism of texts, while at the same time the theory of language has illuminated literary theory. *Linguistic Criticism* is an introduction to the subject by one of its most experienced practitioners. Roger Fowler sets out clearly and simply a variety of analytic techniques whose application he demonstrates in discussion of a wide range of texts from fiction, poetry, and drama. He concentrates on structures which relate literature to ordinary language, stressing the importance of the reader's every-day language skills.

An OPUS book

CAUGHT IN THE WEB OF WORDS

James Murray and the Oxford English Dictionary

K. M. Elisabeth Murray

Preface by R. W. Burchfield

K. M. Elisabeth Murray tells the story of how James Murray, a largely self-educated boy from a small village in Scotland, entered the world of scholarship and became the first editor of the *Oxford English Dictionary*

'One of the finest biographies of the twentieth century, as its subject was one of the finest human beings of the nineteenth. Everybody who speaks English owes Murray an unpayable debt. Everybody even dimly aware of that debt ought to devour, as I have done, this most heartening story of learning, energy, faith and sheer simple humanity.' Anthony Burgess

'She has put together a gripping engaging story; endearing too. The daily round of a big Victorian family, with its jokes, games and treasured seaside holidays, is entrancingly evoked.' *Sunday Times*

THE PROBLEM OF STYLE

J. Middleton Murry

Many are troubled today by the ever-increasing spread of various forms of jargon. In this book, based on his lectures delivered at Oxford in 1961, Murry attempts to define the enemy of all jargon—style.

'Style is not an isolable quality of writing' he remarked, 'it is writing itself.' Where style is exact, jargon blankets experience with a web of formulas and second-hand phrases; where style is sensuous, jargon is most often generalized and impersonal; where the concision of style is the result of critical thought, the prolixity of jargon is itself an evasion of thought, in a vain desire to impress.

This is far from being a polemical book. But in his firm grasp of principles, his desire for clarity, his deep belief that the structure of the finest literature must be meaningful not only to literary writers but to ordinary readers, Middleton Murry shows his own acute critical sense and contributes much to keeping good writing alive.

MODERN ENGLISH LITERATURE

W. W. Robson

This is a critical account of a wide selection of writers from Shaw and Wells to Pinter and Hughes. The emphasis is on the prose fiction, poetry, and plays of the period; but from time to time the author discusses non-fiction writers, so as to suggest the general movement of twentieth-century thought. Mr Robson's critical standards are broad and humane. At the same time his preferences are clear and he gives reasons for them.

An OPUS book

THE OXFORD GUIDE TO WORD GAMES

Tony Augarde

This is a unique guide to all kinds of word games and word play, from crosswords and scrabble to acrostics, rebuses, and tongue-twisters. Not only does it reveal the origins of games, outlining their fascinating history, but it describes how to play them, and their often equally interesting variants. Illustrating his descriptions with examples and diagrams, Tony Augarde builds up an intriguing and amusing picture of the British love of verbal ingenuity.

'very good value and fun' *Sunday Telegraph*

THE OXFORD LITERARY GUIDE TO THE BRITISH ISLES

Edited by Dorothy Eagle and Hilary Carnell

This is the paperback edition of the best-selling *Oxford Literary Guide to the British Isles*. It lists hundreds of places in Britain and Ireland and gives details of their connections with the lives and works of famous writers. It provides maps, precise directions, and opening times for the tourist. Not only is it an indispensable companion to every journey, but also a delight for the armchair traveller with its endlessly fascinating facts and anecdotes.

'Anyone who can read or write will find the *Guide* a sure way of wallowing unashamedly in a rich nostalgia for . . . our literary heritage.' *Times Literary Supplement*

THE OXFORD PAPERBACK DICTIONARY

Edited by Joyce M. Hawkins

This dictionary was first published in 1979 and became an immediate success, attracting world-wide attention and praise for its clear definitions, up-to-date coverage of vocabulary, straightforward system of pronunciation, and especially for its notes on correct English usage. In this new enlarged edition these features have been retained and the coverage has been increased, especially in the field of computers, which have recently invaded not only the office but also the home.

'Every home, office, secretary and boss should have one' *The Good Book Guide*

Oxford Paperback Reference

THE OXFORD–DUDEN PICTORIAL ENGLISH DICTIONARY:

Leisure and the Arts

Certain kinds of information are better conveyed visually than by written definitions. *The Oxford–Duden Pictorial English Dictionaries* offer more than an ordinary illustrated dictionary; they present the vocabularly of a particular subject alongside a picture illustrating it. An alphabetical index is also provided for easy cross-reference.

This volume ranges from fine art and the theatre to sports, fashions, and the home, covering a wide-ranging vocabulary of use in everyday life.

Oxford Paperback Reference

THE OXFORD–DUDEN PICTORIAL
ENGLISH DICTIONARY:
Science and Medicine

Certain kinds of information are better conveyed visually than by written definitions. This dictionary offers more than an ordinary illustrated dictionary; it presents the vocabularly of a particular subject alongside a picture illustrating it. An alphabetical index is also provided for easy cross-reference.

This vocabulary of Astronomy, Geography, Dentistry, Mathematics, Natural History, and much more is given in this dictionary.

Oxford Paperback Reference

THE CONCISE OXFORD DICTIONARY OF
PROVERBS
Edited by John Simpson

Many proverbs come to us with the wisdom of ages behind them, while new ones are continually being created. John Simpson's compilation embraces over 1,000 English-language proverbs in current use, and those who love words will be fascinated to trace the origins—both old and new—of many familiar phrases.

'brilliantly arranged in alphabetical order by the first significant word in each quotation with cross-references by later significant words ... I recommend it without hesitation to all students of the English language and lovers of literature, as well as to pedants, crossword fanatics and those who like to prove people wrong in argument.' Auberon Waugh, *Sunday Telegraph*

'a work of scholarship and good humour, which deserves a place on the shelves of anyone interested in twentieth-century English usage' *British Book News*

THE KING'S ENGLISH

Third Edition

H. W. Fowler and F. G. Fowler

Generations of students, scholars, and professional writers have gone to *The King's English* for answers to problems of grammar or style. The Fowler brothers were particularly concerned to clarify the more problematic and obscure rules and principles inherent in English vocabulary and composition, and also to illustrate with examples the most common blunders and traps. They wrote with characteristic good sense and liveliness, and this book has become a classic reference work.

A DICTIONARY OF MODERN ENGLISH USAGE

H. W. Fowler

Second Edition

Revised by Sir Ernest Gowers

This is the paperback edition of Fowler's *Modern English Usage,* which for over fifty years has been the standard work on the correct but easy and natural use of English in speech or writing. It deals with points of grammar, syntax, style, and the choice of words; with the formation of words and their spelling and inflexions; with pronunciation; and with punctuation and typography. But most of all Fowler is renowned for the iconoclasm and wit with which he writes.

'Let me beg readers as well as writers to keep the revised Fowler at their elbows. It brims with useful information.' Raymond Mortimer, *Sunday Times*

'Fowler is still the best available authority. For those who think that it matters to make their writing shipshape and water-tight, there is still no alternative. Apart from that, we read him because he was a funny, quirky, witty man, who used words to express complicated meanings with beautiful conciseness.' *Books and Bookmen*

THE OXFORD DICTIONARY OF CURRENT ENGLISH

Edited by R. E. Allen

This is the most authoritative, comprehensive, and up-to-date dictionary of its size available, specially designed to be quickly and easily used in everyday life. Among its main features are:

* over 70,000 definitions

* senses arranged in order of comparative familiarity and importance

* pronunciations given in the International Phonetic Alphabet

* special markings for disputed and racially offensive uses

* extensive treatment of idioms and phrases

* generous coverage of terms used in technology and the information sciences

* clear layout and presentation with a minimum of special abbreviations and symbols

THE OXFORD GUIDE TO THE ENGLISH LANGUAGE

Edited by E. S. C. Weiner and Joyce M. Hawkins

This is the ideal concise handbook for everyone who cares about using the English language properly. Combining between one set of covers Edmund Weiner's *Oxford Guide to English Usage* and a compact Oxford dictionary compiled by Joyce Hawkins, it is comprehensive and exceptionally convenient for regular quick consultation.

The dictionary contains nearly 30,000 words and phrases, and provides a compact and up-to-date guide to contemporary English—spelling, pronunciation, and meaning.

AFTER BABEL

Aspects of Language and Translation

George Steiner

George Steiner presents the first systematic investigation of the phenomenology and processes of translation inside language and between languages since the eighteenth century. Taking issue with the principal emphasis of modern linguistics, Steiner finds the root of the 'Babel problem' in our deep instinct for privacy and territory. He notes that every people has, in its language, a unique body of shared secrecy. With this provocative thesis he analyses every aspect of translation, from fundamental conditions of interpretation to the most intricate of linguistic constructions.

'He is saying things we cannot afford not to take note of . . . I greatly admire the intellectual venture which this book represents.' Donald Davie, *Times Literary Supplement*

'As a critic, Dr Steiner is an original, rather like the Ancient Mariner. Arresting one with a glittering, bold thought, he draws one into expositions of deep and diverse illumination . . . a masterly and impressive work.' Jan Marsh, *Daily Telegraph*

ACADEMIC YEAR

D. J. Enright

Introduced by Anthony Thwaite

Three expatriate Englishmen teaching in Egypt towards the end of King Farouk's splendid and shabby reign live through the academic year of this novel. Apostles of an alien culture, they stand somewhere between the refined English aesthetics of Shelley and T. S. Eliot and the chaotic squalor of the Alexandrian slums, trying to balance the unattainable against the irredeemable, the demands of scholarship against the dictates of reality, while making a modest living for themselves. Their consequent adventures and misadventures are either hilarious or tragic, and sometimes both. And, we suspect, as near the truth as makes no difference.

'This first novel is funny, extremely funny; it is an Alexandrian *Lucky Jim* with much more humanity and much less smart lacquer.' *Daily Telegraph*

ON DIFFICULTY

and Other Essays

George Steiner

What do we mean when we say that a text is difficult? These stimulating essays by Professor Steiner raise this and other questions at the frontier of our understanding of language and society. Underlying them is a fundamental theme which Professor Steiner has explored in such books as *Language and Silence*, *Extraterritorial*, and his major study of human speech, *After Babel*: in what ways are the classical and humanistic ideals and values which have animated Western literature and habits of thought now being eroded? How has our ability to read been affected by the decline of privacy, the changing weight of emphasis between the public and the private sectors of personality and speech? Questions such as these make *On Difficulty* essential reading for the inquiring layman as well as for the specialist.

'Since the publication of the essays in *Language and Silence* . . . we have witnessed the growth of a major critical presence in the work of George Steiner.' Richard Holmes, *The Times*